Europe in Crisis

Series Editor
Martin A. Schain
Center for European Studies, The Vernom
New York University
New York, New York
USA

The current crisis in Europe has often been depicted as an economic/currency crisis that poses a danger for European economic unity and its common currency, the Euro. Monetary union, it has been argued, has outrun fiscal union, depriving the EU of an important means of dealing with the pressures on the currency. It has also been understood as a crisis of governance, of institutions with the decision-making capacity to deal with the crisis. Finally, the impact of the economic emergency has altered the political landscape in different EU countries in different ways. The crisis appears to be creating changes that will endure, but cannot yet be predicted entirely. This series fills an important gap in scholarship by supporting a level of analysis that is more thoughtful than the periodic media coverage and less complicated than much of the deep theoretical analysis. These books are timely and concise with the promise of a long lifetime of relevancy.

More information about this series at
http://www.springer.com/series/14975

Michael Minkenberg

The Radical Right in Eastern Europe

Democracy under Siege?

Michael Minkenberg
Frankfurt/Oder, Brandenburg,
Germany

Europe in Crisis
ISBN 978-1-349-95147-5   ISBN 978-1-137-56332-3 (eBook)
DOI 10.1057/978-1-137-56332-3

Library of Congress Control Number: 2016956864

© The Editor(s) (if applicable) and The Author(s) 2017
This work is subject to copyright. All rights are solely and exclusively licensed by the Publisher, whether the whole or part of the material is concerned, specifically the rights of translation, reprinting, reuse of illustrations, recitation, broadcasting, reproduction on microfilms or in any other physical way, and transmission or information storage and retrieval, electronic adaptation, computer software, or by similar or dissimilar methodology now known or hereafter developed.
The use of general descriptive names, registered names, trademarks, service marks, etc. in this publication does not imply, even in the absence of a specific statement, that such names are exempt from the relevant protective laws and regulations and therefore free for general use.
The publisher, the authors and the editors are safe to assume that the advice and information in this book are believed to be true and accurate at the date of publication. Neither the publisher nor the authors or the editors give a warranty, express or implied, with respect to the material contained herein or for any errors or omissions that may have been made. The publisher remains neutral with regard to jurisdictional claims in published maps and institutional affiliations.

Cover illustration: Abstract Bricks and Shadows © Stephen Bonk/Fotolia.co.uk

Printed on acid-free paper

This Palgrave Pivot imprint is published by Springer Nature
The registered company is Nature America Inc.
The registered company address is: 1 New York Plaza, New York, NY 10004, U.S.A.

Foreword

In this remarkable short book, Michael Minkenberg presents an important new analysis of the radical right in Eastern Europe. There is an abundance of literature on radical right parties in Western Europe, much of which is cited in this book for comparative purposes. The emergence of what appears to be similar parties in the East, however, has been frequently noted, but rarely studied in depth. Therefore, this is a groundbreaking analysis at a time when these parties and their policies have become increasingly visible and dominant in some of the major countries in Eastern Europe.

What are most remarkable in this analysis are the sharp differences between Eastern and Western Europe. Twenty-five years after the fall of Communism, and more than a decade after most of the countries of Eastern Europe were integrated into the European Union, East vs. West remains an important basis for analysis. The parties and movements of the radical right in the East are far more radical in their actions and their objectives than those in the West. They are also more organizationally unstable and volatile, and more closely linked to ancient nationalist issues.

The rise and electoral success of the radical right in Western Europe is generally related to reactions to immigration and the increased presence of immigrants. The rise of the radical right in the East, Minkenberg argues, is rooted in historical animosities and conflicts with ethnic minorities. The recent influx of refugees is not at the root of these tensions, but has exacerbated them. Voters in the East have been far more sensitive to ethnic differences than even those in the West, but most of these differences have been ethno-nationalist. Moreover, there is a considerable chasm between the party worlds and systems of the East, compared with those in the West. The electoral strength of the radical right in the East is weaker than that in the West, but, because it is more profoundly radical and nationalist, its presence is more deeply felt.

Michael Minkenberg has written a troubling and important book. He demonstrates the fragility of democracy in Eastern Europe, as well as the durability of nationalist issues that link the past to the present, even after all that has happened—or perhaps because of all that has happened. Moreover, this analysis helps us to understand more about the powerful hostility that greeted the recent wave of refugees in Eastern Europe during the past two years, in a region where few immigrants had settled before. If the radical right in the West reflects fear about the future, these same movements in the East reflect the continuing importance of the unresolved past.

Martin A. Schain, Series Editor
Professor of Politics, Emeritus, New York University

Acknowledgments

This book represents the end of a long journey—but not its final destination; for that, another leap will be needed. So far, many people have accompanied me on this journey, and I hope many of them will continue. For the company, intellectual and otherwise, I want to thank first and foremost an inspiring institution and its people that lies right on the border between two countries, between what is considered "the West" and "the East," or the "Central East," of Europe, that is to say the European University Viadrina and my team at the Chair of Comparative Politics.

Special thanks go to: Malisa Zobel who read and commented on the entire draft of the book and Christopher Fritzsche whom I have kept busy researching on the radical right in Eastern Europe; my colleagues at the European University Viadrina who taught me, a newcomer to the field of East European studies, the basics needed to start my work, in particular Timm Beichelt and Jan Wielgohs (the latter having left us much too early); and my (former) doctoral students in the field of East European politics who despite my constant criticism did not give up on their projects, finished them with flying colors or are still joyfully busy with them and provided me with inexhaustible and valuable feedback, in particular Anja Hennig, Bartek Pytlas, and Oliver Kossack.

I also thank my research network that extends all over Central and Eastern Europe as well as in selected places elsewhere in the world for their support in developing my research. My thanks also go to Elaine Fan and Chris Robinson at Palgrave Macmillan who made sure I stayed on track and steered me through the production process.

Contents

1 Introduction — 1

2 Concepts: Analyzing the East European Radical Right — 9

3 Contexts: Legacies and the Transformation Process — 35

4 Contents: Organizational Patterns and Ideological Profiles — 67

5 Configurations: Mobilization and Performance — 99

6 Consequences: Interaction and Impact — 121

7 Conclusions — 143

Bibliography — 151

Index — 177

ABBREVIATIONS OF COUNTRIES

AT   Austria
BE   Belgium
BG   Bulgaria
CH   Switzerland
CZ   Czech Republic
DE   Germany
DK   Denmark
EE   Estonia
FR   France
GB   Great Britain
HU   Hungary
IT   Italy
LT   Lithuania
LV   Latvia
NL   The Netherlands
NO   Norway
PL   Poland
RO   Romania
RU   Russia
SK   Slovakia
SW   Sweden

Abbreviations of Parties and Movements (Country in Parentheses)

AfD	Alternative für Deutschland (Alternative for Germany) (DE)
AN	Alleanza Nazionale (National Alliance) (IT)
ANS	Aktionsfront Nationale Sozialisten (Action Front of National Socialists) (DE)
AWS	Akcja Wyborcza Solidarność (Solidarity Electoral Action) (PL)
BNP	British National Party (GB)
BSP	Bulgarska Sotsialisticheska Partiya (Bulgarian Socialist Party) (BG)
BZÖ	Bündnis Zukunft Österreiches (Alliance for the Future of Austria) (AT)
CCS	Comités Chrétienité-Solidarité (Committees Christianity-Solidarity) (FR)
CD	Centrumdemocraten (Center Democrats) (NL)
CD	Christian Democrats (various countries)
CVP	Christliche Volkspartei (Christian People's Party) (CH)
DF	Dansk Folkepartiet (Danish People's Party) (DK)
DPS	Dvizhenie za Prava i Svobodi (Movement for Rights and Freedoms) (BG)
DS	Dělnická strana sociální spravedlnost (Workers' Party of Social Justice, until 2010 *Workers'* Party) (CZ)
DVU	Deutsche Volksunion (German People's Union) (DE)
EI	Eesti Iseseisvuspartei (Estonian Independence Party) (EE)
FANE	Fédération Action National-Européen (Federation of National-European Action) (FR)
FAP	Freiheitliche Deutsche Arbeiterpartei (Free German Workers Party) (DE)
FDP	Freie Demokratische Partei (Free Democratic Party) (CH)

FI	Forza Italia! (Go Italy!) (IT)
Fidesz	Fidesz—Magyar Polgári Szövetség (Fidesz—Hungarian Civic Alliance) (HU)
FKGP	Független Kiszgazda, Földmunkás és Polgári Párt (Independent Smallholders, Agrarian Workers and Civic Party) (HU)
FN	Front national (National Front) (FR)
FPÖ	Freiheitliche Partei Österreichs (Freedom Party of Austria) (AT)
FrP	Fremskridtsparti (Progress Party) (DK); Fremskrittsparti (Progress Party) (NO)
GERB	Grazhdani za Evropeysko Razvitie na Balgariya (Citizens for European Development of Bulgaria) (BG)
HZDS	Hnutie za demokratické Slovensko (Movement for a Democratic Slovakia) (SK)
JSN	Jeudg Storm Nederland, Stormfront (Netherlands Youth Storm) (NL)
KDH	Krest'anskodemokratické hnutie (Christian Democratic Movement) (SK)
KDNP	Kereszténydemokrata Néppárt (Christian Democratic Party) (HU)
KNP	Kongres Nowej Prawicy (Congress of the New Right) (PL)
KPN	Konfederacja Polski Niepodleglej (Confederation for an Independent Poland) (PL)
KzB	Koalicija za Balgarija (Coalition for Bulgaria (BG)
LDPR	Liberal Democratic Party of Russia (RU)
LMP	Lehet Más a Politika! (Politics can be different!) (HU)
LN	Lega Nord (Northern League) (IT)
LPF	List Pim Fortuyn (NL)
LPR	Liga Polskich Rodzin (League of Polish Families) (PL)
L'S-HZDS	Ľudová strana – Hnutie za demokratické Slovensko (People's Party – Movement for a Democratic Slovakia) (SK)
LTS	Lietuvių tautininkų sąjunga (Lithuanian Nationalist Union) (LT)
MDF	Magyar Demokráta Fórum (Hungarian Democratic Forum) (HU)
MG	Magyar Gárda (Hungarian Guard) (HU)
MIÉP	Magyar Igazság és Élet Pártja (Hungarian Justice and Life Party) (HU)
MNR	Mouvement National Républicain (National Republican Movement) (FR)
MÖM	Magyar Önvédelmi Mozgalom (Hungarian Self-Defense Movement) (HU)
MOST	Most-Híd (Bridge (in Slovak) - Bridge (in Hungarian)) (SK)
MS	Matica Slovenska (a cultural association for language and culture) (SK)
MSI	Movimento Sociale Italiano (Italian Social Movement) (IT)

MS-FT	Movimento Sociale Fiamma Tricolore (Social Movement—Tricolore Flame) (IT)
MSZP	Magyar Szocialista Párt (Hungarian Socialist Party) (HU)
NA	Nacionālā apvienība (National Alliance) (LV)
ND	Noua Dreaptă (New Right) (RO)
ND	Ny Demokrati (New Democrats); Nationaldemokraterna (National Democrats) (SW)
NDSV	Nacionalno dviženie za stabilnost i văzhod (National Movement for Stability and Progress) (BG)
NF	National Front (GB)
NNP	Nieuwe Nationale Partij (New National Party) (NL)
NO	Národní Odpor (National Resistance) (PL)
NOP	Narodowe Odrodzenie Polski (Polish National Rebirth) (PL)
NPD	Nationaldemokratische Partei Deutschlands (National Democratic Party of Germany) (DE)
NSDAP	Nationalsozialistische Deutsche Arbeiterpartei (National Socialist German Workers' Party) (DE)
NSS	Nové Slobodne Slovensko (New Free Slovakia) (SK)
NVU	Nederlandse Volksunie (Dutch People's Union) (NL)
ODS	Obedineni Demokratichnite Sili (United Democratic Forces) (BG)
ONR	Obóz Narodowo-Radikalny (National-Radical Camp) (PL)
ÖVP	Österreichische Volkspartei (Austrian People's Party) (AT)
PD	Partidul Democrat (Democratic Party) (RO)
PDSR	Partidul Democratiei Sociale din România (Party of Social Democracy in Romania) (RO)
PiS	Prawo i Sprawiedliwość (Law and Justice) (PL)
PNL	Partidul Naţional Liberal (National Liberal Party) (RO)
PO	Platforma Obywatelska (Civic Platform) (PL)
PRM	Partidul Romania Mare (Party for Greater Romania) (RO)
PSD	Partidul Social Democrat (Social Democratic Party) (RO)
PSL	Polskie Stronnictwo Ludowe (Polish People's Alliance) (PL)
PSM	Partidul Socialist Român (Socialist Party of Romania) (RO)
PUNR	Partidul Unităţii Naţionale a Românilor (Romanian National Unity Party) (RO)
PVV	Partij voor de Vrijheid (Party of Freedom) (NL)
PWN-PSN	Polska Wspólnota Narodowa: Polskie Stronnictwo Narodowe (Polish National Union) (PL)
ROC	Romanian Orthodox Church (RO)
ROP	Ruch Odbudowy Polski (Movement for the Reconstruction of Poland) (PL)
RN	Ruch Narodowy (National Movement) (PL)
RP	Reformu partija (Reform Party) (LV)

SD	Sverigedemokraterna (Sweden Democrats) (SW)
SDKU	Slovenská demokratická a krest'anská únia (Slovak Democratic and Christian Union) (SK)
SLD	Sojusz Lewicy Demokratycznej (Social Democratic Alliance) (PL)
SMK	Strana mad'arskej koalície (Hungarian Coalition Party) (HU)
Smer-SD	Smer–sociálna demokracia (Direction—Social Democracy) (SK)
SN	Stronnictwo Narodowe "Ojczyzna" (National Front Party of the Fatherland) (PL)
SNJ	Slovenská Národná Jednota (Slovak National Union) (SK)
SNS	Slovenská Národná Strana (Slovak National Party) (SK)
SO	Samoobrona (Self Defense) (PL)
SP	Slovenská Pospolitost' (Slovak Togetherness) (SK)
SPR-RSČ	Sdružení pro republiku—Republikánská strana Československa (Coalition for Republic—Republican Party of Czechoslovakia) (CZ)
SVP	Schweizerische Volkspartei (Swiss People's Party) (CH)
SzDSz	Szabad Demokraták Szövetsége (Alliance of Free Democrats) (HU)
TB/LNNK	Tēvzemei un Brīvībai/Latvijas Nacionālās Neatkarības Kustība (For Fatherland and Freedom/Latvian National Independence Movement) (LV)
UDC	Unione de Centro (Union of the Center) (IT)
UDMR	Uniunea Democrată Maghiară din România (Democratic Alliance of Hungarians in Romania) (RO)
UKIP	UK Independence Party (GB)
VB	Vlaams Belang (Flemish Interest), until 2004: Vlaams Block (Flemish Blok) (BE)
VL	Visu Latvijai! (All for Latvia!) (LV)
VR	Vatra Romaneasca (Romanian Cradle) (RO)
ZChN	Zjednoczenie Chrześcijańsko Narodowe (Christian National Union) (PL)
ZRS	Združenie robotníkov Slovenska (Union of the Workers of Slovakia) (SK)
ZZS	Zaļo un Zemnieku savienība (Union of Greens and Farmers) (LV)

LIST OF FIGURES

Fig. 2.1	Modeling the role of the radical right in the political process and its impact	32
Fig. 3.1	The fusion of religion and national identity in Europe, East and West (2003)	48
Fig. 3.2	European public opinion and immigration, 2011 and 2015	49
Fig. 3.3	Xenophobia in Europe	52
Fig. 6.1	Spatial shifts in East European party systems, 2002–2010	133

List of Tables

Table 2.1	In-group/out-group criteria in right-wing radical discourse (following W. Heitmeyer's concept of group-based enmity)	15
Table 3.1	Interwar regime change and religion in Western and Eastern Europe	47
Table 3.2	Ethnic homogeneity in East European countries (%)	51
Table 3.3	Ethnocentric prejudice in selected European democracies, 2008 (% approving)	54
Table 3.4	Party membership ratios in selected West and East European countries (% of electorate)	58
Table 3.5	Context factors for the radical right in Eastern Europe	62
Table 4.1	Major radical right actors in Eastern Europe (1990–2000)	69
Table 4.2	Major radical right actors in Eastern Europe (2001–2010)	72
Table 4.3	Major radical right actors in Eastern Europe (after 2010)	74
Table 4.4	The anti-democratic impulse of the East European radical right—regime references	80
Table 4.5	The radical right and their religious agenda in Western and Eastern Europe (since the 1990s)	87
Table 4.6	Stratification of right-wing radical party voters in Slovakia, Poland, and Hungary (over and under-representation by percentage of voters)	89
Table 4.7	Strength of radical right-wing movements in Europe, pre-2004 and 2014	92
Table 4.8	Trends in officially recorded racist crime, 2000–2013	94
Table 5.1	Radical right election results (%) in national parliamentary elections in Eastern Europe in comparison to Western Europe, from 1990 (average per five years, chambers of deputies)	101

Table 5.2	Life span of radical right parties in Western and Eastern Europe (1990–2016)	103
Table 5.3	Party strength and movement strength of the radical right and context factors in Western Europe (c.2000)	107
Table 5.4	Context factors and radical right actors in Eastern Europe (2000–2004)	109
Table 5.5	Context factors and radical right actors in Eastern Europe (2010–2014)	110
Table 5.6	Religious diversity, pluralization, and the radical right in Western Europe (1980–2000)	112
Table 5.7	Ethnic pluralization and the radical right in Eastern Europe (1990–2015)	113
Table 5.8	The radical right in Eastern Europe: Patterns of interaction in selected arenas (post-2000)	117
Table 6.1	The radical right in European national government, 1990–2016	124
Table 6.2	Radical right parties in Eastern Europe: Impact in selected arenas (post-2000)	135

CHAPTER 1

Introduction

Abstract After discussing the observation that, despite the successful integration of the new post-communist democracies into the European Union, the quality of democracy has suffered setbacks in some countries and that ultranationalist politics remains pervasive in the region, the author presents the following central argument of the book. While there are commonalities between East and West, the nature of the post-communist transition process and the unfinished nation-building in the region have made the radical right in Eastern Europe a *sui generis* phenomenon, being both organizationally more fluid and ideologically more extreme than its Western counterpart. In the Introduction the author outlines the organization of the book, which begins with a conceptualization of the radical right as one grounded in modernization theory and the specification of the particular East European context, before addressing the ideological and organizational mapping of the field of radical right actors and their interaction with other actors, and finally considering the resulting effects on the politics and policies in the region.

Keywords Transformation process · Democratization · Convergence · Most similar systems · EU

With the Eastern enlargement of the European Union many observers concluded that the transformation process in Eastern Europe[1] had finally reached its climax of establishing stable democracies firmly rooted in a European community and sharing the same liberal and democratic values. But the quality of democracy has suffered setbacks in some countries and the European integration process is now seriously challenged. At the beginning of 2016, nationalist politics and the agenda of the radical right attained new levels of support in Europe and in particular in the new democracies of the post-communist East. For example, liberal democratic standards in Hungary have been corroded by the Fidesz government, a development which was influenced by the radical right parties of MIÉP and its successor Jobbik: both contributed to the transformation of Fidesz into a right-wing populist party. Likewise and more recently, Poland's new national-conservative governmental party PiS, once the senior partner in a coalition government which included the radical right LPR and which today is the inheritor of the LPR ideology and its electorate, is restricting the independence of the judiciary and public broadcasting in order to prepare further far-reaching reforms. Unlike in Hungary, the European Commission has decided to investigate the condition of Poland's constitutional state. Also, in other East European countries radical right actors have been influential in shaping the transformation process and political development of these societies (see the contributions to Minkenberg 2015a).

That the clocks tend to tick differently in large parts of Eastern Europe can also be seen in these states' reaction to the increased refugee influx over the last year. The quarrel over the appropriate handling of the refugees and their distribution within the EU is now stalling the European integration process. This problem has been highlighted by several countries refusing to accommodate asylum seekers at all; the majority of these states are in Eastern Europe. On top of this, the Hungarian prime minister Viktor Orbán initiated and led a coalition of governments in the region in early 2016 which tried to establish a counter-movement within the EU to what they call "liberal, mainstream Europe."[2]

In sum, it seems the agenda of the radical right has reached the mainstream. When in the 1990s the regime change led to a rush to democracy among the mainstream left and right, the radical right's ultranationalist agenda appeared rather marginal. As Cas Mudde observed in 2005: "racist extremist parties are not really a major political force in Central and Eastern Europe. Indeed, if compared to their 'brethren' in Western

Europe, they look somewhat pathetic: (far) more extremist, but (far) less successful" (2005a, 269). However, the constant calls for a strong nation did not subside with democratic consolidation; rather they traveled across the political board. It is therefore important to take a closer look at the role, and possible impact, of the radical right in Eastern Europe. If those parties and movements stabilize their position and gain even more traction in the region, the EU and its institutions, along with the respective democratic order, will face major problems.

These developments can be seen as a sign of an all-European trend. In fact, such a trend regarding the radical right has been suggested by a number of authors who argue that, with the growing consolidation of East European democracies and ongoing European integration, a convergence of party systems, and in particular of radical right politics, is occurring which renders obsolete a region-specific focus and categories (see Mudde 2007; Umland 2015; von Beyme 2015). While recent developments in East *and* West indeed testify to a radicalization of national politics in policy fields such as immigration, integration, and the handling of refugee and border issues, the view that this leads to "closing the gap" between the East and West (see Beichelt 2012) is misleading, because radicalization runs contrary to the assumed linear trend of further liberalization and democratization and in the East it encompasses large parts of the political spectrum.

The radical right in contemporary Eastern Europe claims a prominent place in these processes. Seen from a historical angle, there are three different views on the difference or similarity between East and West. Some observers draw analogies between the post-1989 radical right and interwar fascism, in terms of a "Weimarization" of Eastern Europe (or Europe in its entirety) and the return of the pre-1945, ultranationalist, or even fascist past—the "return of history" (see e.g. Umland 2008). Others argue that since some East European party systems increasingly resemble their Western counterparts, so does the radical right—the "return to Europe" (see Bustikova 2014, 2015; Reynié 2013, 301–313). A third line of thought sees the radical right in the region as a *sui generis* phenomenon, inherently shaped by the historical forces of state socialism and the transformation process and, as a result and in contrast to Western Europe, ideologically more extreme and anti-democratic while organizationally more a movement than a party phenomenon (see Minkenberg 2002a; Stöss 2010).

Against the argument of convergence, then, in this book I attempt to demonstrate the persistence of differences between East and West when it comes to the politics of the radical right; the roots of recent developments in the East precede the various all-European crises, such as the "refugee crisis" of 2015 or the "financial crisis" of 2008. Liberalization and democratization were always challenged by radical right (and other) actors who put into question the new political order and, hence, fundamentally endangered the rights and status of minorities and immigrants. Instead, ultranationalist politics in the region and its most articulate carrier, the radical right, should be seen in a larger context, especially in light of the region's particular historical legacies, the dynamics of the regime change after 1989, and the dynamics of the political process in the new democracies.

As the Hungarian situation illustrates, there is difficulty in assessing whether a definitive democratic consolidation has taken place once EU membership is achieved. This difficulty is complicated by the unresolved question as to whether the politics of ultranationalism and the radical right in the region have been successfully "tamed" by the new political order, its elites, and European integration. While the force and plausibility of (post- or reformed) communism seems to retreat with time, hence contributing to a consolidation of the democratic regime and capitalist economy (see Beichelt 2001, Chapter 5), the same cannot be said for that other systemic opposition, that is the radical right (see Minkenberg 2002a, 2009a, 2013a; also Mudde 2007). In most countries in the region, the radical right continues to play a significant albeit not persistent role in the politics of democratic governance. It may be too much to take their existence as an indicator of an unsuccessful democratic consolidation (which would raise some interesting questions about democracy in *Western* Europe). But their anti-systemic thrust in the context of young democratic regimes with under-institutionalized party systems and unresolved ethnic cleavages does point at a fundamental challenge to the process of democratization.

It is the purpose of this book to provide a comparative analysis of the post-communist East European radical right, both in terms of party and non-party formation, by using the West European radical right as a baseline. I will offer insights into the political field of the radical right following the onset of democracy in the region and I will elicit region-wide and country-specific characteristics. I will argue that, due to the nature of the transition process from Soviet hegemony to national independence, and from communist to democratic societies and to the unfinished process of nation-building in the region, the radical right in Eastern Europe is a *sui generis* phenomenon; that it is both organizationally more fluid and ideologically more extreme than its Western counterpart. I will also argue that the fluidity and limited electoral success of these parties do not render them less significant; quite the contrary. The specific contexts in which they operate, along with a multitude of right-wing movements, sometimes competing and sometimes cooperating with the mainstream parties, permit a considerable degree of impact on their respective political systems.

The analysis presented here draws on a set of country cases which qualify as the most similar systems (see Przeworski and Teune 1970, 32–34). The strategy of comparison, however, proceeds in a two-fold way: by comparing the radical right within this set of countries, and by comparing this radical right with that in Western Europe. The country cases include those new democracies in the region which: have a communist past; were under Soviet, that is foreign, control prior to 1989; have established democratic regimes since then; and have officially concluded their transformation by becoming members of the European Union in 2004 or 2007. The underlying logic of the case selection follows the reasoning that the radical right in a democratic process can only be meaningfully studied if the democratic game has been in town for more than just a few years. Hence, the countries covered are Poland, the Czech Republic and Slovakia, the Baltic Republics, Hungary, Romania, and Bulgaria (the successor states of Yugoslavia are not included because of different starting points and transition processes). Occasionally references to other cases will be made in the comparative contributions, where suitable. The methods employed consist largely of historical and comparative political sociology, in combination with electoral research and analysis of public opinion trends. In order to study the role of the radical right in the political process and its impact on the political system, an analytical model derived from movement research will be applied. The analysis in the book proceeds in five steps.

The first task involves the conceptual clarification and the composition of the analytical models (Chapter 2). The concept of "radical right" is discussed and situated in the current academic debate between alternative concepts such as fascism, populism, and extremism. In this chapter I ground the concept in modernization theory and develop an operational definition centered on the ideological core of exclusivist ultranationalism (with different ideological variants). I advance the argument that the term "radical right," when applied to countries with democratic settings and an open political space, can best capture the various actors on the far right in all parts of (democratic) Europe, and that party actors, as well as non-party or movement-type actors, can be included in such a term. In other words, despite the different contexts in which the radical right has operated in Eastern Europe up until today, as compared to its counter-part in Western Europe, it is unnecessary to develop a distinctly "East European" concept for these actors. The analytical model of the radical right as a collective actor is then spelled out by employing process-analytical approaches from movement research.

In a second step (Chapter 3), the specific contexts for the East European radical right will be identified and operationalized. An overview of "legacies" which make the region distinct from Western Europe with its own set of legacies will provide some historical depth to the analysis. These will include distinct ways of nation-building: all of today's East European democracies were parts of multinational empires in the heyday of European nation-building in the late nineteenth and early twentieth century. Following historians and social scientists such as Tony Judt (2005) and Andrew Janos (2000), it will be argued that most East European countries have followed a distinct path into modernity which included (a) the failure of democracy in the interwar period (except for Czechoslovakia) and (b) incorporation into the communist bloc after World War II, which interrupted the nation-building processes until the Velvet Revolution of 1989. The second and third sections of this chapter address the most relevant cultural and structural context factors for the radical right in the region. These include in particular a political culture with low levels of trust, no societal rooting of the party systems and diverging cleavage patterns, a different set of issues feeding the radical right, and elites which are more sympathetic towards nationalism than those in Western Europe. This will be corroborated with survey data and other material. It will become clear that the set of issues driving the West European radical right, that is immigration and insecurity, does not correspond to the agenda in the East which is much more centered on historical grievances or narratives, the role of national minorities (in the face of very low levels of immigration), and border questions (irredentism).

The third step of the investigation (Chapter 4) involves a detailed analysis of the entire field of radical right actors in the region. The central question to be asked is to what extent the radical right in East European democracies differs from that in the West, especially in its organizational and ideological characteristics. The analysis of parties will show that the platforms of most of the radical right in the region are more openly anti-democratic, anti-liberal, racist, and historically revisionist than those of the (successful) parties in Western Europe. On the movement level, the analysis will point at the porous borders between radical right parties and militant or violent activists, although here comparative data on the organizational strength of movements and their protest events in the region are hard to come by, and case studies and secondary evidence will be used for elaborative purposes.

In the following step (Chapter 5), the performance of the radical right and its determining factors are addressed. The chapter will bring out the high degree of volatility of the radical right over time, in particular in the party sector. With a few exceptions and in stark contrast to Western Europe, radical right parties have relatively short lives, and their electoral results fluctuate enormously. But weak party organization and inconstancy at the polls do not translate into political irrelevancy, once the radical right's interaction with its political environment is taken into account. The chapter shows that conventional context factors are weak predictors of radical right successes; yet the radical right is helped by slow but noticeable processes of ethnic pluralization. Finally, it will be seen that interaction between parties and movements is persistent, as is the competition between the radical right and its main competitors in the party system with programmatic spillover effects into the mainstream.

The final step (Chapter 6) concerns the question of the effects of the radical right. Starting from some scholars' observations of the limited effects of the radical right overall, controversially debated in the literature, in this chapter I will make the point that the East European radical right has lasting effects not only on nearby competitors but also on the larger political system. The level of government participation and policy making in coalition government (as in Poland, Slovakia, Romania, and more recently Latvia and Bulgaria) will be complemented by an analysis of interaction patterns between the radical right and the mainstream actors, including the state. Here, some fresh research on particular countries in the region is available for a more comparative approach. The major effect is not the implementation of a distinct set of radical right policies but rather the radicalization of parts of the mainstream, instead of a mainstreaming or "taming" of the radical right. This poses severe challenges to the democratic quality of the political systems in question.

NOTES

1. Eastern Europe denotes "the region, defined as the lands between the Gulf of Finland in the North and Greece in the South, and between Germany in the West and Russia in the East" (Bernhard and Jasiewicz 2015, 314). More specifically and for the purpose of this study, Eastern Europe after 1989 encompasses all EU member countries which formerly had communist regimes and were part of the Soviet Union or under its hegemony (see Minkenberg 2015a).
2. See Keno Verseck, "Orbáns Verbündete blasen zum Kampf gegen liberales Europa." *Der Spiegel* 7, January 2016 (http://www.spiegel.de/politik/ausland/viktor-orban-und-der-aufstand-gegen-das-system-eu-a-1070728.html; accessed November 21, 2016).

CHAPTER 2

Concepts: Analyzing the East European Radical Right

Abstract After a discussion of alternative terms and concepts such as fascism or populism, the author develops an operational definition of the "radical right" as exclusivist ultranationalism, grounded in modernization theory. He argues that this term can best capture the various actors on the far right in all parts of (democratic) Europe, covering party as well as non-party or movement-type actors. Despite the different contexts in which the radical right has operated in Eastern Europe up until today (the ramifications of the political transformation), as compared with its counterpart in Western Europe (the post-industrial context), a distinctly "East European" concept for these actors is not necessary. The chapter concludes with the presentation of an analytical model for studying the role of the radical right in the political process and its political impact.

Keywords Ultranationalism · Populism · Extremism · Modernization · Process model

Scholarship on the radical right employs a plethora of terms, concepts, and analytical models. For any comparative study it is essential to clarify key terms and concepts, and this is even more imperative when applying a concept which has been developed in the context of Western democracies to a region which has undergone—and still is experiencing—a profound regime change and the accompanying social, economic, and cultural changes. After a discussion of alternative terms and concepts, I develop an operational definition of the "radical right," one which is grounded in modernization theory, and I explain its applicability to Eastern Europe, as well as Western Europe. This term can best capture the various actors on the far right in all parts of (democratic) Europe, and party actors, as well as non-party or movement-type actors, can also be included in such a term. In other words, despite the different contexts in which the radical right has operated in Eastern Europe up until today (the ramifications of the political transformation), as compared to its counterpart in Western Europe (the post-industrial context), it is unnecessary to develop a distinctly "East European" concept for these actors. I also aim to provide an analytical model of the radical right as a collective actor in a more dynamic way than can be found in the typical demand-and-supply-side approaches and I suggest a process model for analyzing the political role and effects of the radical right.

1   A Concept of the Radical Right in Comparative Perspective

In the last two decades, a vast body of comparative literature on the radical right in established democracies has been published.[1] Most of the existing literature is preoccupied with the organizational and ideological features of these parties as well as explaining their success or failure at the polls after the revival and renewal of the radical right in the 1980s and 1990s. Typically, these explanations proceed by the logic of identifying relevant factors of demand and supply, with an increasing emphasis on the supply side (for example in Art 2011; Mudde 2007; Rydgren 2007).

Research on the radical right in Eastern Europe (for the regional label, see Chapter 1, note 1), though more recent and thus more limited in scope and quantity, looks at the phenomenon through the same lens. For a long time, only a few comparative and case studies existed; and they have become rather dated by now (see Ramet 1999; Mudde 2005b). While the number of case studies has certainly increased during the last decade (see e.g. Bíró Nagy et al. 2013; Mareš 2011; Mesežnikov and Gyárfášová 2008; Pankowski 2010; Sum 2010), many of these works still lack clear-cut references to or the application of the—admittedly limited—comparative approaches to the radical right in the region. So far, only the all-European study of the populist radical right by Cas

Mudde (2007) stands out as a systematic comparative analysis, yet here Eastern Europe is not treated as a distinct region (see also Bustikova and Kitschelt 2009; Minkenberg 2002a, 2010). Recently, new comparative scholarship has emerged which adds fresh data and insights into radical right interaction and dynamics in East European party systems, though it focuses only on overviews or a limited number of country cases (see the contributions to Minkenberg 2015a; Pirro 2015; Pytlas 2016).

The country-specific literature often points out particular characteristics of the radical right in the region, which distinguishes it from its West European counterpart. This can be generalized in a wider comparative fashion with the following specificities. East European radical right parties are characterized by a higher degree of movement-like features (weak structures, propensity for street politics), a more extreme and anti-democratic ideology, and more fluctuation or less success at the polls (see Minkenberg 2002a, 336; Mudde 2005a). Moreover, the movement sector appears more lively and violence-prone, and radical right violence in the East is met with less counter-mobilization and state vigilance than in the West (see Mudde 2005a). Yet, these results from the small body of literature are often rather vague and tentative—as the authors admit themselves—because they are based on scarce empirical data. Further, though the finding that the East European radical right is less successful than its West European counterparts (Stöss 2010) might still hold true, it is the case that several radical right parties have been able to stabilize their position as significant parliamentary forces over the last decade; in no less than five East European countries, radical right parties are or have been members of coalition governments or supported minority governments, that is once in Poland and Romania, twice in Bulgaria and Latvia, and three times in Slovakia (see Chapter 6 and Minkenberg 2013a, 2015b; Mudde 2007).

The consequences of radical right parties in power, as well as the impact of the radical right in general, that is their role in the process of post-communist transformation and consolidation, has only recently attracted the attention of scholarly research (see Minkenberg 2015a; Pytlas 2016). So far, the bulk of this kind of research has mainly focused on Western Europe. Various studies demonstrate, for example, how the radical right changed or radicalized public opinion and discourse, altered the positions and strategic behavior of mainstream parties, affected government policies, or induced counter-activities by state actors and civil society.[2]

Despite its late start and cursory findings (see Minkenberg 2002a, 361; Mudde 2005a, 267), research on the East European radical right has progressed considerably in recent years. Due to the contribution of pioneering comparative works as well as the recent increase of in-depth case studies, the mapping of the field has developed significantly. Yet, recent developments call for more attention. Besides outlining demand- and supply-side factors in the development of the region's radical right, a look at the effect of radical right parties and their corollaries on politics and society is necessary. This concerns in particular the interplay of the strategies of radical right parties' and the reaction of mainstream parties' (in the vein of such studies as McAdam 1999; Minkenberg 1998, Chapter 9; Tilly and Tarrow 2006). So far, evidence for the impact of the radical right and its interaction with its social and political environment are largely absent from the literature on the East European radical right (with exceptions such as Mudde 2005b, 2007, Chapter 12; and recent works by Minkenberg 2015a; Pirro 2015; Pytlas 2016).

In the research on the radical right, definitions of right-wing radicalism vary widely and terminology remains contested. Despite the rapid growth of this research field, the "war of words" (Mudde 1996) or the "taxonomic chaos" (Olsen 2000) persists. However, this debate will not be continued here. Following my earlier conceptualization of the radical right, the term includes all variants of collective actors (parties, movements, sub-cultural milieus) which emerge in times of accelerated political, socioeconomic, and cultural change and which fight such change by radicalizing the inclusionary and exclusionary criteria of national or in-group belonging (see Minkenberg 1998, 29–47, 2013a; see also Carter 2005, 14–20; Kitschelt 2007, 1179). Such a modernization-theoretical approach attempts to avoid the widespread practice of using ad hoc definitions which often read like shopping lists of the main definitional criteria (see discussion in Minkenberg 2000).

An early explanatory approach of the success of right-wing radicalism, which explicitly dwells on concepts of social change, is provided by German sociologists Erwin Scheuch and Hans-Dieter Klingemann (1967). Their model is based on the assumption that the potential for radical right-wing movements exists in all industrial societies and should be understood as a "normal pathological" condition. In all fast-growing modernizing countries there are people who cannot cope with rapid economic and cultural development and who react to the pressures of readjustment with rigidity and closed-mindedness. If the available supply by the mainstream parties loses its persuasiveness or alignments weaken, these reactions can be mobilized by right-wing movements or parties, which offer political philosophies that promise an elimination of pressures and a simpler, better society. These philosophies do not contain just any thinkable utopia but are usually a romanticized version of the nation before the first large wave of modernization. That is, the two sociologists postulate that the core of the problem consists of a specifically asynchronous dealing with the past, especially a dissent from an evaluation of modernity in the respective societies.

Cas Mudde in his response to the "normal pathology thesis" (2007, 296–297, and 2010; see also Pytlas 2016, 6–7) argues that the thesis postulates the radical right as an outsider or anomaly in liberal democracies; instead it should be seen as a "pathological normalcy" in terms of a radicalization of mainstream ideas. But this critique rests on the assumption of a disconnect between the radical right and the mainstream. It overlooks the fact that the concept of the radical right (as romantic ultranationalism or similarly defined) does not postulate a clear-cut difference between the democratic center and the far right—unlike concepts such as fascism or extremism theory (see below, where the distinctions between the radical right, the extreme, fascism, etc. will be addressed and clarified). As has been shown elsewhere (Minkenberg 1998, 2002b, 2013a), the radical right can be conceptualized in a more dynamic way as a bridge or hinge between the mainstream and an extreme right which is clearly disconnected from the mainstream, but whose success still rests on the condition of accelerated social change which "sets free" the normal pathological potential.

Many explanatory approaches include—implicitly or explicitly—arguments derived from modernization theory; and they persuasively indicate the conditions for a successful mobilization of right-wing radicalism (see Betz 1994 for an early account). However, they tell us rather little about the ideology of the radical right itself. It seems useful to build on modernization theory not just in terms of the societal context for mobilization but also in order to identify the core ideology of the phenomenon, not least because these theories might provide some conceptually grounded criteria for such analyses which might help to overcome the arbitrariness of the shopping list approaches (see Minkenberg 2000). This is not the place, however, to review the vast amount of literature on modernization theory (see Knöbl 2003). Suffice it to say that even if modernization is thought of as a concept capturing European or more generally Western processes, it can be applied to political developments in Eastern Europe. Broadly, modernization can be understood as a growing autonomy of the individual (status mobility and role flexibility) and an ongoing functional differentiation of society in combination with rationalization and a growing autonomy of societal subsystems (see Rucht 1994, 54). In this light, right-wing radicalism can be defined as the radical effort to undo such social change (Minkenberg 1998, 35–47). The counter-concept to social differentiation is the nationally defined community; the counter-concept to individualization is the return to traditional roles and the status of the individual in such a community. It is this overemphasis on, or radicalization of, images of social homogeneity which characterizes radical right-wing thinking. Understood in this way, the historical origins of right-wing radicalism can be seen in the interdependence of nation building, democratization, industrialization, and the growing importance of the natural sciences (see Minkenberg 1998, 39–43; Smith 2001, 21–42), though some trace the origins back to early modernity (Greenfeld 1992; Marx 2003).

Hence, right-wing radicalism will be defined primarily by the ideological criteria of a populist and romantic ultranationalism, a myth of a homogeneous nation which puts the latter before the individual and his or her civil rights and which therefore is directed against liberal and pluralist democracy (though not necessarily in favor of a fascist state), its underlying values of freedom and equality, and the related categories of individualism and universalism (see Minkenberg 2000; also Mudde 2000a, Chapter 7). This definition focuses explicitly on the idea of the nation as the ultimate focal point, situated somewhere between the poles of *demos* and *ethnos*. The nationalistic myth consists of the construction of an idea of nation and national belonging by radicalizing criteria of exclusion. These can be ethnically based, but also cultural, that is religious, and aim at an extreme cultural or ethnic homogeneity of the primary group and a congruence between the state and the nation (Smith 2001, 34). Whatever the criteria, this ideology involves a radical in-group/out-group distinction, to which can be added the propensity for a regime that strictly enforces these distinctions, that is an authoritarian order or strong state. Indeed, right-wing radical thinking, in its modernization-theoretical conception espoused here, is thoroughly intertwined with an authoritarian, that is fiercely anti-egalitarian and anti-emancipatory, view of the world which includes a top-down approach to politics and the corresponding emphasis on strong leadership as well as the absence of internal democracy in radical right groups and organizations (see Minkenberg 1998, 37–47; Mudde 2007, 22–23). This concept echoes the social theory developed in the grid/group model, the two political dimensions of which consist of boundary drawing between the in-group and the out-group, with the emphasis of a high level of in-group homogeneity on the one hand, and the level of strictness in enforcing the rules (strong or authoritarian state) on the other (see Douglas and Wildavsky 1982; Kitschelt 2007, 1179).

A list of such group boundaries drawn in radical right discourse and their underlying logic is provided in Table 2.1.

Analytically, these criteria are distinct and have their own rationale. In the real world, however, they are often mixed together, and it is the task of the researcher to disentangle them and reveal the respective or prevailing rationale of right-wing thinking. The concept of "nativism" here corresponds to its use in Mudde's and other definitions, as a version of xenophobia directed at all threats—imagined or real—to the native population's identity and homogeneity (see Mudde 2007, 18–19). Nativism then becomes a radical right ideology when its components

Table 2.1 In-group/out-group criteria in right-wing radical discourse (following W. Heitmeyer's concept of group-based enmity)

Criteria of exclusion	Core argument
Racism	Inferiority of the "other" on the grounds of biological difference ("natural" hierarchy)
Anti-Semitism	Special case of racism (here understood as modern as opposed to traditional anti-Semitism)
Ethnocentrism	Superiority of own collectivity on the grounds of cultural and economic achievements (developmental differentiation)
Xenophobia	Defensive reaction against ethnic and cultural "others" (fight for resources, fear of "cultural mixing")
Nativism	Special case of xenophobia (in immigration countries the rejection of foreign influences regardless of ethnicity)
Religiocentrism (Fundamentalism)	Superiority of own collectivity on the grounds of a particular faith and exclusionary access to "truth"
Heterophobia	Intolerance to deviation from mainstream norms (unacceptability of moral "others," also within own ethnicity)

Sources: Minkenberg (1998, 119); Heitmeyer (2005, 14–15); Zick et al. 2011. An expanded list of in-group/out-group distinctions can be found in Heitmeyer (2012).

of nationalism and xenophobia are complemented by authoritarian features (ibid., 24) which translate the populist impulse of right-wing radicalism, that is the anti-establishment thrust and the identification of "the people" as the only source of political authority, into a top-down relationship between the leader of the party (movement) and the masses (see Griffin 1991, 36; Minkenberg 1998, 44).

Historically, the radicalized notion of national homogeneity resulted from the transformation of an emancipatory nationalism to an integral or official version (see Alter 1985; Anderson 1983) and culminated in a romantic ultranationalist myth of belonging by the end of the nineteenth century; as such, it borders on or even inhabits chiliastic, that is quasi-religious, characteristics, especially when moral qualities of the nation and the notion of a national rebirth are added (see Griffin 1991, 32–33). Some authors insist on including anti-system attitudes or opposition to democracy as an essential definitional criterion (Backes and Jesse 1989; Ignazi 1992, 2003). But these attributes are often under-specified since there is a significant difference between those who reject the entire democratic order and those who want less democracy but more state, or less state and more democracy (see Carter 2005, 42). According to the definition used here, right-wing radicalism is not the antithesis of democracy per se. In other words, the radical right as defined here is not necessarily in favor of doing away with democracy but wants government by "the people" in terms of *ethnocracy* (see Griffin 1999, 308–315).

In sociological terms, the radical right may be an "extremism of the center" (Lipset 1963), or some alliance between the working and middle class (Kitschelt 1995; Rydgren 2013), but here it is primarily understood in an ideological way and part of the political-programmatic spectrum in distinction to other party families, most of which constitute the "mainstream" (see Meguid 2005, 2008). In light of the logic of party families, the labels "populist right" or "right-wing populism" without any further specification (see Albertazzi 2009; Decker 2006; Mény and Surel 2000; Wodak 2015) do not add much analytical traction, since populism is a rather elusive category. While some, like Margaret Canovan, stress the ideological components such as a political program organized around anti-elitism and an appeal to "the people" to justify criticism of representative democracy (see Canovan 1981, 289–294; also Berlet and Lyons 2000, 4–13), others see it more as an issue of style than of substance and as of temporary quality. In the words of Paul Taggart:

populism is a reaction against the ideas, institutions and practices of representative politics which celebrates an implicit or explicit heartland as a response to a sense of crisis; however, lacking universal key values, it is chameleonic, taking on attributes of its environment, and, in practice, is episodic. (Taggart 2000, 5; see also Kazin 1995)

The characterization of "chameleonic" and "episodic" clearly does not fit such groups as the French Front National, the Danish People's Party, or the Slovak National Party. Even the more clearly specified version of an "Alpine populism" combining xenophobia, market liberalism, and the celebration of the Alpine region's alleged cultural distinctiveness (see Betz 2005) contains more ideology and endurance than being an episodic protest against accelerated change and therefore can be situated squarely in the concept of the radical right as used here.

Other authors prefer the label right-wing extremist or extreme right, pointing out that radicalism has its roots in the political left during and after the French revolution and that the far right groups exhibit anti-system, that is anti-democratic, attitudes (see Ignazi 2003). The term right-wing extremism is particularly widespread in the German debate. Several political scientists such as Uwe Backes or Eckard Jesse (1989) use the concept as applied by the German Offices for the Protection of the Constitution and their annual reports (for an application to Eastern Europe, see Thieme 2007). These concepts are rooted in a theory of extremism which defines the radical or extreme right as a variant of a more general and genuine extremism, the polar opposite of liberal, constitutional democracy. Thus, the key definitional criterion is the extremists' opposition to the constitution. However, this definition is heavily centered on judicial criteria which are generated by public institutions and state actors and stem from the particular German concept of *wehrhafte Demokratie*, or militant democracy (see Jaschke 1994, 25–31). For comparative research, the German concept is only of limited use (for comparative versions of militant democracy, see Capoccia 2013; Müller 2012). As in Mudde (2007, 25), "extremism" will be preserved for the explicitly anti-democratic and/or violent right.

This also holds true for the contested concept of fascism which is still widely used though more as a politically charged term than as an analytical category—except in historical studies. Postwar history of the research of fascism has undergone a massive transformation, from Seymour M. Lipset's (1963) famous definition of it as the "extremism of the center" (i.e. an anti-liberal protest of the middle classes against capitalism and socialism) to the revival and readjustment of the concept by Roger Griffin (1991), Wolfgang Wippermann (1983), and others. Their reading of fascism as a generic anti-liberal movement of palingenetic ultranationalism subsumes a diverse group of actors from historical fascists of the interwar period to the current parties of the radical and populist right in West and East. Here, fascism will be confined to those organizations, individuals, and ideologies which use historical fascism as their reference and, hence, are clearly anti-democratic.

It should have become evident that the concept of the radical right does not suggest a homogeneous group of actors, such as the family of communist parties. The radical right needs to be differentiated in ideological as well as organizational terms, especially regarding the issue as to where to draw the line between the margin and the mainstream, and how and under which circumstances the radical right can move from the former to the latter, or transform (in segments) from one kind of actor (such as a party or a movement organization) to another. Here, the comparative literature offers various approaches, such as Ignazi's (2003) distinction between the classical extreme right and the post-industrialist extreme right; Kitschelt's typology of fascism, welfare chauvinism, anti-statist populism, and the new radical right (1995); or Carter's five-group typology of neo-Nazi parties, neo-fascist parties, authoritarian xenophobic parties, neo-liberal xenophobic parties, and neo-liberal populist parties (2005, 50–51).

In a similar vein and following my earlier work, a fundamental ideological dividing line can be seen in the question as to whether today's radical right embraces historical (interwar) movements, ideologies, or regimes of Nazism, fascism, or other clearly anti-democratic, right-wing, authoritarian ideas or leaders, or whether it advocates a more contemporary, racist, or ethnocentrist nationalism, allowing for a less extreme version of the radical right and introducing non-ethnic elements of exclusionist ultranationalism, such as religion (see Table 2.1). The latter version has been seen as an expression of a new radical right (see Prowe 1998; Minkenberg 1998, 2000, 2013a; Ignazi 2003; Bornschier 2010) to be explained by accelerated modernization processes in Western societies that occurred during the 1960s and 1970s. Across all national differences, similar societal developments correspond with a rise of the radical right in many countries and cannot be discussed here in full. They include, along with the more specific issues of immigration and multiculturalism, reform of the welfare state and the advent of neoliberal politics and globalization—rather far reaching social and cultural changes which have been identified by numerous authors as "post-industrialism," "value change," "late capitalism," "the other modernity," and so on (see Beck 1992; Inglehart 1977, 1997; Minkenberg 2000). In this modernization shift, the following factors dominate: cultural orientations, a sharpened sense of crisis, the primacy of the "life world" (*Lebenswelt* in Habermas's reading), and the central role of education, language, and communication. The process can be read as a new phase of individualization and pluralization, following the above definition of modernization, and as the de-emphasis of established authority, both religious and rational-legal in the Weberian sense.

The political consequences of this modernization shift have been interpreted in various ways with regard to the democratic order in Western societies. Some see it as a "democratization of democracy," that is a narrowing of the distance between the democratic state and the citizens, a reformulation of citizenship, and an increase of responsiveness (Offe 2003; Dalton 2008, 255). Others point out the "overload of democracy" which is confronted with growing demands, alongside a more individualistic culture, which cannot be met by the established system and which result in a decoupling of citizens and the state and a "post-democratic" situation which consists of a reduction of politics to the merely symbolic (Crouch 2004). It remains controversial whether these developments amount to a real crisis of democracy (see Merkel 2014; Blühdorn 2013). But what they signify is a new complexity of contemporary Western societies and changes in the democratic quality of their political orders which provide opportunities for a radical populist critique of political elites and the representative system.

This admittedly very brief characterization may suffice to illuminate the fact that, in Western societies since the 1970s, a new dynamism and pace of social and cultural change has occurred, the very ingredient which helps to manifest the "normal pathology" of right-wing radicalism mentioned earlier. But the mobilization now occurs in the context of a new cleavage of political forces. The "silent revolution" of post-materialist value change, new social movements, and left-libertarian or Green parties is now followed by a "silent counter-revolution," a materialist-authoritarian reaction of radical right parties and movements (see Minkenberg and Inglehart 1989; Ignazi 1992; Minkenberg 1993). The new radical right differs from its right-wing predecessors as well as from conservatism both in terms of its ideology and its support patterns. It is the right-wing pole of a new conflict axis which cuts across the established party spectrum. That is, in both ideological and social respects, it is the polar opposite of the post-materialist New Left, new social movements, and related parties or party factions (see Minkenberg 1993, 1998; Kitschelt 1995; Bornschier 2010). In other words: the new complexities of the latest modernization shift has resulted in a rearranged political spectrum in which traditional alignments of voter groups (e.g. the working class and the lower strata with left-wing politics, the middle class with conservative parties) weaken and political space opens up for parties and movements of the new radical right, among others. At the same time, political participation declines and becomes socially more selective in terms of an emerging "elitization" of politics, that is the increasing role of education and cultural capitals in the new "mini publics" of political debates and decisions (see Shapiro 2003). Only in the context of this structural change and its accompanying processes of realignment and dealignment of voters do single issues like immigration, which are not new issues per se, gain new significance and a mobilizing function.

2 Conceptual Enlargement: The Radical Right and the East European Context

The application of the modernization-theoretical argument to post-1989 Eastern Europe rests on the assumption of a comparable political-historical framework of consolidating democracies, which share many political, social, and cultural legacies of European history such as Christianity and the Enlightenment, industrialization, the idea of the nation-state, and the democratic reference. These characteristics can also be found in the new democracies in Eastern Europe but to varying degrees and in the particular context of lower levels of industrialization than in most of Western Europe, a limited experience with democracy as a political regime, and a post-communist past completely absent in Western Europe (see Jowitt 1992; Janos 2000). Therefore the application of the concept is not without problems. However, the proposed main origin of radical right thinking and mobilization, a profound and accelerated modernization process, is very obvious in the form of the political and social transition these countries have experienced since 1989.

In general, the transformation process in Central and Eastern Europe is more far-reaching, deeper, and complex than the current and previous modernization processes in the West; and it occurred at a high pace (see Von Beyme 1994, 12–14; also Ekiert and Hanson 2003; Elster et al. 1998; Kornai 2006). First, it includes the collapse not only of political regimes but also of their legitimating ideologies. Thus, a simple return to left-wing or socialist ideas as a recourse by the "losers" of this modernization process is only a limited option. Right-wing groups, or those which combine socialist with nationalist ideas, can benefit from this constellation. Second, the democratization of regimes has been accompanied by an economic and social transformation which touched all aspects of life, thus making it different from earlier waves of democratization or "redemocratization" such as the German and Italian cases after World War II. The complexity of the transformation process produces large "transformation costs" (see Nelson 1998), which can benefit the radical right. Third, the exchange of entire social systems has caused high levels of social disorientation and ambivalence towards the new order. Again, political entrepreneurs who offer simple solutions and appeal to "the people" or the nation rather than a particular social class or a universal vision of progress have a competitive advantage. In addition, the accompanying cultural change challenges the acceptance of the new order in that the socio-cultural conflict has taken over the regime divide as the most prevalent cleavage structuring political competition (see Pytlas 2016, 4–7). "Identity politics" or "value wars," that is enduring debates on national identity and other collective identities, controversy about moral norms, and accompanying conflicts between traditionalists and modernizers, have superimposed other conflict dimensions such as the socioeconomic one after the initial phase of transformation and the mitigation of the regime divide (see Ágh 2009; Beichelt 2001; Ekiert and Kubik 2014; Huber and Inglehart 1995; Pytlas 2013).

In sum, these transformation-induced opportunity structures, which lie behind the institutional settings of liberal democracy as they are put into place in most Eastern European countries, must be seen as generally favorable to ultranationalist appeals of the radical right. It is also clear that these processes are fundamentally different from the Western transition from industrial to post-industrial society, one of the key context factors for the emergence of a new, or post-industrial, radical right. The transformation process is a multiple modernization process, that is the transition to a liberal democracy and to market capitalism along with elements of a change from industrialism to post-industrialism, which often involves aspects of simultaneous nation and state-building as well. As a result, the radical right in the region combines post-industrial aspects such as the use of modern mass media, issue politics, and the decreasing role of mass (party) organizations with the legacies and ideologies of a particular past, that is the mix of traditional nationalism in the East and the residues of state socialism.

Regarding the region-specific varieties of right-wing radical ideologies and historical references, the experience of state socialism and the lack of any long-lasting democratic practice must be taken into account. In fact, it has been suggested that new typologies of right-wing radical parties in Central and Eastern Europe be created, for example by classifying them according to the origins of their ideological identity. Cas Mudde (200b) proposes distinguishing between pre-communist radical right parties which are rooted in the political culture and ideas of the period before communism (such as the Russian Pamyat or Polish PWN-PSN), communist radical right parties which are characterized by a combination of nationalism and nostalgia for the communist past (like the Romanian PRM and PUNR), and post-communist radical right parties which are newly established and focus on current issues (like the Serbian Radical Party or the Russian LDPR) (see also Shafir 2000). But characterizing such parties according to their *historical* origins does not automatically translate into ideological types. Radical right parties which emerged in Eastern Europe after 1989 may or may not have a strong longing for some part of the country's past; they may focus on current issues *and* cultivate the (reinvented) nationalist image of some part of the country's non-democratic past. That is, the categories of pre- and post-communist radical right seem ideologically unspecified.

However, distinguishing variants of the radical right, whether in Western or Eastern Europe, remains important. Following the above definition and the fundamental distinction between clearly anti-democratic, or fascist or otherwise extremist, versions and those which play, more or less, by the rules of the game, the concept of the radical right here includes the populist radical right à la Mudde (2007) as well as the not so populist radical right. These considerations lead to a typology for Eastern Europe which follows the modernization-theoretical argument in that the ideological variants can be identified according to the respective concept of nation and the exclusionary criteria applied (see Minkenberg 1998, Chapter 1, 2013a). The fundamental distinction between an extreme and a non-extreme radical right, as outlined above, provides the basis for the categorization. Racist, xenophobic, nativist, and ethnocentric criteria of exclusion, as spelled out in Table 2.1, will be subsumed under the category of a non-extreme radical right. If, however, ethnocentrism occurs in combination with the justification or application of political violence, the advocacy to abolish liberal democracy, or the celebration of past dictatorial regimes or leaders it will be regarded as the extreme variant. In addition, another, not necessarily xenophobic or racist, version of the radical right is that of religious ultra-nationalism which usually occurs together with "heterophobia" (Table 2.1, which turns into the specific expression of homophobia in a moral-religious context). This operation leads to a threefold typology of the radical right:

1. An extremist or autocratic-fascist right, usually anti-democratic in terms of opposition to the new democratic order or support for past dictatorial regimes/leaders, often including racism or xenophobia and exhibiting more militancy and/or an affinity to violence;
2. A racist or ethnocentrist right, but neither fascist nor clearly anti-democratic or anti-system, with democracy as a political regime for the "true nationals" only, i.e. in an ethnocratic sense;
3. A religious-fundamentalist right, in which nationalism merges with religious rigidity in an anti-liberal and anti-pluralistic way. (Minkenberg 1998, 237–240, 2008, 12–20; also Carter 2005, 41–50; Mudde 2007, 41–50)

All three variants have in common a strong quest for internal homogeneity of the nation as the primary "we-group"—a rejection of difference and pluralization—and a populist anti-establishment political style (see previous section and Minkenberg 1998, Chapter 7; also Kitschelt 2007, 1179–1180). More versions can be established, such as in Carter's fivefold typology (2005, 50–51). However, her distinction between radical right parties which want more democracy and less state and those which want less democracy and more state is hard to operationalize since "more democracy" often translates into less democracy for the out-groups. Furthermore, the difference between neo-Nazi and neo-fascist groups, with both being defined as outwardly anti-democratic but the latter having no ethnocentrist or anti-immigrant agenda, may be more conceptually than empirically relevant: in Western Europe, only very small groups in Spain are detected as neo-fascist, except for the Italian MSI. In Eastern Europe, immigration has not been a significant issue at all until very recently, but ethnocentrism is pervasive; hence such a distinction does not apply (see Chapter 3). As to a category of a "populist right" as opposed to a radical right (see Minkenberg 2013a; also Kitschelt 2007, 1179), one can distinguish two versions: (i) those which emerged from a transformation within the party (FPÖ, AfD) and (ii) those which emerged from a transformation due to outside forces (PiS, Fidesz). The first belongs to the party family of the radical right and seems more prevalent in Western Europe; the second, contrary to Pankowski (2010), should not be grouped into this party family because it remains ideologically more diverse and diffuse than the first one.

For Eastern European democracies, it has been suggested furthermore to distinguish between fascist-autocratic and nationalist-communist ideologies, depending on the radical right's point of reference to interwar fascist or right-wing authoritarian regimes such as Horthy's in Hungary or to nationalist communist regimes as they evolved in Ceauşescu's Romania (see Beichelt and Minkenberg 2002; Ishiyama 2009). However, with the growing historical distance to 1989 and the retreat of communist ideology, such a distinction has become increasingly difficult to uphold. The Romanian case illustrates the problem of such a distinction as significant parts of the radical right since the 1990s have embraced both the legacies of Ceauşescu and the interwar fascist leader Antonescu (see Frusetta and Glont 2009; Cinpoeş 2013). Hence, such a category seems superfluous.

The second dimension of differentiating variants of radical right actors consists of organizational typologies. Conventionally, radical right parties are distinguished by their strength as measured in terms of organizational features, membership, and electoral support (see Art 2011). Variations are explained in the party and electoral research literature by pointing both at ideological variations and the degree of fragmentation of the radical right party sector and the political and electoral system on the one hand, and at other parties' strategies, that is the "political space" for the radical right, on the other (see for example Betz 1994; Kitschelt 1995; Norris 2005). These are primarily institutional or political-structural explanations which do not make reference to cultural variables such as political or other traditions. Moreover, they ignore the non-party sector of right-wing radical mobilization, which may have repercussions for the electoral performance of these parties. Already in 1988, Klaus von Beyme had argued that future studies of right-wing extremism will have to pay more attention to the whole political context of this political movement instead of being preoccupied with traditional party and electoral studies. (Von Beyme 1988, 16)

Following this pledge, the organizational variants of the radical right will be distinguished by their approach to institutional political power and public resonance (for details, see Minkenberg 1998, Chapter 7, 2015b). The most obvious and most frequently studied are parties and electoral campaign organizations which participate in elections and try to win public office. Next to these are social movement organizations that try to mobilize public support as well but do not run for office; rather they identify with a larger social movement (a network of networks with a distinct collective identity) and offer interpretative frames for particular problems (see Tarrow 1994, 2012; Benford and Snow 2000). Finally, smaller groups and socio-cultural milieus operate relatively independently of parties or larger social movements and do not exhibit formal organizational structures, though they can also be characterized as networks with links to other organizations and a collective identity which tends to be more extreme than that of the parties or movement organizations (including higher levels of violence). They represent a "micro-mobilization potential" for the radical right (Bergmann 1994; Kaplan and Lööw 2002).

Since the radical right is conceptualized here as a collective actor rather than a party family, such a perspective requires the combination of party research with movement research. But even if the radical right is treated as a party family, movement research can inform the analysis because radical right parties almost by definition engage in "contentious politics" (Tilly and Tarrow 2006), challenging all other parties, that is the entire party system, and even the political order rather than merely seeking office or a change in policy (see Minkenberg 1998, Chapter 1, 2003). On this account, most of the parties of the radical right blur the lines between political parties and movements and can be interpreted as "movement parties" which according to Kitschelt (2006) apply organizational and strategic practices from social movements (without necessarily having originated from social movements, as Kitschelt stipulates). This becomes even more imperative when studying the radical right in the political process, its interaction with others, and its effects (for an application of this research to the West European radical right, see Minkenberg 2002b, 2009b, 2013b).

3 Modeling the Mobilization and Interaction of the Radical Right

Models trying to explain successful radical right mobilization generally follow the logic of highlighting the demand and supply-side factors (as in Mudde 2007), though the factors identified as relevant vary across the literature and research field. This concerns in particular the role of culture which is often absent in party research; instead the institutional context, the electoral market as well as party ideology, organization, and personnel dominate (see Akkerman and de Lange 2012; Carter 2005; Kitschelt 1995; Mudde 2007; Norris 2005). This seems noteworthy, since right-wing radical parties position themselves more strongly around cultural norms and focus in particular on the role of national symbolism and patterns of interpretation, in contrast to liberal or social democratic parties (see Minkenberg 1998, 44–47; Mudde 2007, 119–137). Ultimately, their legitimacy plays a critical role in their mobilization of support, although their critics and opponents constantly question such legitimacy (see also Art 2011). Hence, despite the importance of structure, a cultural dimension of the explanatory variables is reintroduced into the comparison. In contrast, movement research explicitly considers the role of political culture or at least cultural variables. Here political culture will be conceptualized as a measure of ideological schisms and cultural differentiations, or as the influence of particular political traditions (authoritarian, participatory, revolutionary) on the respective conflict cultures and their formal and informal rules in each case (Rucht 1994, 311). On another level, political culture plunges into the concept of "framing" or of "cultural resonance," that is to say into the corresponding measure of the range of social values and of those themes raised by movements and of the construction of "meaning" (Benford and Snow 2000; Gamson 1988). In the words of Tarrow, "social movements are deeply involved in the work of 'naming' grievances, connecting them to other grievances and constructing larger frames of meaning that will resonate with a population's cultural predispositions and communicate a uniform message to powerholders and others" (Tarrow 1994, 122), which is precisely what radical right parties do.

In a comprehensive sense, political culture constitutes the "subjective dimension" of politics. It bestows meaning in political action (Almond and Powell 1966, 50), bringing symbols and political meanings together. The concept of cultural resonance or "framing" connects the meaning of cultural symbols, with respect to their availability, with strategies and power relations among social actors. The "framing" marks a double act of connection, that is the endeavor to unite collective actors with individual cognitive orientations, and a cultural adoption of identifiable "resonant" ideas or traditions in the broader public or particular subcultures with those of collective actors (Tarrow 1994, 122; McAdam 1994, 37–38; see also Benford and Snow 2000). In this context, cultural resonance does not mean the effect of collective action, but instead a condition for the possibility of establishing these connections altogether.

According to the definition of the radical right proposed here, the cultural resonance of themes of a right-wing radical discourse is based, above all, on the specific national understanding of a society. With this understanding, a radical right can mobilize public support while simultaneously demarcating themselves from the discourse of the prevailing elites and drafting a counter-discourse. The necessity to challenge the ruling national elites' interpretation of national interests by their own "genuine" interpretation generally contributes to the radicalizing of nationalist discourses and the construction of conspiracy theories (see Minkenberg 1998, 53–57).

A final aspect of cultural constraints and opportunities for right-wing radical mobilization are dominant religious traditions. The literature often refers to the constraining or facilitating roles of particular traditions regarding the resonance of radical right-wing appeals. For example, scholarship on Germany stresses that, while in the last years of the Weimar Republic the NSDAP did not succeed in mobilizing many Catholic voters, Protestants were more receptive to their message (see e.g. Falter 1991). In other countries, such as Spain and Italy, Poland and Slovakia, the Catholic Church facilitated the rise of ultranationalism in the nation-building period or even the establishment of fascist regimes (see Anderson 2003; Grzymała-Busse 2015). The radical right's use of cultural codes of "otherness" or "us vs them" can therefore be tied to the nexus between nation-building or national identity and the dominant religious traditions—and these interconnections should be tested regarding their implications for ideological and organizational variants of the radical right in each country (see Minkenberg 2017 forthcoming).

Besides these culture-bound factors shaping radical right-wing party formation and movement mobilization, there are also structural aspects which inform these processes. In the party research the cleavage model and electoral systems are widely used (see Carter 2005; Norris 2005) while movement research often draws on the concept of opportunity structures, which can be distinguished according to the proximity of the collective actors (see Tarrow 2012, 80–83). Some authors have endeavored to connect both models (Kriesi et al. 1995; Kitschelt 1995; Minkenberg 1998). Generally, it can be assumed that the chances for new movements and parties to mobilize their latent support increase as existing cleavages weaken and new polarization arises that cannot be integrated into the existing conflict structures (see Kriesi et al. 1995, 5–6). This means that the mobilization chances for new collective actors are greatest when some traditional elites lose control over their clientele and old ties weaken, and also when old conflicts are strongly institutionalized and hence become less significant to public controversies. According to Kitschelt (1995) and others, the convergence of established actors along older cleavages contributes to freeing up the right fringe in political space, which can then be successfully mobilized by some radical right-wing actor. But a weakening of existing conflict lines contributes above all to mobilization, if a new polarization occurs across the entire political spectrum and not just as a weakening on the right-wing pole (see Inglehart 1997; Minkenberg 1993, 1998). Political opportunity structures can be understood generally as "consistent, but not necessarily formal or permanent, dimensions of the political environment that provide incentives for people to undertake collective action by affecting their expectations for success or failure" (Tarrow 1994, 85). Among these, formal institutions, the role of authority, in particular the role of the state, and the strategies of established elites must be counted—this accounts for movement as well as for niche party mobilization (see Meguid 2005; Tarrow 2012, 77–87).

Given the "outsider role" of radical right actors, the organizational structures of the state and its approach to outside actors appear also important, as has been acknowledged in movement research for a long time. Kriesi et al. isolate three arenas of collective action upon which opportunity structures have an effect: the parliamentary arena, the administrative arena, and the arena of street-level participation: "the strength of the state is, first of all, a function of two general structural parameters...: the degree of the state's (territorial) centralization and the degree of its (functional) separation of state power" (Kriesi et al. 1995, 28; see also Minkenberg 1998, Chapter 7, and 2008, 28–30).

Therefore attention should be paid to specific aspects of institutional structures, such as the state in its entirety, as for example the structure of party systems or the degree to which parties are either open of closed to the bringing of demands from outside of the system into it

(Rucht 1994, 308–309). In addition, the possibilities of state institutions to repress new collective actors, as well as the application of repressive measures in concrete cases, must be assessed, especially given the foundations and rules of the game for existing political systems which are explicitly or implicitly challenged by the radical right:

> Representative states' commitments to pluralism make it easy to marshal support for repressive measures against those who do not share pluralism's values. Liberal systems can be ferociously illiberal when challenged by those who do not share liberalism's values. (Tarrow 1994, 94; see also Bleich 2011)

Since repression can also lead to increased solidarity among those affected and to amplification of collective identity, the effects are not definite. Still it can be generally anticipated that, although repression does not necessarily affect the degree of mobilization, it still makes an impact on the action repertoire: "like facilitation, repression is typically selective. By focusing on more radical organizations and actions, it will reduce the amount of radical mobilization" (Kriesi et al. 1995, 39). As the most extreme expression of collective action, violence approaches a critical function in the use of state repression and movement mobilization. Principally the violence of collective actors, like the state repression of violence, generates a delegitimization of the actor, often mobilizing the general public. In the forum of mobilization processes in elections, other strategies and supporters of action must be considered in the context of the party system, which are summarized here as external conditions of mobilization, similar to the "external supply side" in Mudde (2007). They affect not only the mobilization of the radical right (such as electoral results) but also, and possibly more importantly, its role in the political process and its impact.

A model which helps explain the particular role of the radical right in these processes must take into account the dynamics of interaction between the radical right and other political actors (political parties, civil society, police forces) as well as the cultural and institutional context in which such interaction takes place (see McAdam 1999: xiv). More specifically, the impact of the radical right, configured as "interaction effects" and influenced by the strategic response of other actors as well as the cultural and institutional context, does not occur linearly but takes place on various levels and to varying degrees, for example agenda setting and policy making levels, as well as the degree of activity or passivity of public response patterns (see Downs 2012; Minkenberg 2001, 2002b, 2009b, 2013a, 2013b; Mudde 2005a, 2007; Williams 2006).

The processes and patterns of interaction and resulting effects in the different arenas are influenced by specific strategic options of the political system and its agents as well as other actors and the public vis-à-vis the radical right, including the timing of their application. The strategic reactions are situated between the poles of demarcation and confrontation on the one side and co-optation and incorporation on the other, supplemented by a strategy of ignoring potential contenders on the right-wing fringe (Downs 2001, 2012; Meguid 2005, 2008). Moreover, parties do not only compete with the radical right by co-opting their issue positions, but also by taking over their narrative framing of specific issues (Pytlas 2016). Interaction is however not only limited to political parties; the state and civil society also interact with the radical right. Following Downs (2012), co-optation or collaboration strategies by mainstream actors may reduce the votes for and the mobilization potential of the radical right. Yet, this short-term gain is likely to be outweighed by long-term effects which pose risks for democracy, such as a radicalization of the mainstream. This mechanism is of utmost importance to the democratic development of the young democracies in Eastern Europe since mainstream parties and discourses are often already more radicalized than in Western Europe (see Minkenberg 2002a, 2013a; Mudde 2005a; Pankowski 2010; also various contributions in Minkenberg 2015a). As will be shown further below (Chapters 3 and 6), the radicalism of parts of the mainstream in the region can be attributed to particular contextual factors such as the interrupted nation-building processes and legacies of the communist past (see Minkenberg 2009a; Bernhard 2015).

Based on these considerations and earlier work (Minkenberg 2015a), the impact of the radical right is modeled here as "interaction effects." Regarding these effects, a distinction will be made between direct impact, that is effects which can be directly attributed to the radical right, such as policies or administrative acts executed by radical right parties in government, and indirect effects which occur through the influence of radical right groups' on other actors, for example by exercising pressure and lobbying activities on policy makers. The most straightforward policy effects may take place when the radical right is in government. Yet, even then pivotal bargaining processes are at work since no radical right party has been the leading party of a governing coalition (yet), let alone a single governing party. Regarding the impact of parties outside government or parliament, the radical right impact is likely to be even more intermediary and less easy to trace.

An analytical model with a limited set of factors relevant to determining radical right impact, for example on national minorities and migrants (and indirectly also on democratic quality), is presented in Fig. 2.1 which exemplifies a number of interaction patterns.

First, while radical right movements are an important force in many East European countries, based on earlier findings (Minkenberg 2015a) parties can be expected to matter more when it comes to influencing policy making. To a large degree, their role depends on whether they can be considered relevant according to Sartori's criteria of "blackmail potential" and "coalition potential" (Sartori 1976), with blackmail potential not being restricted to a presence in parliament but also including significant levels of electoral support below the existing electoral thresholds (see Minkenberg 2003, 154; also Pederson 1982). Second, both the direct and indirect effects of the radical right are related to the strategic reactions of the remaining competitor parties. As mentioned earlier, various strategies can be distinguished: those of positive engagement (co-optation and collaboration), negative engagement (demarcation and confrontation), and disengagement (e.g. ignorance and non-cooperation) (Minkenberg 1998, Chapter 9, 2002b; Downs 2001, 2012). If the mainstream parties choose a strategy of complete disengagement—a so-called cordon sanitaire—the radical right will have only insignificant influence. Vice versa, the absence of a cordon sanitaire feeds back into the policy-making process by increasing the radical right's credibility and room to maneuver vis-à-vis other parties. Third, the timing of strategic reactions and interplay with other actors, such as state actors (police, courts, bureaucracy) and civil society, is also very important.

On the level of interaction with the state, that is the forces of "law and order," negative effects by the radical right on the status of national minorities are largely determined by the legal contexts and their application. In contrast to Western Europe, East European democracies have implemented the arsenal of "militant democracy" only rudimentarily: parties of the radical right are seldom banned (Mareš 2012, 2015) and even violent activities by radical right-wing actors are only inconsistently met with active prosecution and counter-measures (see also contributions to Minkenberg 2015a). Applying repression or severe restriction always results in a fundamental problem: by doing so, authorities inevitably enter

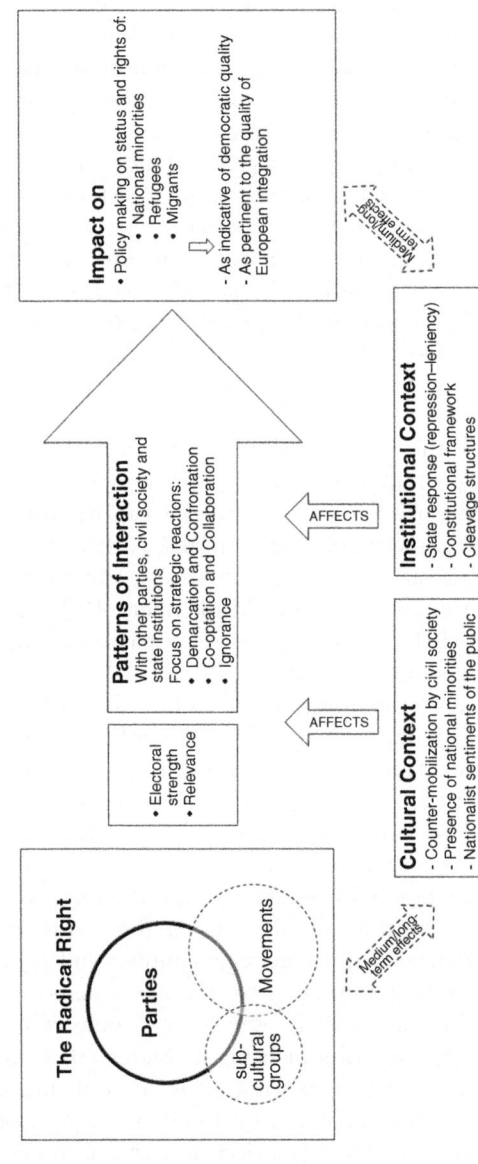

Fig. 2.1 Modeling the role of the radical right in the political process and its impact (*Source:* Author with Oliver Kossack and Malisa Zobel (European University Viadrina), based on Beichelt and Minkenberg (2002), Minkenberg (2013b and 2015b))

the "democratic dilemma" of protecting democracy by curtailing democratic rights such as freedom of speech or assembly (see Fennema 2000).

With regard to national minorities, an escalation of confrontation is likely to ensue between the radical right and networks of pro-minority advocates and anti-racist groups. They may have negative side effects in the sense that recognition of national minority rights in significant segments of the larger public will be damaged (i.e. a dynamic of polarization in the public), depending on the political reputation of the radical right's opponents, their tactics, and leadership (see Minkenberg 2002b; also Koopmans and Statham 2000; Koopmans et al. 2005). In a more general vein, the effects on national minorities vary also with the organizational type of the radical right actors (see Minkenberg 2009b, 2013b). Political parties are most likely to exercise direct negative effects if no cordon sanitaire exists and state authorities pursue a liberal or lax approach towards the radical right as party.

Notes

1. See e.g. Art 2011; Arzheimer 2008; Betz 1994; Bornschier 2010; Carter 2005; Eatwell and Mudde 2004; Hainsworth 2008; Ignazi 2003; Kitschelt 1995; Minkenberg 1998, 2008; Mudde 2000a, 2007; Norris 2005; Rydgren 2013; Van Der Brug et al. 2005.
2. See e.g. Akkerman 2012; Akkerman and de Lange 2012; Bale et al. 2010; Carter 2005; Downs 2001, 2012; Meguid 2008; Minkenberg 2002b, 2006; Mudde 2007; Schain 2006; Williams 2006.

CHAPTER 3

Contexts: Legacies and the Transformation Process

Abstract The third chapter identifies and operationalizes the specific contexts of the East European radical right. An overview of "legacies" from the nineteenth century through the communist regimes shows the distinctiveness of the region as a whole compared to Western Europe. The author suggests that most East European countries followed a distinct path into modernity which included (i) the failure of democracy in the interwar period (except for Czechoslovakia) and (ii) incorporation into the communist bloc after World War II, which interrupted the nation-building processes until the Velvet Revolution of 1989. The last section addresses structural and cultural context factors such as the patterns of party competition, the role of ethnic minorities, and the political culture, and ends with a summary table of all relevant variables in all countries under consideration.

Keywords Nation building · Legacies · Regime change · Minorities · Xenophobia · Opportunity structures

The previous chapter outlined the general model of the radical right as a collective actor in a democratic context and made the case for using it in research on Eastern Europe, bearing in mind that the differences make it a phenomenon that is sui generis yet also comparative with its West European counterpart. This chapter continues the discussion by specifying the region-specific context factors of the East European radical right which consist of particular historical legacies (late nation-building, lack of a democratic experience, communist regimes), the Brubakerian "triad" coming from the particular trajectory of nation-building and the accompanying cultures, and the structural patterns of under-developed cleavages in electoral politics as well as an under-institutionalized party system.

1 THE RETURN OF THE PAST OR THE RETURN TO EUROPE—THE QUESTION OF LEGACIES

As indicated in the previous chapter, the central commonality and, in an all-European perspective, fundamental distinctiveness of the region under consideration lies in its communist past between 1945 and 1989. To this can be added, according to some authors, a specific version of nationalism which centers on ethnic rather than civic, or territorial rather than voluntary, dimensions (see Kohn 1944; Smith 2001, 39–42). Such East–West dichotomies have been criticized as too schematic (see Shulman 2002) but, as will be shown below, more—and more subtle—differences can be added to the context of the post-1989 radical right in Eastern Europe, and particular nationalist traditions cannot be excluded (see Minkenberg 2002a). But the bottom line of an East–West difference remains irreducible: the "common denominator of the communist past" (Bernhard and Jasiewicz 2015, 314), regardless of other historical legacies or the region's historical diversity. The communist experience in all of Eastern Europe cannot be deconstructed, likewise the particular experience of regime change after 1989.

As a starting point, the historical moment of 1989 denotes a radical break in political terms, which opened opportunities not just for democracy and capitalism but for many new (and not so new) actors and ideas. As one of the experts of the region puts it: "the ideological extinction of Leninist formations left behind a vacuum that has been filled by syncretic constructs drawing from the region's precommunist and communist heritage" (Tismaneanu 2007, 35).

Among these "syncretic constructs" Vladimir Tismaneanu lists "nationalism in both its civic and ethnic incarnations, liberalism, democratic socialism, conservatism, populism, neo-Leninism, and even more or less refurbished fascism" (ibid.). This list resembles more or less the inventory of Western party politics minus the Green movement, plus a somewhat reconstructed Leninism. However, the emphasis here is not on the equivalence of the situation with "the West" but with "the past", the region's heritage. And equally important, almost half of the phenomena identified as filling the post-Leninist vacuum constitute what can be summarily described as the radical right (see Chapter 2). Here, in a nutshell, can be found a central topos in the study of the region's contemporary politics in general, and of its radical right politics in particular: the emphasis on the extraordinary relevance of history and geography. It is this intersection of history or particular legacies, and the nature of the transformation process, which provide the characteristic context for the mobilization and impact of the radical right in the region.

A quick glance at the literature about the process reveals an interesting transformation of the concept itself, if not a paradigm shift (see Carothers 2002; Ekiert 2015). Early transformation literature about the countries in post-1989 Eastern Europe typically employed a focus which organized the analyses with an assumed *telos* of the transformation, that is a transition from autocracy to the establishment of liberal democracy (see O'Donnell et al. 1986; Bank 2010, 34–36; Albrecht and Frankenberger 2010a, 43–47). In the meantime, the completion of regime transformation is not equated anymore with the consolidation of democracy; instead one authoritarian regime might be replaced by another, a pathway which has been increasingly discussed in the more recent literature (see Hadenius and Teorell 2007, 145; Albrecht and Frankenberger 2010b; Bunce et al. 2010).

But by locating these new regimes, variously labeled "electoral authoritarianism" or "hybrid regimes" (see e.g. Diamond 2002; Schedler 2006), outside the European Union, the teleological logic—in this instance the politically charged assumption that EU membership is equal to a complete transformation and consolidated democracy—reenters the picture. A number of comparative case studies show that transformation is not only an open but also an uneven process. For example, Romania and Slovakia in the 1990s, despite the demise of the old regimes, underwent a period of "deviation" into a nationalist-authoritarian or national-communist phase before joining the other post-communist countries in Eastern Europe on their path to democracy and EU membership (see Mungiu-Pippidi 2010, 66). It is hardly coincidental that this phase of retardation involved radical right parties in government and the persistence of a strong identity-based cleavage (see Ekiert and Kubik 2014, 52; Elster et al. 1998, 267). But the most compelling evidence for the "openness" of the transformation process as well as that of accession to the European Union can be found in the recent rise of illiberal politics in Hungary and Poland, to which can be added Bulgaria. These cases undermine the teleological perspective underlying the project of European integration as well as much of the respective literature, and are now labeled as instances of "defective" or "illiberal democracy" or the breakdown of the "liberal consensus" (see Dawson and Hanley 2016; Koenen 2015; Merkel 2004).

The entire transformation process after 1989 is often clothed in terms of historical and geographical categories, either as a "return of history" or a "return to Europe," or both (for the following, see Minkenberg 2009a, 446–450). On the one hand, historical analogies are invoked which cast the various countries' development after the fall of communism in light of the remapping of the region in the wake of World War I and the 1919/1920 peace treaties. Some authors see it even as the belated conclusion of the Wilsonian project of state and nation-making after that war (see e.g. Judt 2005, 637–638). As is well known, Europe's Wilsonian order after World War I ended in the rise of fascism and a period of totalitarian politics and wartime destruction, and yet the "legacy" of 1919 seemed to persist until and well beyond the 1989 upheavals. On the other hand, post-1989 Central and Eastern Europe is characterized as a region catching up with its Western counterpart—the "return to Europe"—while still being identified in terms of a distinct "otherness" which often includes notions of backwardness (see Wolff 1994; also Janos 2000; Kopstein 2003). Whether this return can ever be completed under such a conceptual premise, remains an open question.

Either way, the radical right in contemporary Central and Eastern Europe claims a prominent place in this post-communist "politics of return" at the nation-state level (see Hirsch and Miller 2011; Minkenberg 2010), and the study of this current echoes the more general concern, in the analyses of the region, with historical analogies and the role of legacies. Some liken the post-1989 radical right to the rise of interwar fascism and point at the fate of the Weimar Republic. The scenario which is summarized as "Weimarization" includes such aspects as the overlap of presidential, parliamentary, and plebiscitary elements in the system, a fragmentation of the party system, political polarization, the rise of extremism, and problems in coalition building (see Gusy 2008; Seefried 2016). The appearance of such and related symptoms in the transformation countries is interpreted as the return of the pre-communist, ultranationalist, or even fascist past and the accompanying insecurity of the international order, that is the "return of history" (see e.g. Andor 2000, 165; also Kovàcs 1998; Umland 2008). Another interpretation argues that an increasing convergence of political systems between East and West and the growing resemblance of East European party systems with their Western European counterparts applies also to the radical right, at least where it is electorally successful—an aspect of Eastern Europe's "return to Europe" (see Bustikova 2014, 2015; Grescovits and Bohle 2001; Öhlén 2014). Both perspectives can claim some credibility, as will become more apparent later on and in Chapter 4, but in contrast to either perspective, the argument here is that the radical right in the region is not simply an aspect of a historical "return" but a sui generis phenomenon, shaped by the legacies and varieties of state socialism and the particular paths of the transformation process, but also responding to the current context of political development in the respective countries (see Minkenberg 2002a, 2010).

However, while these historical arguments or the reference to legacies are widespread in the comparative analysis of the radical right in Central and Eastern Europe (not to mention the single-case country studies which all too readily explain the radical right's features and mobilization by the respective country's particular past and heritage), there remains a fuzziness as to how this past is operationalized and what kind of legacies are held relevant (see Minkenberg 2009a; Wittenberg 2015). To clarify, one must distinguish more sweeping claims that "history matters," or that long-range historical processes matter, from a narrow focus on a particular legacy, such as the experience of Leninism. In both versions, path dependency affects spatial variation, that is the range of events at one point in time is constrained by events at an earlier point in time (see Tilly 2006, 421; see also Mahoney and Schensul 2006).

Applied to the radical right in Eastern Europe after 1989, this logic and distinction raises the question as to whether historically long-range pre-communist or the more immediate pre-1989 patterns in politics and society are relevant to explaining the rise and variation of the radical right in Eastern Europe, as compared to Western Europe. The first approach can be found, for example, in the writing of Andrew Janos (2000) who explains the "borderlands" position of East Central Europe by linking pre-communist paths of socioeconomic development to the post-communist trajectories in politics. The second approach, formulated in its original version by Kenneth Jowitt (1992), starts from the observation that the same Leninist realities had shaped politics and society in the entire region and that this legacy, shared by all former Eastern Bloc countries in Europe, favors an authoritarian rather than liberal, democratic, and capitalist way of life (p. 293). Jowitt anticipated troubling effects of this system of rule on the prospects for democracy in the region:

> The Leninist legacy in Eastern Europe consists largely—not exclusively—of fragmented, mututally suspicious, societies with little religio-cultural support for tolerant and individually self-reliant behaviour, and of a fragmented region made up of countries that view each other with animosity. The way Leninists ruled and the way Leninism collapsed contributed to this inheritance. (p. 304)

As the only effective way out of this situation, Jowitt hoped for a massive intervention of Western Europe and the United States.[1]

The two versions' legacies and their relative weight have been analyzed recently by Grigore Pop-Eleches (2015) who found that the explanatory power of pre-communist and communist legacies varies according to issue areas, with political attitudes largely shaped by the communist experience, and regime trajectories more dependent on pre-communist pathways. Since radical right parties and movements constitute the transmission belt between the general public and accordingly the attitudinal level of politics and the regime level, this finding requires further specification regarding the legacies' effects on such collective actors.

In addition, it is important to note how this legacy concept in the study of post-1989 East European politics developed over time (see Tismaneanu et al. 2006; Ekiert 2015). On the one hand, a number of scholars, though at times quite critical of Jowitt's own approach and pessimism, followed the logic of his argument and focused on the communist era as the independent variable in studying the prospects of liberalization, capitalism, and democracy in the region (see Ekiert and Hanson 2003; and various contributions to Tismaneanu et al. 2006). Here, the variation of post-communist outcomes (e.g. successful or unsuccessful regime change) is related to the nature of post-communist regimes. A particularly instructive application of this approach is the comparative analysis of party competition in selected countries, relating the degree of structured party systems to the role of bureaucracy and rationality in the old regime (Kitschelt et al. 1999). On the other hand, in a critical essay Herbert Kitschelt (2003) warns of two "excesses" in the explanation of post-communist regime diversity. The first is that of deep explanations, which means going back far into history and accounting for a variety of causes next to Leninist legacies, such as religion and geographic location. The second is that of shallow explanations, that is a focus on the set of patterns, among other things, by the transformation process itself, by bargaining dynamics and so on. In his conclusion, Kitschelt seems to follow Tilly's recommendation of focusing on both macro- and micro-processes, on path dependency and agency, to combine causal mechanism with causal depth, including cultural mechanisms (ibid., p. 80).

That the legacy concept is rather slippery has been observed many times; it may encompass anything that precedes the post-communist regime change. But "if the weight of the past affects the present, at a minimum it is necessary to specify which past" (Kopstein 2003, 233). With regard to Eastern Europe and the radical right and following Wittenberg (2015, 370–375; see also Minkenberg 2009a), three basic layers are of importance:

1. The period 1989–1992, i.e. the immediate post-communist context;
2. The period 1949–1989, i.e. the experience of Leninism as a political and cultural regime;
3. The pre-1949 period, i.e. the Wilsonian order after World War I, the experience of largely non-democratic interwar regimes, and the history of nation-building that preceded the Wilsonian order.

The question of the relevant legacies and pathways becomes particularly important for the analysis of the radical right in the region. Clearly, this is a shift in the application of the legacy approach which, in all its variety, was conceptualized for explanations of regime change, not for a particular movement or party family. Yet, measures of successful regime change often include as an indicator the support for anti-democratic, or anti-system, parties or movements (see Auer 2000; Beichelt 2001). Already Jowitt himself had identified—as one of the outcomes of the "Leninist extinction"—nativist and violent reactions to the costs of the transformation process (1992, 275; see also Howard 2006, 39). But the conceptual links and causal connections warrant further specification.

Regardless of its particular historical positioning, the radical right is, almost by definition, a prime agent, as well as a target, in the business of reinventing or instrumentalizing a country's past. In any of these interpretations, history—in its more recent (state socialist and regime transformative) and more distant (pre-communist) manifestations—can be accredited with a crucial role in the shape and development of the radical right. It seems that, in contrast to its Western European counterpart, whether it is catching up or not, the East European radical right is particularly conditioned by the force of history, that the histories of state socialism and of pre-communist (non-democratic) experiences can be seen as major factors in shaping both the contents and the opportunities of the radical right in these new or emerging democracies (see Minkenberg 2009a, 450).

The argument that the East European radical right is particularly susceptible to historical legacies is related to the characteristics of both the region and, as outlined in the second chapter, the radical right. The latter's effort to construct an extremely homogeneous idea of nation and national belonging includes by definition a historical component or narrative which must be considered and related to historical realities (see Pytlas 2016, Chapter 3). The comparative literature on the radical right in post-1989 Eastern Europe employs some or most of the definitional characteristics discussed in Chapter 2 and combines them with the region's experience of regime change and transformation and its particular state-socialist or Leninist past (see Minkenberg 2002a, 2009a; Mudde 2000b; Ost 2005; Ramet 1999). But while the importance of history or particular legacies for the trajectory of the radical right in the region is regularly emphasized in the literature, there is vagueness in the application of the legacy concept. If at all, the role of the past is typically operationalized in sequential terms, as historical reference points, such as when some experts suggest creating new typologies of right-wing radical parties in Eastern Europe by classifying them according to the (historical) origins of their ideological identity. As discussed before, Cas Mudde (2000b) distinguishes pre-communist radical right parties, communist radical right parties, and post-communist radical right parties.

While it is plausible to characterize such parties according to their *historical* origins (except for most cases of the pre-communist radical right), it makes less sense *ideologically*. Most radical right parties which emerged in Eastern Europe after 1989 nurtured a strong longing for a particular part of their country's past; but they also focused on current events and political opponents while attempting to reinvent nationalist traditions and not-so-democratic symbols of the country's past (see Chapter 4). In his classic study on the radical right in Europe, Mudde (2007) not only drops this typology but refrains altogether from testing regional effects on, or the relevance of the East–West divide for, the radical right—let alone distinct legacy effects, which could be subsumed under regional effects. The regional particularities of post-communist Europe are only marginally identified when Mudde compares levels of democratic support and ethnic diversity in the region's aspiring democracies during the 1990s, finding but little evidence for a causal effect on the electoral success of the radical right (ibid., 205–216). And the argument for the effect of an authoritarian or Leninist legacy on the radical right is settled with a few remarks and a broad brushstroke: "the obvious problem with this general thesis is that it cannot account for the striking absence of populist radical right success in most of the post-communist world or for the intra-regional differences" (ibid., 217).

Indeed, when held at such an abstract and general level, the legacy argument evaporates. But the obvious next step would be to ask if different "pasts" or legacies account for the variation of radical right success, or of radical right formations, in light of the legacy approaches which strive to explain variations of regimes (as the systemic equivalent to types of radical right groups) and the success of democratization (equivalent to the electoral success of the radical right). In other words: differences in legacies may translate into different effects, both in terms of the comparison of Western and Eastern Europe, that is their divergent post-World War II legacies and the particularities of each region's radical right, and in terms of the types of legacies and their impact on the types and performance of the radical right within Eastern Europe. Moreover, success is defined by Mudde in rather narrow terms as electoral success (ibid., p. 216); when taking into account the radical right's radiation into its political environment, for example changes in the political climate, other actors' strategic reactions, or policy effects, there might be less absence of success, as will be shown in Chapter 6.

2   Cultural Context: Nation-building and Nationalism

Following the conceptual outline offered in Chapter 2 and the discussion of legacies, the remainder of this chapter provides the empirical contours of the radical right in the region with a special emphasis on East European specifics as compared to the West or all-European context as provided by Cas Mudde (2007) and other comparativists. Among the cultural context factors, nationalism, nation-building and national identity, and the related issues of in-group and out-group distinctions deserve special attention.

In all communist states prior to 1989 there were tendencies to compensate the weakening legitimacy of the regime by bringing up national issues, thus seeking to enhance political legitimization via recourse to national traditions (see Ishiyama 2009, 489–490). Socialist parties without real efforts to reform their programs to a pro-democratic direction are still enriching their ideologies with nationalist issues. Here, a direct link exists between the "communist nationalism" of the communist period and potentially right-wing radical positions in the post-communist period. In this regard, Eastern Europe differs markedly from Western patterns.

One of the most important aspects of any collective mobilization rests in the "cultural resonance" of particular issues as a condition for the possibility of mobilization. The concept of right-wing radicalism as populist and romantic ultranationalism suggests that the type of nation, which exists in a given society, is particularly relevant. It is possible to situate types of nations—"imagined communities" in Benedict Anderson's term (1983, 160)—in modern European history along the dimension of *demos* versus *ethnos* and to summarize them in three distinct types, according to the degree of openness/closedness of the criteria for membership in the nation (Meinecke 1908; Alter 1985; Brubaker 1992; see also Minkenberg 1998, Chapter 2): a *political nation* in which the belief in common political values and institutions in a well-defined territory dominates; a *cultural nation* in which the belief in cultural, especially religious, characteristics, irrespective of the political design, dominates; and an *ethnic nation* in which the belief in a shared culture is accompanied by the belief that one can only be a member by being born into this national community, or a belief in the "natural," that is biological, roots of a nation.

A large part of historical research on nationalism in the nineteenth century converges on pointing out that, in Western Europe and in the Americas, nation-building occurred in independent nation-states, or colonies struggling for independence, and was closely allied to politically strong liberal forces and accelerated in the bourgeois revolutions (see Alter 1985; Anderson 1983; Hobsbawm 1990; Smith 2001). Nation-building in Western Europe followed mainly a trajectory in which a "political nation" had emerged and combined with some cultural or ethnic aspects. As is well known, the German path to national unity and the subsequent national identity diverges from this "Western model" by its heavy emphasis on the German *Kulturnation* which after unification in 1871 was recast into the myth of an ethnic community of Germans, or *Volksnation* (ethnic nation). In Eastern Europe, political nation-building occurred later or was blocked while nationalism took on a distinct cultural or ethnic flavor and, with few exceptions such as Czechoslovakia (which did not gel as a nation-state after all), democratization occurred in a fragmentary fashion (see Smith 1995, 140–142; also Thompson 2002).

It has been argued that this comparison of a Western and an East European type of nation-building is an outdated notion and makes little, if any, sense, and that there are multiple paths to modernity (see Auer 2000; Eisenstadt 2000; Hroch 2005; Shulman 2002). The notion of multiple modernities is not disputed here and the French model is one of several. But even though East European publics may also exhibit civic elements in their national imaginings, ignoring the relevance of particular historical trajectories of nation-building or democratization in certain parts of Europe seems overly ahistorical. At the time when in Western Europe the processes of nation-building entered a phase of consolidation and liberalization (the last third of the nineteenth century), all of Eastern Europe was subject to multinational empires, that is the Habsburg, the Russian, and the Ottoman empires (Szücs 1990). Nation-building here was always of the Risorgimento type (Alter 1985), directed against the existing order and dependent upon its collapse, irrespective of some East European nationalists' own dreams of empire (see Trencsényi 2001, 63). The dates of national independence were 1881 for Romania, 1882 for Serbia, 1908 for Bulgaria, and 1919 for all the others. Hungary after the "Ausgleich" of 1867 achieved autonomy in domestic affairs; the compromise led to the recognition of civil rights and parliamentary representation in both Vienna and Budapest on the one hand, but was accompanied by a turn away from political liberalism towards ethnic nationalism among the Magyars as well as the Germans in Austria on the other (Smith 1995, 142). Apart from Russia, the dominant pattern was the emergence of a national identity without the nation-state, that is a primarily ethnic nationhood, and the establishment of a nation-state along with democratization after World War I, that is in the context of the first wave of democratization (Huntington 1991).

This wave ended with the fall of liberalism and the establishment of dictatorial regimes in all newly democratized countries in Eastern Europe, except for Czechoslovakia, as well as in parts of Western Europe. Besides political and ethnic divisions, in addition to the economic slump of the 1930s, the region-wide version of nationalism, in which weak liberal elements mixed with strong ethno-cultural ingredients, facilitated this new wave of regime change (see Hobsbawm 1996, 135–141). Religious or clerical nationalism, decidedly anti-liberal and often tied to the Catholic Church's vehement opposition to the secular nation-builders, was an all-European phenomenon that found particularly weak resistance in Eastern Europe (see Spohn 2003a, 6; also Brubaker 2012; Jaffrelot 2009).

The uneven development of democracy in the interwar period is illustrated in Table 3.1 which shows that, with the exception of the Weimar Republic in Germany and Belgium, democracy survived "the Slump" (Hobsbawm) in Protestant Western Europe, while all of Eastern Europe transformed their post-World War I—regime into right-wing dictatorships.

The pattern in Table 3.1 corresponds to recent comparative research about the breakdown of democracy in interwar Europe, which emphasizes political and cultural causes instead of economic ones (see Berg-Schlosser and Mitchell 2002). With the exception of Belgium, there was not a single Catholic or Orthodox country which did not undergo a regime change and establishment of a fascist or right-wing dictatorship. In most cases, the major church in the country remained passive or became supportive of the new regime. This can be explained by the affinity between the church structure and radical-right ideology:

> Catholicism, Orthodoxy and, to a lesser extent, Lutheranism, with their insistence on the primacy of the institution of the church, are much more likely to see the state of the political embodiment of "the people" as a community, rather than as the expression of the preferences of individuals. (Bruce 2003, 110)

While after World War II, in most of Western Europe, Protestant and Catholic churches came to terms with liberal democracy and human rights, in particular in the wake of the Second Vatican Council (1962–1965), the East European communist regimes drove churches into opposition and strengthened a fusion of nationalism and religion in a number of countries, thereby carrying on illiberal traditions into the post-1989 world. The degree of fusion between national and religious identity in Western and Eastern Europe on the eve of EU enlargement in 2004 is shown in Fig. 3.1.

These data demonstrate a similar variation between countries in West and East, albeit with a larger range in Eastern Europe between the maximum value in Bulgaria (76%) to a minimum in Latvia (23%) or even East Germany (13%). They reflect both a religiously exclusionist nationalism in

Table 3.1 Interwar regime change and religion in Western and Eastern Europe

	Democracy	Right-wing authoritarian regime
Catholic countries	Belgium Ireland* Czechoslovakia**	Austria (1934—supportive) France (1940—supportive) Italy (1922—supportive) Poland (1938—supportive) Portugal (1933—initially supportive) Spain (1939—supportive) Croatia (1941—supportive) Hungary (1920s—supportive) Poland (1938—supportive) Slovakia (1939—supportive)
Protestant or mixed Protestant countries	Denmark (occupied by Germany 1940) Finland (occupied by Germany 1944) The Netherlands (occupied by Germany 1940) Sweden Switzerland United Kingdom	Germany (1933—passive) (Baltic States—"benign despotism" in the 1930s)
Orthodox (or mixed) countries		Bulgaria (1918—supportive) Romania (1923/38—supportive) Kingdom of Serbs, Croats, and Slovenes (1929—supportive)

Note: Beginning year of non-democratic regime and attitude of major church towards regime in parentheses.
*Ireland underwent a transition to full independence from the UK after World War I which by 1937 resulted in a democratic constitution with substantial privileges for the Catholic Church, thus adding a dose of illiberalism to the regime.
**Czechoslovakia had a numerical majority of Catholics in the interwar period but mixed religious traditions; moreover in the first decade of its existence, the country experienced a cross-partisan wave of anti-Catholicism, led by the first president Tomas Masaryk.
Sources: Anderson (2009, 49–54); Bruce (2003. 97–111); Grzymała-Busse (2015, 188–189).

some countries and their mono-confessional past; as will be shown below, this is not without consequences for out-groups.

A concomitant factor of nation-building and national identity in the region relates to the existence of the nation states' borders, many of which cut across the settlement areas of national or ethnic communities. Here, particular legacies of the multinational empires and the subsequent

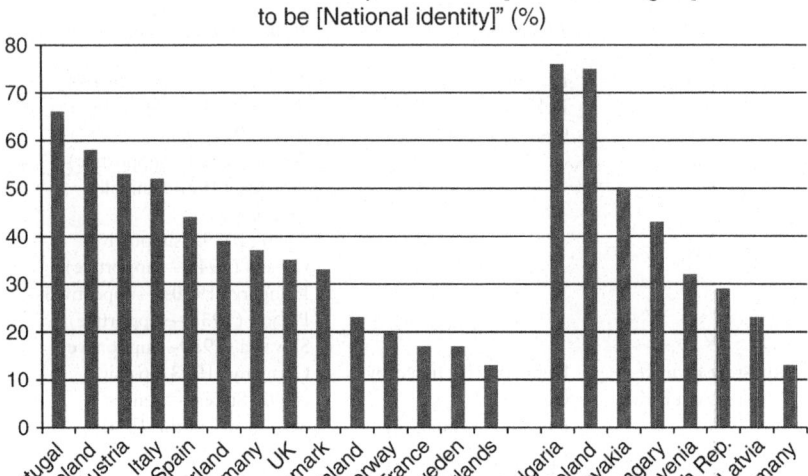

Fig. 3.1 The fusion of religion and national identity in Europe, East and West (2003) (*Source*: ISSP Data 2003 in countries where such data were available (Grzymała-Busse 2015, 359))

nation-building processes exist which date back to the remapping of the region in the wake of World War I and the Paris peace treaties. Some authors see the post-1989 regime change as the belated conclusion of the Wilsonian project of state and nation-making after that war (Judt 2005, 637–638). Yet, this deficit of the Wilsonian order, which caused much turbulence in the interwar period and was left untouched by the communist order after World War II, continued into the post-communist era, the "legacy" of 1919 seeming to persist until and well beyond the 1989 upheavals (see Brubaker 1997; Bochsler and Szöcsik 2013). It is most visible in Hungary today where in 1994 and in 2005 almost 20% of Hungarian voters supported the revision of the country's borders as determined by the Treaty of Trianon in 1920 (see Pytlas 2016, 171). This factor is very closely related to the third cultural context factor, majority–minority relations.

While, in Western Europe, immigrants take the role of scapegoats for resentment and are a core element in the political agenda of the radical

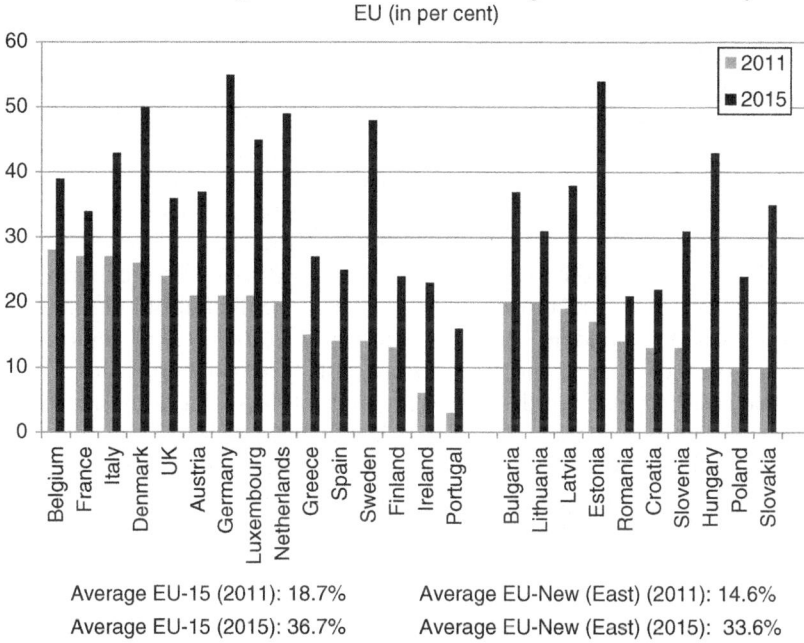

Fig. 3.2 European public opinion and immigration, 2011 and 2015 (*Source*: Eurobarometer May 2011, May 2015 (Perrineau 2016, 192))

right, these are not readily available in Eastern Europe. In the region, immigration is neither a significant social fact nor a political issue, at least until recently (see Barnickel and Beichelt 2013). Eurostat data from 2008 show that the proportion of foreigners in East European countries (excluding the Baltics) ranges from 0.1% (in Poland) to 3.9% (Czech Republic), with all other countries falling in-between (Juhasz 2010).

In contrast to the real numbers of immigrants in East and West, Fig. 3.2 shows similar levels and variations of concern over immigration in 2011 in West and East, despite the absence of large-scale immigration to Eastern Europe. The proportion of those considering immigration a particularly significant issue more than doubled in a number of countries between 2011 and 2015, most notably Germany, the Netherlands, Denmark, and Sweden, due to the influx of refugees and asylum seekers from the Middle East and Africa (with Germany, France, and Sweden taking in the largest numbers of asylum seekers; UNCR data from 2013), but well before the massive increase from the summer of 2015 onwards. It is noteworthy that, even before the jump in numbers and the usage of the "Balkan route" from 2015 on, concern over immigration increased enormously in Hungary and Slovakia, but also in Poland and Estonia. This can be read as a sign of a particular anxiety related to the more traditional ethnic conflict configuration.

Instead of immigrants, national minorities and neighboring countries have been assigned the role of scapegoats in Eastern Europe—a context for which the roots are to be found in the particular nation and state-building process in the region. More specifically, many post-communist nations can be characterized by a "triadic" configuration of nations between nation-building processes, the existence of national minorities within the new states, and the existence of "external homelands" (see Brubaker 1997; also Smith 2001). The role of "external homelands" or "lost territories" signifies one of the key characteristics of the region's nation-building process—and current condition—with particular relevance to the radical right. It is in this arena where the process of nation-building might well override other issues and thus help explain more than other factors the mobilization of right-wing radicalism (Stein 2000). If there exist numerically significant national minorities of more than 1 or 2% of the population conflicts of a national scale can be expected to emerge along an ethno-cultural axis.[2] In countries like Estonia, Bulgaria, Romania and Slovakia, constitutional conflicts which threatened the process of democratic consolidation have developed around issues which, in the absence of such minorities, would not have entered the political agenda: the attempts to ban ethnic parties, citizenship and language laws, issues of territorial autonomy, and education (see Beichelt and Minkenberg 2002, 9–11). Moreover, in a number of countries in Central and South Eastern Europe, the large presence of Roma feeds into the majority–minority relations, most notably in Romania (with an estimated 1.3 million Roma), Hungary ($c.$650,000), and Slovakia ($c.$500,000) (Jenne 2000; Grienig 2010). Finally, as Table 3.2 illustrates, a number of countries in the region have experienced an increase in ethnic homogeneity between the interwar and the immediate post-communist periods, notably Poland and Romania, due to territorial changes, and the successor states of Czechoslovakia and Yugoslavia due to the breakup of their countries. While in Bulgaria, the ethnic make-up appears to have remained stable, the Baltic States of Estonia and Latvia saw an increase in ethnic heterogeneity resulting from the politics of Russification during the Soviet era

CONTEXTS: LEGACIES AND THE TRANSFORMATION PROCESS 51

Table 3.2 Ethnic homogeneity in East European countries (%)

Country	Majority population	Censuses*			Estimate/Census
		1920	1930	1993	2000ff.
Stable approximate nation-states: stable definition of the majority nationality; large majorities					
Lithuania	Lithuanians	81 [1923]		80 [1992]	87 [2015]
Hungary	Magyar		97	89 [1990]	84 [2011]
Bulgaria**	Bulgarians	83	87 [1934]	85–90	80
Newer approximate nation-states: stable definition of the majority nationality; large majorities in the early 1990s but smaller majorities in the interwar era					
Poland***	Poles	70	70	99	97
Romania	Romanians		72	88	85 [2015]
Recent approximate nation-states: devolved from "mini-empires", large or medium-large majorities in the early 1990s					
Czechoslovakia	"Czechoslovaks"	66 [1923]	67		
The Czech Rep.	Czechs			81	88 [2016]
Slovakia	Slovaks			86	81 [2011]
Yugoslavia	"Serbo-Croats"	74 [1923]	77 [1931]		
Serbia	Serbs			80 [1991]	66
Slovenia	Slovenes			99 [1991]	88
Croatia	Croats			78 [1991]	92
Former approximate nation-states with a decreasing majority population until the early 1990s					
Estonia	Estonians		86 [1934]	62 [1992]	65
Latvia	Latvians		77 [1935]	53	69 [2011]

Note: Census ratings in terms of the relative size of the regime-proclaimed majority nationality.
*The censuses of the interwar period are generally unreliable in their estimates of the size of ethnic minorities. The figures are, nevertheless, interesting as expressions of perceived size of regime-proclaimed core populations.
**The 1993 Bulgarian census data suggests that ethnic minorities account for more than 10% of the population.
***The Polish interwar estimates are highly questionable. Polish nationality was at least partly determined by the ability of the respondent to understand the census-taker when addressed in Polish.
Sources: The entire Table except for the last column is taken from Berglund et al. (2013, 29); data in the last column from Pan and Pfeil (2000) or census data (with year added in parentheses) if available (www.worldpopulationreview.com, accessed August 26, 2016).

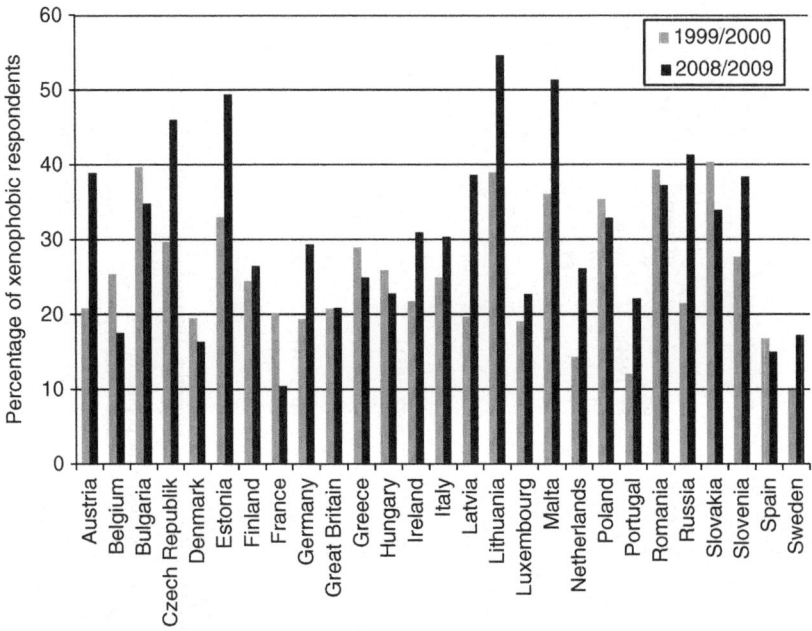

Fig. 3.3 Xenophobia in Europe (*Note*: A respondent in this survey is categorized as "xenophobic" when he or she mentioned at least one of the categories "Muslims," "Immigrants," or "People of a Different Race" in response to the question "Could you please sort out any that you would not like to have as neighbors?" (European Value Study, 2008, p. 3). (*Source*: European Value Study, 1999 and 2008: MASTER QUESTIONNAIRE2008 FINAL VERSION, in: http://www.gesis.org/unser-angebot/daten-analysieren/umfragedaten/europ ean-values-study/4th-wave-2008/ (accessed October 31, 2013))

(see Melvin 2000). In some countries ethnic diversity has increased during the 1990s, most notably in Bulgaria and Hungary.

The distinctive patterns of hostility towards ethnically and culturally defined "others" in Europe are depicted in Fig. 3.3 where levels of xenophobia are measured in two waves of the European Values Survey. The data show that there is a relatively large pool of xenophobia, in most countries around or clearly above 20%. No clear-cut trend can be observed between 1999 and 2008/2009; however, the rejection of ethnically or religiously defined others was significantly higher in the new democracies in Eastern Europe (except for Hungary). Overall, there is an average 10% difference between West and East. Interestingly, Austria takes a "middle position" between West and East with regard to these numbers in 2008/ 2009. Moreover, xenophobia is particularly pronounced in the Baltic States; in Estonia and Latvia large Russian minorities (see Table 3.2) have become the targets of scapegoating since these countries' independence.

This impression of an East–West difference in xenophobia is confirmed by more recent data in selected countries (see Table 3.3): while in Poland and Hungary more than 40% of the population believes that there is "a natural hierarchy between black and white people" and more than 23% believe that "blacks and whites should not marry," the numbers in these and other questions are significantly lower in West European countries (Zick et al. 2011, 68–69).

3 STRUCTURAL CONTEXT: REGIME CHANGE AND MODERNIZATION

Alongside these cultural context factors, a number of structural factors can be identified as particularly relevant to the degree and kind of right-wing radical mobilization in East European countries. Comparative studies of the radical right in Western democracies single out institutional factors (such as the strength of the state as measured, e.g., by the degree of centralization) and the patterns of party competition and cleavage structures summarily referred to as "political opportunity structures" in the literature (see Minkenberg 1998, 37–45, 2008, Chapter 2; also Mudde 2007, Chapter 10). Of particular concern here are the cleavages in the party system and the state reaction to oppositional politics. State strength as a variable, identified as a key factor explaining differences in movement mobilization in the West (Tarrow 1994; Kriesi et al. 1995), can be discounted as a relevant explanatory factor, since there is no variation: none of the East European member states in the EU are decentralized or federally organized.

The East European party systems differ a lot from those in Western Europe, where changing cleavage structures, dealignment, and realignment processes have been shown to significantly affect the electoral success of the radical right, in particular the emergence of a new politics or a left-libertarian/authoritarian axis that cuts across the old cleavages

Table 3.3 Ethnocentric prejudice in selected European democracies, 2008 (% approving)

	Germany	Great Britain	France	Netherlands	Italy	Portugal	Poland	Hungary
"There exists a natural hierarchy between black and white people"	30.5	34.6	38.5	32.4	18.7	45.1	41.6	41.8
"Blacks and whites should better not marry"	13.5	10.6	13.6	4.7	7.5	17.9	23.5	30.3
"We have to protect our own culture from the influence of other cultures"	51.9	59.2	54.8	54.1	49.4	70.1	69.0	78.5
"There are too many Muslims in [country]"	46.1	44.7	36.2	41.5	49.7	27.1	47.1	60.7
"Muslims in [country] demand too much"	54.1	50.0	52.8	51.8	64.7	34.4	62.3	60.0
"There are too many immigrants in [country]"	50.0	62.2	40.3	46.0	62.5	59.6	27.1	58.7
"The many immigrants here sometimes make me feel like a stranger in my own country"	37.6	45.8	31.0	37.7	27.0	19.1	19.4	44.6

Note: Shading indicates different attitude dimensions, which are distinct from each other but correlate highly internally: the upper gray cells denote racism, the lower gray cells xenophobia (see Table 2.1). The dimension of Islamophobia is in the middle (no shading).
Source: Zick et al. (2011, 62–70).

(see Minkenberg 1993, 1998; Kitschelt 1995; Bornschier 2010). In Eastern Europe, there is no distinction between old politics and new politics and an absence of the immigration issue. Instead, all cleavages are new (or renewed) and must be seen in the context of the transformation process. If Lipset and Rokkan's "freezing hypothesis" (1967, 168) was already questionable for Western party systems in the 1970s and 1980s, then it is even more difficult to apply to Eastern Europe. The party systems were short-lived and unstable in the 1920s, and the one-party regimes that followed the war eradicated the feeble cleavage structures that might have existed. It is first and foremost the regime divide which structured party competition in Eastern Europe in the course of the transformation process (see Beichelt and Minkenberg 2002, 11–12). Traditional cleavages or those with renewed salience have taken over the role of structuring party competition only in those countries where the most dominant issue, the regime conflict between supporters of the old regime and supporters of the new order, retreated and democratic consolidation had advanced (see Kitschelt et al. 1999; Beichelt 2001). However, with the accession to the European Union, the regime divide lost much of its salience—except where it is kept alive by parties such as Fidesz in Hungary and PiS in Poland which aim to benefit from an ongoing polarization along these issues. But here, it is particular political actors' narratives of the regime divide and not the divide itself which superimpose the other conflicts (see Pytlas 2016, 48–68).

With regard to the radical right, it is not only the regime divide which constitutes a difference between Eastern and Western European party systems and cleavages but also the quality of other cleavages (for an overview see Evans and Whitefeld 2000, 48–51). For example, Geoffrey Evans points out that:

> In contemporary Central and Eastern Europe, the debate about class politics takes on a very different form than in the West: it concerns not whether class divisions have declined with the transition from industrialism to postindustrialism, but whether they have increased as the ex-communist countries—with their former ideology of classlessness—undergo the uneasy transition from command economy to free market democracy. (Evans 1999, 18)

Part of the scholarship (see Sztompka 1992) proposed a *"tabula rasa"* hypothesis, arguing that programmatic party creation along cleavage lines will not emerge for a long period of time, being instead dominated by charismatic and clientelist parties; however, this assumption was soon proven wrong (see Evans and Whitefeld 2000). Political cleavages also did not simply "unfreeze" in their pre-authoritarian shape, as could be inferred from earlier democratization waves, for example in Latin America. The next wave of scholarship constituted a "middle path" position, emphasizing the important but not deterministic role of "classical" or pre-authoritarian cleavages, adjusted and reframed in the course of post-communist transition (Von Beyme 1996; Stöss and Segert 1997; Beichelt 2001). In an early assessment, Klaus von Beyme identified eight cleavages in the East but hastened to add that the older, pre-communist ones (urban–rural, state–church, monarchist–republican) had been eroded by state socialist modernization policies (Von Beyme 1996, 424f.). This leaves four others. Among these are center–periphery and workers–owners, which von Beyme suggested were irrelevant for the radical right, as well as Westerners–indigenists and internationalists–nationalists which are better seen as two sides of the same coin than two distinct cleavages (Stöss and Segert 1997).

In the meantime, some scholars have returned to the Lipset and Rokkan frame and identified the socioeconomic competition between forces which promote the ideas of market liberalism and those which favor political redistribution, or between modernizers and opponents to modernization, as the most pervasive, although the ideological labels "left" and "right" cannot be transferred without modifications from West to East (see Berglund et al. 2013; Deegan-Krause 2013, 48–49; Kitschelt et al. 1999; Tavits and Netki 2009; Whitefield and Rohrschneider 2009). The idea of a dual modernization conflict along a socioeconomic axis and along a socio-cultural or value-related axis seems most persuasive because of the distinct logical and historical differences of the two cleavages (see Plasser et al. 1997, 399). Similarly, Kitschelt and collaborators identified as the two main cleavages the one between market liberals and social protectionists on the one hand, and that between secular libertarians and religious authoritarians on the other (Kitschelt et al. 1999). When applied to the radical right in Central and Eastern Europe, this model suggests situating the parties at the authoritarian end of the libertarian–authoritarian axis and closer to the state than the market end of the other axis.

In a further development of his cleavage model and the grid/group concept of the radical right, and by incorporating the legacy debate outlined above, Kitschelt, with Lenka Bustikova (2009), addresses a wide range of phenomena, both in terms of country cases included in their comparative investigation as well as the variables they test as causal factors for the electoral success of the radical right. They follow Kitschelt's earlier work on post-communist party competition (Kitschelt et al. 1999) and the type of communist regimes and suggest a political-economic perspective, rather than one based on cultural and identity politics, for the explanation of voting for the radical right. Their argument is that in countries with a legacy of national-accommodative communism which implemented to a certain degree cross-class social policies and, after 1989, provided a welfare state safety net for the losers of regime change, the radical right received only limited support. The opposite is true for countries with a patrimonial communist legacy. Here, "red-brown" authoritarian and exclusionary programs resonate in significant segments of the public, mixed with anti-capitalist positions (see also Ishiyama 2009). Bustikova and Kitschelt test these propositions for 17 countries and find that these legacies cast a shadow over the processes after 1989 and account for the general patterns of radical right mobilization.

However, other scholars point out that, while socioeconomic conflict may structure the general competition between parties or political camps in Eastern Europe, it is the ongoing nation-building process along with "culture wars," that is a fierce socio-cultural competition, which embed rather than supplement the socioeconomic conflicts (see Blokker 2005; Huber and Inglehart 1995; Rovny 2013; Pirro 2015; and contributions to Minkenberg 2015a):

> It is in the sphere of socio-cultural conflict that these competition phenomena have been most profound. Here, the overarching post-communist change encompassed the axiological pluralization of Central and Eastern European societies and discourses. (Re-) emerging left-liberal values and lifestyle, the pluralization of the mass media, as well as secularization and value individualization, opened up a salient socio-cultural conflict between "modern" and "traditional" views of society. (Pytlas 2016, 6)

This diagnostic does not indicate the return of cleavage politics in the Western, or conventional, sense. Rather, these conflicts unfold in the context of party systems which are characterized by low levels of stability. Party organizations are weak and membership figures in the East point at loose—and loosening—attachments to political parties (van Biezen et al. 2012). In the years following EU enlargement in 2004, the average total party membership as a percentage of the electorate in Eastern Europe was 3.04, as compared to 4.64 in Western Europe (my calculation based on data in Table 1, in van Biezen et al. 2012, p. 28), although in almost all countries membership figures declined dramatically across the East–West divide, as can be seen in Table 3.4.

While Austria, and with some distance Belgium and Italy, exhibit the highest membership ratio in Western Europe around 1990 as well as around 2008, the highest in the East (Bulgaria, Estonia) are significantly lower than in the Western peak countries. Only in Poland did the ratio fall below 1.0 by 2008, closely followed by Hungary in the East and the UK in the West. It seems that West European countries with a strong traditional Christian democracy perform better than those without. In such an environment of skeletal parties, it is to an increasing extent party

Table 3.4 Party membership ratios in selected West and East European countries (% of electorate)

	1990 or proximate	2000 or proximate	2008 or proximate
Western Europe			
Austria	23.71	17.66	17.27
Belgium	9.15	6.55	5.52
Denmark	5.88	5.14	4.13
France	2.98	1.57	1.85
Germany (W in 1989)	3.89	2.93	2.30
Italy	9.10	4.05	5.57
Netherlands	3.19	2.51	2.48
Sweden	8.00	5.54	3.87
UK	2.63	2.63	1.21
Eastern Europe			
Bulgaria	n.d.	6.41	5.60
Czech Republic	7.04	3.44	1.99
Estonia	n.d.	3.34	4.87
Hungary	2.11	2.15	1.54
Latvia	n.d.	0.74	n.d.
Lithuania	n.d.	2.05	2.71
Poland	n.d.	1.15	0.99
Romania	n.d.	n.d.	3.66
Slovakia	3.29	4.11	2.02

Note: Averages calculated on the basis of a full set of countries.
n.d. no data
Source: van Biezen et al. (2012, 43–46, Appendix Table 1).

leadership, rather than the organizational resources or the programmatic appeals of the parties, which accounts for electoral success, although professionalization of the (remaining) members also counts (see Tavits 2013). The weakening ties to parties can also be seen in the region's voting behavior; parties are facing the challenge to compete over an ever larger cohort of unaligned voters which results in a high level of fluidity of the party systems and a wide spreading of voter appeals across the programmatic board (see Pytlas 2016, 6; Rudi 2010; Walczak et al. 2012).

On a more general level, electoral volatility in Eastern Europe is remarkably high and the party systems are under-institutionalized. Following Mainwaring and Scully (1995), who identify as the most important criterion of institutionalization a regularity in patterns of party competition, followed by the parties having stable roots in society (i.e. a cleavage pattern in voting behavior) and adherence to and respect for the rules of the electoral game, the new democracies in Eastern Europe fall behind other democratic regions (see Bielasiak 2002; Casal Bértoa 2012). Electoral volatility since the inauguration of democracy in Central and Eastern Europe was four times as high as in established democracies (see Savage 2016, 504). Also, the under-institutionalization of East European party systems can be measured by the number and vote share of new parties: between 1990 and 2004, there was an average 5.6 new parties per election, with an average vote share of 19% (ibid.; also Powell and Tucker 2014). Part of the explanation lies in political and ethnic fragmentation in some countries; other factors are the economic and institutional contexts of the elections (Mainwaring and Zoco 2007; Powell and Tucker 2014; Sikk 2005; Tavits 2008). These explanations have been complemented by new findings pointing at the role of corruption: while historically derived corruption reduces electoral volatility and support for new parties, due to the clientelist structures which bind voters to old parties, the increased perception of corruption leads to a loss of trust in the established elites and provides opportunities for new parties, thus raising electoral volatility (Engler 2016). Since levels of political trust are generally lower in Eastern Europe than in the West, electoral volatility should remain higher in the East.

Political-cultural differences between East and West also persist in other respects. Survey data show an East European average of 17% of the population in 2013 who trust the national parliament (national government 22%, political parties 13%), as compared with 39% in Western Europe (national government 37%, political parties 25%), 63% in Northern Europe (national government 48%, political parties 38%), and 19% in Southern Europe (national government 19%, political parties 14%). Except for Southern Europe, where the fiscal crisis led to a severe drop in the levels of trust after 2008 (minus 19% in the case of trust in parliament), the levels and differences have remained relatively stable over time with only single-digit decreases in percentage points (Mungiu-Pippidi 2015, 10; see also Macek and Marková 2004). This East–West pattern corresponds to the larger political-cultural frame, in particular support for democracy, on a number of levels from general or abstract to the specific democratic order of the respective countries to civil liberties and political participation. Democratic support and culture are generally lower in the new democracies in the East than the older democracies in Western Europe, although there are signs that the gap is slowly closing (see Almond et al. 2009, 22–41; Fuchs and Roller 2006; Klingemann 2014).

Finally, state response to oppositional politics or the politics of contention and the role of civil society may be more consequential for right-wing radical mobilization than patterns of party competition alone (see Stepan and Linz 1996; Kopecký and Mudde 2003; Mudde 2005a). On the one hand, civil society in the region consists of a number of groups in many countries which, in the classical literature on civil society, could be summarily labeled as "un-civil society," that is less of a quality enhancing democracy and more of a quality challenging democracy; hence there is no clear boundary between civil and uncivil society (see Mudde 2003). Moreover, comparative studies document a universal under-development of civil society in the region across several indicators (except in the Czech Republic, Slovenia, and Estonia), compared to the West European average (Merkel 2010, 423–429; also Weßels 2003). Recent studies show "a large and temporarily resilient post-communist deficit in civic participation" (Pop-Eleches and Tucker 2013, 63), which can be explained by both living through communism—this is the argument made by Howard (2003)—and by living through the collapse of communism. In his seminal study on civil society in post-communist countries in Eastern Europe, Marc M. Howard demonstrates that, in post-communist democracies, the average number of organizational membership of individuals is significantly lower (a mean of 0.91) than in the older democracies of Western Europe and beyond (a mean of 2.39) and in post-authoritarian democracies in Southern Europe, Latin America, and Asia (a mean of 1.82), and that this situation may not simply reflect a (temporary) weakness but can be seen as a decline in the post-communist period (2011, 63–73). At the same time, other studies point at a divergence of post-communist civil societies reflecting historical legacies and different outcomes of the post-communist transformation (see Ekiert and Kubik 2014).

On the other hand, state reaction to contentious politics by the radical right is closely tied to the above-mentioned porous borders between the political mainstream and the margins, particularly concerning the spread of nationalism. In the course of the transformation process, most states in the region have introduced the arsenal of "militant democracy," that is the restriction of rights and political organization such as party bans and censorship in the name of defending democracy (see Capoccia 2013; Müller 2012). But with few exceptions, its implementation and application has been rather deficient, insofar as it is rarely used against the racist and radical right (see Jesse and Thieme 2011, 437–439; Mareš 2012, 2015; Mudde 2003, 158–163, 2005a, 274–277; also Priban and Sadurski 2006; Sajó 2004).

Following these considerations and earlier work (Beichelt and Minkenberg 2002; Minkenberg 2002a, 2009a), Table 3.5 provides a summary of the relevant context factors for the Eastern European radical right and suggests that the countries under consideration dispose of different opportunity structures for the emergence of the radical right. Due to the resistance to the Ottoman Empire (political sphere) and the guidance of the Greek Orthodox Church (socio-cultural sphere) Bulgaria has clearly developed as a cultural nation, which since the late nineteenth century had been organized independently, even if official independence from Ottoman rule only came in 1909. The possible roots of right-wing radicalism have to be seen mainly in the conflict structure of today's society, which manifest themselves in the ongoing regime conflict in conjunction with the existence of an easily identifiable (Turkish) minority. This pattern can also be observed in some neighboring countries, notably Moldova, Romania, and Slovakia. The minority issue in these countries had been included in the regime conflict during the 1990s, with post-communist actors willing to instrumentalize ethnic interests in the battle against handing over the power to "democrats" and the new capitalist order. In contrast to Bulgaria, Romania should be seen as an ethnic nation, in particular because of the cultivation of Romanian ethnicity under the fascist-autocratic Antonescu and the communist-nationalist Ceauşescu regimes at the expense of the Hungarian minority in Western Romania— a conflict which is still carried on today.

Table 3.5 Context factors for the radical right in Eastern Europe

	Historical and cultural conditions				Opportunity structures		
	Nation type (Main mode of reference)	Fusion of religious and national identity [a]	Existence of external national homelands	Ethnic homogeneity in the early 1990s [b]	Regime conflict: Regime contested by major political forces in 1990s	Party competition (Clear distinction between political camps)	State repression or containment of radical Right [c]
Czech Rep.	Ethnic	Low	No	Medium	No	Yes	Yes
Hungary	Ethnic	Medium	Yes	High	No	Yes	No
Estonia	Ethnic	Low	No	Low	No	Yes	Yes
Latvia	Ethnic	Low	No	Low	No	Yes	No
Lithuania	Ethnic	High	No	Medium	No	Yes	No
Poland	Culture	High	No	High	Yes	No	No
Slovakia	Ethnic	High	No	High	Yes	No	Yes
Bulgaria	Culture	High	No	High	Yes	No	No
Romania	Ethnic	High	Yes	High	Yes	No	No

[a] According to Fig. 3.1 (for Romania, see Andreescu 2015; for Estonia and Lithuania, see Kilp 2009, 226).
[b] Based on census data (see Table 3.2): high = 85% or more belonging to the ethnic majority population; medium = 70–85% belonging to the ethnic majority population; low = less than 70% belonging to the ethnic majority population.
[c] Based on country chapters in Mudde 2005b.
Source: Beichelt and Minkenberg (2002), updated.

At first view, the situation of the Slovak and Czech Republics appear to be rather similar due to their common history and the experience of their 1993 partition (see Beichelt and Minkenberg 2002, 15; Table 3.2). However, there are important differences in cultural and political terms. The revival of Czech culture and ethnic nationalism in the nineteenth century referred to Bohemia mainly. Tomas Masaryk, Czechoslovakia's first president after World War I, was a Slovak himself and his argument that Czechs and Slovaks constituted a joint nation was politically motivated; his initial goal before the war was to establish an autonomous province within the Habsburg Empire. The only period of reference for an independent Slovakia is the clerical-fascist regime of Jozef Tiso during 1939–1945. The "velvet divorce" of 1992, then, changed a lot more for the Slovaks than for the Czechs.

The Slovaks, the majority of whom opposed the divorce (Vodicka 1994, 175–186), had to reorient themselves both politically and culturally. In religious terms, they "gained" a higher congruence between nation and (Catholic) religion, in contrast to the much more secularized Czechs. But they were faced with a problem the Czechs left behind with the partition: the Hungarian minority. On the other hand, the Czech Republic inherited a small Slovak minority (3%) from the joint nation-state. All this helps explain why the Czechs were able to overcome the regime conflict very quickly, whereas Vladimir Meciar's party, the HZDS, had to rely to a much greater extent on the old elites of the Czechoslovak Republic, especially at the sub-national level. Both countries apply the tools of militant democracy but in the Czech Republic it is used more consistently and forcefully as repression (see Mareš 2012), while in Slovakia the state strategy can be classified as containment, aiming occasionally at particular groups.

During the 1990s, the regime conflict also lingered on in Bulgaria and Romania; the latter experiencing, like Slovakia, a coalition government, including the major radical right party of the country. Likewise, the quasi-establishment of the Orthodox Church in both countries after 1989 led to a high level of fusion between religious and national identity, in the face of significant national minorities who belong to a different creed (Hungarians in Romania, Turks in Bulgaria). The countries diverge concerning external homelands: like Hungary in 1920, Romania also lost some territory after World War II. This lost region was called Bessarabia and today constitutes the country of Moldavia.

The remaining countries are all characterized by the fact that the regime conflict has been largely resolved. Estonia and Latvia (like Lithuania, not shown here) gained independence in the early 1990s but experienced a period of statehood between the wars. The rule by Nazi Germany and the Soviet Union and the deliberate migration of Russians to Estonia during the Soviet period left deep traces and fostered a clearly ethnic sense of nationhood in these two nations. Their entire political sphere has been marked by the elite's will to escape Russian power as much and as soon as possible; thus instead of a regime conflict there is an unusual elite consensus concerning political and economic questions. In Hungary, an ethno-cultural sense of nation developed under the auspices of the Dual Monarchy. However, due to the Treaty of Trianon in 1920, the country lost two-thirds of its former territory with several millions of Hungarians (one-third of the pre-1920 Hungarian population) living outside their native state. The question of external homelands heavily burdened the interwar regime and eventually led to an authoritarian regime with fascist traits. Therefore, defining oneself as Hungarian today has a strong ethnic ring (see Fischer 1999, 138–146). The Polish nation is marked by a strong sense of cultural nationhood and a high fusion of national and religious identity (see Grzymała-Busse 2015; Porter-Szücs 2011). The main contributing factors include the long history of partition and foreign rule, the role of the Catholic Church in providing a focus of national identity, and the results of World War II, in particular the territorial and population shift to the West and the disappearance of ethnic minorities (see Davies 1986, 283–287). In Poland, the character of the interwar regime seems to be more heavily debated than in some other Central European states where authoritarian rulers took over the weak democracies in the interwar period: after 1989, the antagonism between pro-Russian Roman Dmowski and anti-Russian Józef Piłsudski experienced a remarkable revival (see Pankowski 2010; Stankiewicz 2002; Zubrzycki 2006).

To summarize: this chapter has shown the usefulness of the legacies approach to understanding current politics in Eastern Europe. To these belong distinct ways of nation-building, the failure of democracy in the interwar period (except for Czechoslovakia), and the incorporation into the communist bloc after World War II, which interrupted the nation-building processes until the Velvet Revolution of 1989. I have also expounded the problems of the teleological assumptions of much of the literature on transformation and democratic consolidation which appeared in the 1990s. Against the particular historical backdrop, I outlined the particularities of the East European context structures of the radical right, as opposed to those in Western Europe. These include a political culture with low levels of trust, a weak rootedness of the party systems in society and diverging cleavage patterns, a different set of issues feeding the radical right, and a mainstream which is more sympathetic towards nationalism than in Western Europe. The set of issues driving the West European radical right, that is immigration and insecurity, does not correspond to the agenda in the East which is much more centered on historical grievances or narratives, in particular political leaders in past dictatorial regimes, the role of national minorities (in the face of very low levels of immigration), and border questions (irredentism). It is the purpose of the next chapter to connect these context factors to the field of the radical right in the countries under consideration and to assess the radical right's particularities within and variation across individual countries in comparison to their Western European counterparts.

Notes

1. Although Jowitt's pessimistic prediction did not come true, his emphasis on the crucial role of the West was seen by some as one of the accomplishments of his analysis (see Howard 2006, 41).
2. Determining the political relevance of ethnic or national minorities based on size is a difficult task, not least because of notable discrepancies in the data depending on the source (government sources, NGOs, minorities themselves). See contributions to Stein (2000) and Pan and Pfeil (2000, xviii–xxi); also more fundamentally Horowitz (1985).

CHAPTER 4

Contents: Organizational Patterns and Ideological Profiles

Abstract The focus in this chapter turns to a detailed analysis of the entire field of radical right actors in the region. The central question to be asked is to what extent the radical right in East European democracies differs from that in the West, especially in its organizational and ideological characteristics. The analysis of parties will show that the platforms of most of the radical right in the region is more openly anti-democratic, anti-liberal, racist, and historically revisionist than those of the (successful) parties in Western Europe. On the movement level, the analysis will point at the porous borders between radical right parties and militant or violent activists, although here comparative data on the organizational strength and protest events of movements in the region are hard to come by.

Keywords Extremism · Territorial revisionism · Racism · Anti-democracy · Party organization · Movement strength

After having established the specific East European context in which the radical right operates, the focus now turns to a detailed analysis of the entire field of radical right actors in the region. The central question to be asked is to what extent the radical right in East European democracies differs from that in the West, especially in its organizational and ideological characteristics. For this, the analysis of parties will focus on the programmatic profile and discuss whether it is more anti-democratic, racist, and historically revisionist than (successful) radical right parties in Western Europe. The discussion also includes an overview of the movement sector, although here comparative data on the organizational strength and protest events of movements in the region are hard to come by.

1 Mapping the Radical Right in the Region

In the first decade following the end of the Cold War, the radical right in the region presented itself as a lively phenomenon but as one widely diverse in success and visibility across the budding new member states. Efforts at the time to capture the patterns of the radical right and to map it for the entire region showed an almost complete absence of such parties in the Baltic States and in Bulgaria in contrast to—as it seemed—electorally firmly settled parties in countries with an already advanced process of democratic consolidation (Czech Republic, Hungary). In two countries (Slovakia, Romania) the radical right had already had government experience in the mid-1990s (see Chapter 6). Besides the parties, an equally lively movement sector had emerged which, as in Western Europe, mobilized more extreme segments of ultranationalists and racists and was accompanied by violent neo-Nazi and racist subcultures in most countries.

Table 4.1 summarizes the situation for the 1990s until the beginning of the new decade. Right-wing radical parties are classified according to their political relevance in terms of their successful electoral performance (with "success" defined here as 5% or more in at least two national elections and/or direct or indirect participation in a government coalition). Classifications such as these are always snapshots at a particular historical moment. Parties can evolve and move out of the designated "box." A textbook case in Western Europe is the Italian Alleanza Nazionale which started as a neo-fascist party under its previous name Movimento Sociale Italiano (MSI) and ended up a conservative party by the late 1990s. Likewise, in Eastern Europe some parties evade easy classifications such as the Polish Samoobrona or the Slovak People's Party-Movement for a Democratic Slovakia. The former combined left-wing economic positions with a nationalist and anti-EU platform, the latter moved from a populist right-wing position in the 1990s towards the mainstream by 2000; (see Mesežnikov 2008; Pankowski 2010, 135–146). In consequence, these parties are not included in Table 4.1.

Table 4.1 Major radical right actors in Eastern Europe (1990–2000)

	Parties	Movements	Subcultural milieus
Extremist right (fascist-autocratic right, often incl. racism or xenophobia)	PWN-PSN (PL) **SPR-RSČ (CZ)** SNJ (SK) **SNS (SK)** **PRM (RO)**	NO (CZ) SP (SK) NOP, ONR (PL) VR (RO)	Neo-Nazis (all) Skinheads (all) Blood and Honour (all)
Ethnocentrist right (racist or xenophobic right but excluding fascism)	**KPN-SN (PL)** **TB/LNNK (LV)** **LTS (LT)** ROP (PL) MIÉP (HU) PSM (RO) PUNR (RO)	Radio Maryja (PL) MS (SK) MÖM (HU)	Neo-Nazis (all) Skinheads (all)
Religious-fundamentalist right (incl. xenophobia)	ZChN (PL)	Radio Maryja (PL)	

Note: Parties in bold have achieved 5% of the votes or more in at least two national parliamentary elections in the 1990s and/or are part of a coalition government (see also Table 5.1).
Source: Minkenberg (2002a, 347, Table 4 revised).

In Romania, easily identifiable right-wing radical parties coexisted with the strongly nationalist successor party of Ceauşescu's communist party. Among the former were the Party for Greater Romania (PRM) and the Party of Romanian Unity (PUNR). The PRM, founded in 1991 by Eugen Barbu and Corneliu Vadim Tudor and led by Tudor, claimed a membership of 35,000 in the mid-1990s and made itself noticed throughout Europe with an openly anti-Semitic and xenophobic, that is particularly anti-Hungarian and anti-Roma, ideology coupled with an anti-democratic and anti-Western doctrine. The latter was derived from a glorification of the Partida Nationala, a nationalist movement of the 1830s, the fascist ideology of the Iron Guards and dictator Marshall Antonescu of the interwar period, and the communist past under Ceauşescu. In the 2000 presidential and parliamentary elections, Tudor and his party reached a peak of support. By comparison, PUNR, founded in 1990 but dissolved around 2000, seemed slightly less extreme. This party was also chauvinist, dirigiste, and particularly anti-Hungarian, but not as openly anti-Semitic and anti-democratic as the PRM. The Socialist Workers Party (PSM) which succeeded the Romanian Communist Party but fared less well than other post-communist parties in Central and Eastern Europe fused nationalist with socialist ideas and openly rejected democracy and Western values and culture. All three parties were temporary members of an informal majority coalition from 1992 to 1994 under the leadership of the Social Democratic Party (PSD) (see Gallagher 1995, 25–47; Minkenberg 2002a, 348–349; Shafir 2000).

As in Romania, the Polish situation was characterized by a high degree of fluidity which often led to a restructuring of the party system and reorganization and renaming of individual parties (see Chapter 3). There were six radical right-wing parties in Poland in the early 1990s but none of them entered parliament in the first elections (see Kalina 2000). The most important ones in the 1990s were the National Front Party of the Fatherland (Stronnictwo Narodowe 'Ojczyzna', SN) which advocated an explicit anti-Semitic and anti-German platform and was oriented at the nationalist ideas of Roman Dmowski of the interwar period (see Walicki 2000; Pankowski 2010), the Movement for the Reconstruction of Poland ROP (Ruch Odbudowy Polski) which joined the alliance with the Solidarity group (AWS) in 1997 but broke apart before the 2001 elections, and the Confederation for an independent Poland (Konfederacja Polski Niepodleglej, KPN) which was ideologically modeled after the ideas of Pilsudski. Finally, as a Polish peculiarity, there was a clerical-nationalist party, the Christian National Union (Zjednoczenie Chrześcijańsko-Narodowe, ZChN), which also followed Roman Dmowski and advocated that Catholic dogma should be the basis of Polish politics and which claims to embrace the interest of ethnic Poles in all of Eastern Europe (see Kalina 2000, 78–82; Ost 1999, 98–100). Unlike in other countries in the region, the Polish radical right parties in the 1990s had a rather limited following which was attributed to the fact "that it lacks a persuasive target against which to mobilize constituents" (Ost 1999, 88). However, with the growing importance of EU accession and the increasing weight of the Western neighbor countries in the process as well as new waves of socio-cultural liberalization, in particular the politicization of gender issues, the Polish radical right found such a target (see Pytlas 2016, 89–92).

In the Czech Republic, the most important party on the radical right was the "Republicans" (SPR-RSČ), founded in 1989 and led by Miroslav Sladek. This party was modeled after Shirinovsky's Russian Liberal-Democratic Party (LDPR) and the German "Republikaner", and was openly xenophobic and the only Czech party which did not accept the secession of Slovakia. Its dreams of an "ethnically pure" greater Czechoslovakia (comprising only Slavic people) were combined with visions of a paternalistic and corporatist, that is authoritarian, state (Szayna 1997, 125). In 1994, the party had about 25,000 members, thus making it the third largest party in the Czech Republic and, compared with the German Republikaner or DVU, an unusually strong radical right-wing party (Brendgens 1998, 60). Nonetheless, in the 1998 parliamentary elections, the SPR-RSČ lost all their seats. In contrast to the Polish and Czech cases in the second half of the 1990s, the situation in Hungary was less volatile. Here, the radical right was dominated by a single and electorally successful party, Istvan Czurka's Hungarian Justice and Life Party (MIÉP). This party split off in 1993 from the conservative Hungarian Democratic Forum (Magyar Demokráta Fórum, MDF), one of the major players in the Velvet Revolution of 1989. MIÉP advocated anti-Semitic and biological-racist and nativist views; one of its major tenets was the undoing of the Treaty of Trianon and the recovery of the old Hungarian territory which now belongs to Romania, Ukraine, and Slovakia, a position supported by 19% of the voters in 1994 (see Minkenberg 2002a, 352; Pytlas 2016, 171).

In the movement sector, Poland and Romania had the most active scenes with a number of fascist or otherwise extremist groups mobilizing the streets against minorities and the political establishment, often using violence. The anti-Hungarian Romanian Cradle (Vatra românească) was led by a former Iron Guardist, Iosif Drăgan, who strove for the rehabilitation of the pre-war leader Marshall Antonescu: he headed two organizations celebrating Antonescu and was instrumental in having several statues of the dictator set up. The Iron Guard also inspired other groups, such as the fundamentalist organizations New Christian Romania and Christian Legion, which were denied official registration and organized locally in several municipalities, and the magazine *New Right* (*Noua dreaptă*). A regular contributor to this magazine was Ion Coja (a university professor and senator from 1992 to 1996) who kept vindicating the Iron Guard and also was co-founder and vice chairman of the Romanian Cradle (see Grün 2002, 294–296; Shafir 2000, 254–261). In Poland, the most important non-party organization of the radical right was and is the ultra-Catholic radio station and media network Radio Maryja, founded and led by Father Tadeusz Rydzyk of the Redemptorist order. With about one million regular listeners and several hundred thousand activists (around 2000), Radio Maryja and its corollaries constitute "a mass social movement" (Pankowski 2010, 96). Prima facie a religious media network, which challenges the alleged liberalization of the Polish Catholic Church, the group sends strong political messages which combine anti-liberal, anti-Western, and sometimes anti-Semitic messages with conspiracy theories and ultranationalism, thereby reanimating the ultra-Catholic and anti-democratc ideology of Roman Dmowski (see Maszkovski 2004; Minkenberg 2002a, 353–355; Mudde 2005a, 269–271; Pankowski 2010, 95–98; Zubrzicki 2006, 81–87).

Finally, in the Baltic States, the alliance between For Fatherland and Freedom (TB) and the Latvian National Independence Movement (LNNK) emerged after 1989 as the most important radical right players in the party system (see Auers and Kasekamp 2015, 139). Their romantic ultranationalism was directed against liberal and pluralistic visions of democracy and society and heavily influenced by the parties of pro-Russian speakers and the fact that, in Latvia, nationalism constitutes part of the mainstream itself (see Minkenberg 2015b, 39). Here the cleavage exists between ethnic Latvians and pro-Russian speaker parties, with the former refusing political collaboration with the latter (see Auers 2013).

During the 2000s, a number of significant changes unfolded in the region's radical right-wing party sector, which is summarized in Table 4.2.

In Poland, the dominant parties KPN-SN and ZChN disappeared and were replaced by a new party, the League of Polish Families (LPR) which took up the banner and reactivated the networks of its defunct predecessors (ZChN, ROP, SN). LPR was founded prior to the 2001 elections and

Table 4.2 Major radical right actors in Eastern Europe (2001–2010)

	Parties	Movements	Subcultural milieus
Extremist right (fascist-autocratic right, often incl. racism or xenophobia)	PWN-PSN (PL) SNJ (SK) **SNS (SK)**	NO (CZ) SP (SK) ONR (PL)	Neo-Nazis (all) Skinheads (all) Blood and Honour (all)
	Jobbik (HU) **Ataka (BG)** **PRM (RO)** VL (LV)	VR (RO) Magyar Garda (HU) VL (LV)	
Ethnocentrist right (racist or xenophobic right but excluding fascism)	MIÉP (HU) LTS (LT)	Radio Maryja (PL) MS (SK) MÖM (HU)	Neo-Nazis (all) Skinheads (all)
Religious-fundamentalist right (incl. xenophobia)	**LPR (PL)**	Radio Maryja (PL)	All-Polish Youth (PL)

Note: Parties in bold have achieved 5% of the votes or more in at least two national parliamentary elections in the 1990s and/or are part of a coalition government (see also Table 5.1).
Source: Minkenberg (2002a, 347, Table 4 revised).

Radio Maryja was instrumental in bringing about the new party: "the endorsement by Father Tadeusz Rydzyk was the single most important factor in securing parliamentary seats for the newly established group" (Pankowski 2010, 111; see also Zubrzycki 2006, 84). While previously the Polish radical right sector was fragmented in various ultranationalist groups, the LPR for the first time since 1989 integrated many of these groups and led them to unprecedented political success, the entry and re-entry into parliament in 2001 and 2005 and government participation from 2005 until 2007 (see Kasprowicz 2015, 164). However, the success story ended as spectacularly as it began: in the 2007 elections, LPR abruptly lost almost all voters and all seats and ended up in demise. In the remainder of the decade, the erstwhile government partner, the Law and Justice Party (PiS), took over much of the electorate and also some leading figures from the LPR, along with the support by Radio Maryja.

Hungary saw a profound transformation of the radical right sector. MIÉP's failure to reenter parliament in the 2002 elections led to its decline and its eventual substitution by the newly established Jobbik (Movement for a Better Hungary). This party, founded in 2003 and since 2009 under the leadership of its founder Gábor Vona, ran together with MIÉP on a list in the 2006 parliamentary elections and failed to enter parliament. Between 2006 and 2010 and after the breakup of the alliance, MIÉP was increasingly marginalized while Jobbik radicalized its agenda. It attacked all other parties as criminal and focused on the alleged "Gypsy crime" and "Gypsy terror," alongside anti-liberal and anti-Semitic messages—a formula which helped it enter parliament in 2010 with a massive 16.7% of the vote (after having entered the European Parliament in 2009 with 14.8%) (see Karácsony and Róna 2011; Krekó and Mayer 2015, 188–192; Pytlas 2016, 191–206). In both Poland and Hungary, the transformation of the radical right party sector was accompanied by the rise of a new movement on the far right, the All-Polish Youth and later Ruch Narodowy in Poland, and the Hungarian Guard in Hungary, the latter being intimately connected to Jobbik.

In Bulgaria, a country with particularly favorable conditions for the radical right but for a long time without a significant party (see Beichelt and Minkenberg 2002, and Figure 3.3), the radical right finally took its place and began catching up with the rest of the region by 2005. Ataka, founded in 2005 in part in reaction to the increasing political activities of the substantial Turkish minority in Bulgaria but also attacking Roma and Jews for the problems in the country, entered parliament in June 2005 with 8.1% of the vote and has kept its seats with slight variations in electoral support up to today (see Pirro 2015, 57–67). In the Baltic States, the situation diverged sharply. While the Estonian Independence Party, which became the most important radical right actor in the 2000s, shifted the focus from blaming the legacies of the Soviet Union to attacking the EU, but failed to receive even 1% in the parliament elections, the Latvian radical right and its standard bearers TB and LNNK held on for a while; however, they moderated their program due to government responsibility and their support began to decline from the mid-2000s (Auers and Kasekamp 2013, 239).

In a number of countries, the shifts in the radical right sector continued after EU accession and into the new decade after 2010 (see Table 4.3). The most significant changes concern the complete disappearance of the Polish LPR and the tentative replacement by a new group, the National Movement (RN) which was created in 2012 in collaboration with various right-wing groups, most notably the All-Polish Youth. This group, modeled after the interwar fascist movement Falanga and following in the footsteps of Roman Dmowski, supported the far right party Kukiz'15 in the 2015 parliamentary elections, thereby gaining five parliamentary seats of the 42 that Kukiz achieved with its 21% of the vote. Next to the RN, another new party on the right is the Congress of the New Right (Kongres Nowej Prawicy), founded in 2011 under the leadership of Janusz Korwin-Mikke who left the

Table 4.3 Major radical right actors in Eastern Europe (after 2010)

	Parties	Movements	Subcultural milieus
Extremist right (fascist-autocratic right, often incl. racism or xenophobia)	Kotleba (SK) RN (PL) **NA (LV)**	SP (SK) RN (PL) VR, ND (RO)	Neo-Nazis (all) Skinheads (all) Blood and Honour (all)
	Jobbik (HU) Ataka (BG) PRM (RO)	Magyar Garda (HU)	
Ethnocentrist right (racist or xenophobic right but excluding fascism)	Kukiz'15 (PL) SNS (SK) LTS (LT)	Radio Maryja (PL) MS (SK) MÖM (HU)	Neo-Nazis (all) Skinheads (all)
Religious-fundamentalist right (incl. xenophobia)		Radio Maryja (PL)	All-Polish Youth (PL)

Note: Parties in bold have achieved 5% of the votes or more in at least two national parliamentary elections in the 1990s and/or are part of a coalition government (see also Table 5.1).
Source: Minkenberg (2002a, 347, Table 4 revised).

party in early 2015. The KNP's platform is considered populist and combines economic libertarianism, social conservatism, and radical Euroscepticism, but unlike most other parties of the radical right it does not favor a strong authoritarian state (see Bachrynowski 2015). While the KNP gained 7% of the vote and four seats in the European elections of 2014, it failed miserably in the Polish parliamentary elections in 2015 with less than 0.1%; however, one KNP candidate gained a seat in the Sejm on the Kukiz'15 list.

In Slovakia, the Slovak National Party SNS re-entered parliament in the March 2016 parliamentary elections with 8.6% of the vote. Under its new leader since 2012, Andrej Danko, the party has moderated some of its positions and distanced itself from the previous leader Jan Slota who sympathized with the fascist regime in the country during World War II (see Gyárfášová and Mesežnikov 2015). This position on the extreme right of the Slovak party system has now been taken by a new party, Kotleba—People's Party Our Slovakia, which is led by Marián Kotleba, an erstwhile activist in fascist movements and an admirer of the pro-Nazi Hlinka Guard which was active during World War II. This party achieved 8% of the vote in the March 2016 elections. Finally, in Latvia, All for Latvia!, which transformed into a party in 2006, merged with the LB/TNNK and formed the National Alliance (Nacionālā apvienība—NA) which after the 2011 elections joined a coalition government (see Auers and Kasekamp 2015, 140–142).[1]

This overview of the radical right in Eastern Europe indicates a considerable level of fluidity in the far right sector, a constant reconstitution of the field with only very few exceptions such as the Slovak National Party or Radio Maryja in Poland which have persisted since the 1990s. This particularity is echoed by the tendency of the more relevant parties to be more ideologically extreme than their West European counterparts.

2 Ideology—Assessing the Democratic Quality

When it comes to the programmatic orientation of the East European radical right, the argument here is that, typically, these parties'—as well as the radical right movements'—ideologies are characterized by a troubled or antithetical relationship to the democratic order in which they operate, if not to democracy as such. In the following, this point will be substantiated in more detail by discussing these actors' prevailing programmatic positions regarding democracy, including their vision of the nation-state and national identity, territorial revisionism, minority and civil rights, and religion. Economic issues, that is whether they espouse more "left-wing" or "right-wing" economic platforms, are of secondary importance here because they are not linked to the core concern of the democratic quality of these programs. Nor can this issue dimension be used to carve out a distinctiveness of the Eastern as compared to the Western European radical right. In fact, right-wing radical parties in East and West are not different in this regard because they share "economic nativism": "while the Eastern European parties are the most extreme in their demands to protect the nation against foreign economic dominance, all European populist radical right parties are characterized by an essentially nativist approach to economics" (Mudde 2007, 127). This insight runs against the prevailing argument that the radical right in the West is economically neo-liberal, as postulated by many experts such as Kitschelt (1995) whose familiar "winning formula" of new radical right parties includes market liberalism (see discussion in Minkenberg 2000).

Instead, a true distinction between the Western and Eastern radical right can be found in these parties' relationship to the pre- and anti-democratic past of their respective nation-states. It has already been pointed out in Chapter 3 that the entire region is characterized by a history of democratic underdevelopment up until 1989 (with the exception of Czechoslovakia). This history and the accompanying narratives color many parties' agendas. Their leaders proclaim nostalgia for the old despotic regimes, and the ethnic and territorial conception of national identity that prevailed under them, following the nation-building struggles before and after World War I (see Hobsbawm 1990). Many of these groups adapt symbols of the fascist movements and regimes of the 1930s and 1940s, such as Hungary's Arrow Cross movement, Romania's Iron Guard and the Romanian Legion, or the revival of Roman Dmowski's anti-liberal, anti-Western ultra-Catholicism in Poland.

Also, history matters in another way. A powerful effect of the past or historical legacies, in which ultranationalist traditions mix with the type of communist regime that existed between 1948 and 1989, can be detected. An analysis of seventeen countries in the former communist East (Bustikova and Kitschelt 2009) shows that, in countries with a legacy of national-accommodative communism and a welfare state safety net for the losers of regime change, the radical right receives only limited support. In contrast, countries with a patrimonial communist legacy witness a resonance of "red-brown" anti-capitalist, authoritarian, and exclusionary programs with considerable segments of the public. This is illustrated by a comparison between Bulgaria and Romania regarding the adaptation of interwar fascist discourse into the contemporary radical right (see Frusetta and Glont 2009). Whereas a Bulgarian fascist ideology was only loosely articulated, Ataka's leader Volen Siderov recycled interwar anti-Semitism, Orthodox mysticism, and fascist slogans and mixed them with a Eurasian vision of a "new order" which opposes American hegemony, a concept very popular among segments of the Russian radical right (see Umland 2007). The party supported the creation of a "nationalist militia" in 2013 with the purpose of confronting alleged immigrant and Roma "terror" on the streets, and in 2014 Siderov and others in the party also engaged in physical violence against police and bystanders at Varna airport (see Avramov 2015, 311–312). Until the party's recent mainstreaming (see Pirro 2015, 60–61), this kind of agenda and action did not add up to fascism but it is clearly outside the boundaries of democratic politics.

The case of a regurgitated authoritarian past is clearer in Romania. While the Party for Greater Romania PRM did not openly embrace interwar fascism, other top figures of the radical right, such as intellectual Ion Coja and PRM member Gheorghe Buzatu, embraced the interwar Legion of Archangel Michael, or Iron Guard, which saw itself as part of a European-wide fascist movement and PRM leader Corneliu Vadim Tudor's anti-Semitism linked up with that of the Legion (see Frusetta and Glont 2009, 563–564). Moreover, Tudor also entertained ties to the Marshal Antonescu Foundation which cherishes the legacy of Romania's right-wing dictator during World War II who brought the Iron Guard into his government (see Shafir 2000, 254). Expressing public esteem for Antonescu seemed a promising strategy, as in the mid-1990s 62% of Romanians asserted that they had a good opinion of him, a view which was still shared by 46% in 2007 (see Turcanu 2010, 4–5). As the Bulgarian–Romanian comparison shows, the key element for the adaptation of the fascist discourse is not the simple "copying" of the interwar movement styles and ideologies. Rather, it is the legacy of the communist era which matters, that is the communists' own approaches to interwar fascism which functions as a "useable past" for the contemporary radical right (see Frusetta and Glont 2009). In both Bulgaria and Romania the radical right presents itself as the heir to interwar fascism while in fact sharing little in common as far as their ideology in a comprehensive sense is concerned. The dual legacies of fascist ideology and communism are merged into a new anti-democratic agenda, suitable for the post-communist arena of competitive politics, by some labeled as the politics of "radical continuity" in the region (see also Grün 2002; Shafir 2000; and above).

In the Hungarian case, Jobbik has shown similar anti-democratic tendencies to recycle symbols and strategies of the interwar period. First, the party used its rise to prominence for a fundamental questioning of every established policy in Hungary, even the democratic order itself (Bíró Nagy et al. 2013, 232). Likewise, the predecessor party MIÉP adopted ideas and usages from Nazi ideology (such as the concept of "*Lebensraum*") or the distinction between creative and generative capital: "these views are evidently sunken cultural goods of Nazi ideology, which are used for political purposes of mobilization against the constitutional liberal-democratic order" (Bayer 2009, 295). Second, Jobbik went one step further than MIÉP by appropriating ideas of the interwar Hungarian Arrow Cross Party, a fascist movement fought by Hungary's strongman Admiral Horthy who ended up allying Hungary with Nazi Germany in World War II and, under German occupation, handing over his power to the Arrow Cross leader. Moreover, Jobbik created the Hungarian Guard in 2007, a paramilitary organization of "self-defense" against the alleged uncurbed "Roma crime" in Hungarian towns and villages (see Krekó and Mayer 2015, 190). The Hungarian Guard wore uniforms and a flag modeled after the Arrow Cross outfit, resorted to violence against unwanted minorities such as Roma or homosexuals (see Bayer 2009, 298–299), and was eventually banned in 2009—only to resurface under different names (see Pirro 2015, 69). In recent years, especially after Jobbik's electoral success in the 2015 parliamentary elections with 20.2% of the vote, the party adopted a strategy of de-demonization. However, this is to be seen more as an image change or stylistic moderation rather than a substantial shift away from its previous extremism; the party stressed that its program remained the same, and party leaders as well as the party base continue with extremist statements, for example when a Jobbik candidate in a by-election shared his opinion on Facebook that the Roma situation could only be settled by killing Roma (see Bíró-Nagy and Boros 2016, 249–251).

In Hungary's neighboring country Slovakia, the troubled history of nation-building in World War II under a fascist regime and in alliance with Nazi Germany provides a particularly precarious frame of reference for attacking the current order (see Mayer and Odehnal 2010, 185; Mesežnikov 2008). Nonetheless, early on after the end of the communist regime, organizations were established such as the Slovak Peoples Party and the Association Andrej Hlinka to promote the interwar nationalistic leader Andrej Hlinka and the clerical-fascist Jozef Tiso (see Cibulka 1999, 115).

These early efforts had no political success but the SNS and its erstwhile leader, Jan Slota, adopted some of the agenda by accommodating nationalists who wanted a rehabilitation of Hlinka and his regime, for example Slota's failed attempt to have a statue erected in honor of Hlinka or the SNS initiative (without success) to pass a special law on the merits of Hlinka (see Gyárfášová and Mesežnikov 2015, 231). Slota's successor Andrej Danko has toned down the message somewhat but Jan Slota has found a worthy successor in Marián Kotleba and his party who continue to celebrate the Slovak War state, was charged for shouting Nazi slogans used by the Hlinka Guard in World War II, and wore uniforms resembling those of the Hlinka Guard (similar to the Magyar Guard in Hungary). While Kotleba stopped wearing the uniforms after he entered parliament, party activists and candidates continue to play with fascist slogans and symbols (see Petková 2016; Tódóvá 2013).

The Polish situation seems reversed in that comparatively unfavorable opportunity structures have allowed for a rather sizable support for the radical right. Here, low levels of formal structuring of the political right and in particular the ambiguous role of the Catholic Church and its lack of a critical position towards anti-Semitism (see Grzymała-Busse 2015, 158–167; Zubrzycki 2006, Chapters 2 and 3) seem to play into the hands of ultranationalist political entrepreneurs. The "lost territories" in the Polish East play no role for nationalistic mobilization here; though in the early 1990s, 60% of Poles claimed there were lost territories in neighboring countries (see Minkenberg 2002a, 345). Instead, the radical right has been influenced by religious fundamentalism and its illiberal politics. Early twentieth-century anti-Semitic politician and ideologue Roman Dmowski, the theorist of "national democracy," had claimed that only ethnic Poles and Catholics made good Poles (Pankowski and Kornak 2013, 158; see also Zubrzycki 2006, 53–60). The Christian National Union (ZChN) insisted in the 1990s that Catholic dogma had to be the foundation of Poland, and that it must defend the interests of all "ethnic" Poles scattered throughout Eastern Europe. In the early 2000s, the LPR continued the ultra-Catholic and illiberal agenda of its predecessor. It did not reject the democratic order as such but insisted on a Catholic foundation for the Polish state—a position which was articulated in a more radical version by Radio Maryja, which regularly broadcasts traditionalist and xenophobic, and at times anti-Semitic and even anti-democratic statements to millions of listeners (see De Lange and Guerra 2009; Maszkovski 2004; Pankowski 2010, 95–126; Pankowski and Kornak 2013).

In the Baltic States, finally, the historical frames of interwar anti-democratic forces such as Nazi activists for Germany as well as the communist ideology and regime play only a minor role among the major radical right actors. In the early 1990s, the Citizens' Congress in Latvia advocated an ultranationalist vision of Latvia, which idolized the pre-war dictatorship of Kārlis Ulmanis and opposed liberal and pluralistic democracy in favor of an ethnically homogeneous Latvian state and nation. This position is still central in the ideology of the National Alliance, while in Estonia the "war of monuments" erupted in the 2000s over efforts to remove Soviet memorials and to honor those Estonians in World War II who fought for their country in German uniform (see Auers and Kasekamp 2013, 237–243).

Overall, a picture emerges in which the radical right's relationship to democracy and historical pre- or anti-democratic frames can be grouped according to the main frame of reference, which is either the legacy of the pre-communist past, which has been labeled the politics of "radical return," or the fusion of communism and nationalism, that is the politics of "radical continuity" (see Shafir 2000, 248–253; also Grün 2002; Ishiyama 2009, 489–492). Table 4.4 attempts a summary of the discussion which also considers the distinction of national identity in terms of religious and ethnic ultranationalism (see Chapter 3).

In general, the references to pre-democratic regimes or leaders play a central role in the East European radical right's ideology, though they do not replace their official commitment to democracy. Furthermore, interwar right-wing regimes and ideologies are more popular among the Central European radical right, while the communist legacies continue into the radical right in Southeast Europe. However, the notion of the

Table 4.4 The anti-democratic impulse of the East European radical right—regime references

		Historical frame of reference	
		Politics of radical return (Interwar regime/ideologies)	*Politics of radical continuity (Communist era)*
Primary national identity	Ethnic nationalism	MIÉP, Jobbik (HU) SNS, Kotleba (SK) NA (LV)	Ataka (BG) PRM (RO)
	Religious nationalism	LPR (PL)	

"politics of radical continuity" does not propose that interwar right-wing politics are irrelevant for the contemporary radical right. Instead of an "either-or" situation, this is an additive relationship since the prewar past has been passed on through the communist era. But most importantly, none of the historically revisionist orientations exist in any of the major parties of the West European radical right (see Minkenberg 2013a): none of the latter advocates the rehabilitation of interwar fascist leaders or the return of such a regime; fascist sympathizers or enthusiasts for right-wing regimes such as Vichy in France or Dollfuß in Austria are marginal currents or individuals in the electorally successful radical right, or constitute electorally marginal parties such as the German NPD (see Minkenberg 1998, Chapter 7, 2000; also Art 2011; Kitschelt 1995; Mudde 2007).

Next to the radical right's position on the significance of past fascist or authoritarian regimes, territorial revisionism and anti-minority attitudes distinguish the East European radical right from their Western counterparts, and again historical narratives enter contemporary politics. Many of these parties' leaders and platforms advocate more backward-looking ideologies, notably with regard to "lost territories" (see Minkenberg 2002a). Unlike "independence movements" in Western Europe (e.g. in the Basque country or Northern Italy), these parties and movements are the most willing in all of Europe to engage in an ultranationalistic politicization of border issues which challenge the current borders of more than one nation state *and* combine this challenge with an anti-democratic, anti-minority agenda.

The now defunct Czech "Republicans" demanded that their country should fit the borders of the former Czechoslovakia, within which only a "homogeneous" population would have the right to reside (see Mareš 2011, 2015). On the other side of the border, the territorial issue plays a different role. The Slovak radical right does not claim any "lost territories"; instead the SNS has repeatedly played the "Hungarian card," that is the cultivation of a territorial threat scenario, with the threat stemming both from within (the Hungarian minority) and from outside (the Hungarian state). The SNS transmits constant reminders that Hungary does not accept the current borders in the region and regards Slovakia as a lost territory: "frames of 'irredentism' and 'Hungarian dominance', perceived as a threat to sovereignty, can be seen as the most important radical right frame in the Slovak discourse on the relations with the Hungarian state and minorities" (Pytlas 2016, 135; see also Pytlas 2013). Moreover, the SNS cultivates ties to Slovak minorities living abroad and claims that Slovaks in Hungary have been assimilated to the point of invisibility (see Pirro 2015, 91–93).

Nowhere is the irredentist issue more important than in neighboring Hungary. Already in the 1990s, MIÉP had raised the issue of the Treaty of Trianon, thereby taking up the politics of Horthy and the Arrow Cross Party during World War II which was abruptly terminated with the establishment of the post-war order and Soviet hegemony in the region. In the early 2000s, the Fidesz government responded to these concerns by passing legislation which expanded labor market, education, and health care access and other benefits to Hungarians living abroad, the so-called Status Law of 2001 (see Kis 2004; also Pytlas 2016, 158–160). Jobbik continued to use the idea of a Greater Hungary by demanding that Hungary play a role as protector to all Hungarians living abroad and calling for the "reincorporation into the national body of both Western and Carpathian-basin Hungarians" (Jobbik Program of 2010, as quoted in Pirro 2015, 74; see also Bayer 2009; Pytlas 2016, 160–174).

In Romania, the Greater Romania Party promotes interwar borders as a way of demanding the annexation of Moldova (see Andreescu 2005). While the party has largely disappeared from the electoral map, movements such as Noua dreaptă (New Right) continue to mobilize for territorial revisions (see Cinpoeş 2013), and stickers can be found in various public places in Bucharest which remind people, for example ATM users, that "Bessarabia is Romania" (my own observation in August 2012). In neighboring Bulgaria, the scenario resembles the Slovak situation: with a sizable national minority in the country which belongs to the titular nation of a neighboring country, the radical right engages in accusations of irredentism. Like the SNS in Slovakia, Ataka claims that Turkey poses a threat and that separatist forces might try to break away from Bulgaria (see Pirro 2015, 61–62).

Again, these issues are largely absent from the radical right in Western Europe. Irredentism was still on the agenda in previous waves of the radical right in the 1960s and 1970s, when in France Tixier and Le Pen demanded the return of Algeria to France, or in Germany the NPD mobilized against the "New Eastern Policy," that is the Brandt government's recognition of the new borders in Central and Eastern Europe (see Minkenberg 2000). Also, in the Netherlands and Belgium in the 1980s, the Belgian Vlaams Blok and the Dutch CP'86 demanded a Greater Netherlands for all Dutch speaking people (see Mudde 2007,

140). But the new radical right in the West has made a clean break with such territorial revisionism.

Likewise, a distinction can be seen when it comes to the ethnocentric platforms in East and West. In Western Europe, immigration has often been the single most important issue in the radical right discourse, and some define these parties as single-issue "anti-immigrant parties" (see e.g. Art 2011; Ivarsflaten 2008; Van Der Brug et al. 2005). Mudde's treatment of out-group construction by radical right parties (2007, Chapter 3) does not systematically distinguish Eastern and Western types, but he does identify some differences in his classification of the radical right's "enemies" (within or outside the nation, and within or outside the state). However, this concept is overly inclusive; enemies are to be found in multiple groups such as elites, people with different life styles, pro-Westerners (in the East), immigrants, minorities, and competitor parties of the radical right. In the end, this leads to similar differences in the empirical examination, since immigration is not an issue in Eastern Europe (see Chapter 2); immigrants do not figure high on the agenda of the East European radical right but national minorities do (see Mudde 2007, 70–73; also Bustikova and Kitschelt 2009; Bustikova 2015; Minkenberg 2002a). While the groups vary from country to country, the stereotyping proceeds in very similar ways.

In Hungary, Roma bear the brunt of radical right mobilization (see Mihálik 2014). The "Gypsy problem" has been addressed by MIÉP and Jobbik alike (see Pirro 2015, 78), but it was Jobbik, which took the ethnocentrism to a new and electorally successful level. These parties argued not simply against the Roma presence in Hungary but introduced the issue of "Gypsy crime" or "Gypsy terror" (thereby creating a distinctly Roma-related category of crime or terror, rather than simply identifying them as perpetrators) to distinguish themselves from their-near competitor Fidesz and force the mainstream to respond (see Karácsony and Róna 2011; Pytlas 2016, Chapter 7). While Jobbik's leader Gábor Vona has toned down the Roma issue in recent years, second-tier party activists and leaders continue to use the issue in an inflammatory way (see Bíró-Nagy and Boros 2016).

As mentioned before, Hungarians are the main target of radical right mobilization in Slovakia. The former leader of SNS, Jan Slota, confessed in 2006 that he envied the Czechs because they had got rid of the ethnic German minority based on the Beneš decrees, insinuating that he would like to do the same with the Hungarian minority (see Gyárfášová and

Mesežnikov 2015, 234; see also Pytlas 2016, 128–131). Another high official articulated his concern that Hungarians, who according to him belonged neither to Slovakia nor to Europe as a whole, "brought Asian blood to Europe" (personal interview, August 2012). As a government party, the SNS has become more cautious in its statements, but the anti-Roma and anti-Hungarian discourse continues in the new Kotleba party (Spáč and Voda 2014). Hateful anti-Roma rhetoric also fuels the Czech radical right, but here the mainstream maintains a cordon sanitaire and strongly rejects this agenda, although on the local level some contagion effects can be detected (see Mareš 2015, 214–215). In Romania, it is the Roma as well as the Hungarian minority who are targeted by the radical right (see Cinpoeş 2013), while in Bulgaria the Turkish minority takes this position. The situation is slightly different in the Baltic States where very few Roma exist but large Russian minorities challenge the nationalists' idea of their respective countries' identity (see Chapter 3). Hence, anti-Russian mobilization is high on the agenda of the Baltic radical right, though the mobilization potential is restricted because it also informs the nationalist view of the mainstream (see Auers and Kasekamp 2015).

Overall, the Roma minority figures as the transnational scapegoat: "in much of Central Eastern Europe, Roma constitute the main enemies within the state but outside the nation" (Mudde 2007, 86). In most countries, the prejudices are quite similar and include the Roma's alleged biological difference, abnormal life-style, high (genetic) propensity to crime, and their being social parasites, all of which are used as arguments as to why this minority cannot assimilate, poses a constant threat to the society, and hence must be dealt with in radical ways. This is illustrated by the Czech radical right leader Sládek when he pronounced jokingly in parliament in 1996 that "the Gypsy's greatest crime" was that they had been born (see Mareš 2015, 214). This radical portrayal of the out-group serves the radical right (and others) with a particular function: "the identification of parasitic enemies... proclaims the ingroup as hard-working and social. In this way, the enemies provide implicit and intuitive substance to an otherwise vaguely defined 'nativeness'" (Mudde 2007, 89).

The mechanism of this stigmatization should be familiar to anyone who has studied anti-Semitism, in Eastern as well as Western Europe. But there are two important differences here: unlike Roma, Jews have been stereotyped as a powerful and intelligent minority, and they are a very small group in Eastern European countries today. Following the Holocaust their number in the region went down, from 4.7 million in 1939 to 70,000 in 2010 (figures in 2010 in the UK: 280,000, in France: 310,000, and in Germany: 230,000; see Pew 2015). Yet, anti-Semitic prejudices flourish, particularly in Eastern Europe. In a comparative survey in late 2008, the proportion of West Europeans who profess that Jews have too much influence in their respective country ranges between 27.7% in France and 5.6% in the Netherlands, with Germany, the UK and Italy falling in-between; the figures are 49.9% in Poland and 69.2% in Hungary (Zick et al. 2011, 65). No matter how small the Jewish population, the anti-Semitic view is that Jews are over-represented in various political, economic, and cultural elite positions, and one person in particular figures as a scapegoat: "with little exaggeration we could say that the famous financial guru George Soros, who maintains close, friendly relations with the leaders of the Alliance of Free Democrats, and who comes from a Hungarian-Jewish family, is worth several hundred thousand virtual Jews" (Karsai 1999, 142; see also Mudde 2007, 79).[2] While, in Western Europe, open anti-Semitism has become rare in the postwar era, most East European parties of the radical right, with the exception of those in the Czech Republic or Slovenia, espouse explicit anti-Semitism, often in terms of anti-Zionist and pan-Slavic versions (see Mudde 2007, 80–81). This relates to a final aspect of ideological difference between the radical right in the East and in the West, namely religion.

Although a number of Western European groups and parties have longtime links to ultra-conservative or fundamentalist currents of Christianity, such as Le Pen's Front National, the Austrian FPÖ, or the Danish People's Party, religion and in particular Christianity has not been high on their agenda in the past (for the following, see Minkenberg 2017 forthcoming). Only recently have they begun to attack Islam as incompatible not only with their countries' democratic order but also their Christian identity (see Betz 2005, 159–164; Minkenberg 2008, 48–50; Skenderovic 2009, 187). Today, Islamophobia and ethnopluralism have entered the platforms of nearly all contemporary radical right parties in the West as part of their mainstreaming efforts (see Art 2011, 130–131; Minkenberg 2013a, 2017, forthcoming; Mudde 2007, 84–86). Where mainstreaming is not sought, as in small cadre parties such as the British National Front up to the late 1990s, radical right groups remain outright racist and/or put more emphasis on anti-Semitism instead of Islamophobia, with the obvious result of finding political allies in anti-Semitic circles in the Muslim world (see Camus 2011, 272–274; Goodwin 2011, 172–173; see also Carter 2005, 35–41).

In contrast, the East European radical right has stood for a merger of the majority religion and ultranationalist platforms since it appeared on the political scene in the 1990s. Most notably, the Polish radical right professes an ultra-Catholicism which recycles the anti-liberal, anti-Semitic, and anti-Western doctrines of interwar ideologue Roman Dmowski (see above and Porter-Szücs 2011, Chapter 9; Zubrzyicki 2006). These anti-modern ideas find particular resonance with listeners of Radio Maryja, in street marches organized by the All-Polish Youth, and parties such as the now defunct League of Polish Families or the current PiS (Law and Justice) party (see Kasprowicz 2015; Pankowski 2010; Pytlas 2016, 86–106). The Slovak National Party stands for a particularly strong fusion of national identity and Catholicism, which in the first phase of national independence in World War II bordered on clerical fascism. These traditions are carried on by today's SNS which, similarly to the Polish radical right, merges Catholicism and nationalism; moreover the previous leader Jan Slota even tried to rehabilitate the fascist priest Tišo and his regime under the aegis of Nazi Germany (see above and Pirro 2015, 89–91; Václavík 2015). In the Hungary of the 1990s, MIÉP and Fidesz took over Catholic voters when the Hungarian Christian Democratic party declined in the wake of internal rivalries (see Kovács 2001, 258). Today, Jobbik echoes other radical right parties in the region by emphasizing that Hungarian national identity and Christianity are an "inseparable concept" (see Pirro 2015, 71–73). Similarly in Bulgaria, Ataka, which was formed as an anti-Turkish and anti-Muslim party, propagates a Bulgarian nation unified by the Orthodox Christian creed (see Avramov 2015, 300–301; Pirro 2015, 61). And in Romania, where radical right parties have declined since 2000, the Orthodox Church of Romania has taken over the role of an anti-liberal safeguard of the Orthodox identity of the country (see Andreescu 2015).

As a summary of the programmatic survey, Table 4.5 illustrates how and to what extent the radical right disseminates a religious agenda, either in terms of affirming a religious identity of the nation they claim to defend (typically Christian or more specifically Catholic, Protestant, or Orthodox) or by attacking "others" on religious grounds. This reasoning leads to three major types: a largely non-religious radical right, a fundamentally religious radical right, and a radical right which has added religion to its repertoire in the course of its existence. The difference between East and West is striking: all relevant East European parties except for the

Table 4.5 The radical right and their religious agenda in Western and Eastern Europe (since the 1990s)

	Party	Movement
No explicit religious reference/agenda from beginning on	NPD/DVU, Republikaner (DE) NA/NNP/NVU, CD (NL) **MSI/AN** (pre-1995) (IT) MS-FT (IT) BNP (GB) **PRM** (RO) SNJ (SK)	ANS/FAP, NPD (DE) Dansk Front (DK) FANE (FR) ANS/JSN (NL) NOP, ONR, PWN-PSN (PL) MG, MÖM (HU) NSS (SK), VR (RO)
Explicit religious reference/agenda as an addition to ethnocentrist platform	AfD (DE) **Vlaams Blok/Belang** (BE) **Front National** (FR) **DF** (DK) **Lega Nord** (IT) **FPÖ, BZÖ** (AT) **SVP** (CH)	
Explicit religious reference/agenda as core of platform from beginning on	**List Pim Fortuyn, PvV** (NL) KPN-SN, ZChN, **LPR** (PL) **SNS** (SK) MIÉP, KDNP, **Jobbik** (HU) **Ataka** (BG)	CCS (FR) New Era (DK) Arhus against the Mosque (DK) Radio Maryja, All-Polish Youth (PL) MS (SK) [ROC (RO)]

Notes: Parties with sustained electoral relevance and/or government participation are in bold; groups in parentheses and in italics are not strictly part of the radical right family, but contain strong radical right tendencies.
Source: Country chapters in Bertelsmann Stiftung (2009), updated.

Romanian PRM addressed religion as a core element of their program, whereas not a single West European party, with the exception of the relatively young Dutch parties, has done so. In combination with the previous aspects of the programmatic core of East European radical right parties, one can say that they are not only more extreme than in the West but also more inherently religious; they are more Christian and more antidemocratic. In that, they also differ from radical right movements in the region, an aspect which completes this chapter.

Recently, East European parties have followed the West European path and added Islamophobia to their religious agenda, except for Jobbik which maintains a favorable view of Islam. But as of now, the presence of Muslims in the region is miniscule aside from Bulgaria and they are unlikely to join the Roma and Jews as targets in electoral mobilization (see Mareš 2014).

These ideological differences between East and West acquire additional weight when compared to the patterns of voting support. As outlined in Chapter 3, cleavages in Eastern Europe are underdeveloped and party systems along with individual parties are somewhat more ephemeral, hence no clear-cut correspondence between particular social groups and party ideologies can be expected. More specifically, the left–right semantics do not work well in the sphere of economic issues (see Tavits and Letki 2009). Whereas in Western Europe the working class is over-represented among radical right voters (see Rydgren 2013), this does not hold for the radical right electorate in Eastern Europe. As a recent study reveals, the longitudinal data on the class composition of radical right parties' electorates in countries where these parties have entered parliaments (Poland, Hungary, and Slovakia) show no clear pattern (see Table 4.6).

Nonetheless, one of the most important observations is that, in Hungary, a clear shift occurred from lower educated, older blue-collar, and self-employed strata supporting MIÉP to higher educated, young, white-collar, and intellectual professionals voting for Jobbik (see Pytlas 2013, 216–218).

A more comprehensive study involving a number of attitudinal items among Eastern and Western electorates of the radical right finds systematic differences in these voters' profiles which correspond accurately with the programmatic differences between radical right parties in West and East (see Allen 2015). While in Western Europe radical right voters are not easily mobilized on religious terms (other than their fear of unwanted religion), Eastern parties can count on the availability of religious voters (see also Minkenberg 2017, forthcoming). Conversely, immigration issues (in contrast to minority issues) work better in the West.[3] Most importantly, however, dissatisfaction with democracy correlates more strongly with a vote for a radical right party in post-communist Europe than in Western Europe (Allen 2015, 9).

In sum: when comparing the mapping of the West European radical right with Eastern Europe, some differences highlight the gap between

CONTENTS: ORGANIZATIONAL PATTERNS AND IDEOLOGICAL PROFILES 89

Table 4.6 Stratification of right-wing radical party voters in Slovakia, Poland, and Hungary (over and under-representation by percentage of voters)

	Slovakia				Poland				Hungary			
	1999	2002	2006	2010	2001	2002	2005	2007	2001	2003	2005	2009
Overall	12	4	12	5	6	13	3	1	3	2	2	3
Education												
Primary	−2	–	–	+2	+1	+9	+1	+0	−1	−1	−1	−1
Vocational	+1	−2	−1	–	+3	+0	+0	+0	+2	+0	+2	+0
Secondary	+1	+1	−1	+1	−2	−5	−1	+0	+0	+0	+1	+2
Higher/university	−2	+0	−4	−2	−1	−7	−2	+1	+2	−1	−2	+1
Occupation												
Unemployed	+1	–	+0	–	+0	+2	+0	+0	+0	+0	+4	+0
Farmers	–	–	−6	–	+3	+2	+0	+0	+2	−2	+2	+0
Manual workers	+2	–	+3	–	+1	−4	+1	+0	+1	+1	+3	+0
White-collar workers	−4	–	–	–	−2	–	−2	−1	−2	+0	+0	+2
Intellectual professionals	−2	–	–	–	−1	–	−2	+0	−1	+0	+0	+3
Self-employed /entrepreneurial	−3	–	−1	–	+2	−3	+0	−1	+1	+0	+2	−1
Management	+0	–	−5	–	−2	−9	–	+0	–	+2	−2	+0
Age												
18–24	+2	−1	+3	+0	−1	+0	+1	+0	+0	+1	+0	+2
25–34	+2	+0	−2	+1	+1	−1	+0	−1	+0	+0	+0	+1
35–54	−1	+1	−1	+1	−1	−3	−1	+0	+0	+0	+1	0
55–64	−3	+2	−2	–	+2	−1	+2	+0	−1	–	–	−1
65–	–	+0	+2	−1	+1	+6	−1	+0	+1	−1	−1	−1

Source: Minkenberg and Pytlas (2013, Table 12.2, p. 215).

East and West since the 1990s. In the East, the following aspects stand out: some extreme types among the radical right parties were electorally successful and even entered national governments (SNS, PRM), thereby preceding some of the Western counterparts which, moreover, were ideologically less extreme and all belong to the ethnocentric category (see Minkenberg 2013a, and Chapter 6); in the East, a number of major players espouse a religious-nationalist agenda, a phenomenon which until the end of the decade was largely absent in Western Europe. And finally, the parties of the radical right underwent several ups and downs, or some parties vanished and new parties appeared.

This scenario of fluidity does not apply to the radical right ideology; here a remarkable persistence can be observed despite some movements and mutations. The persistence was accomplished in two ways. First, in the absence of relevant parties, the radical right agenda is carried on by a plethora of movements and other organizations (see also Kopecký and Mudde 2003). In Poland and Romania, religious actors emerged as the torchbearers of radical right thinking; as outlined in Chapter 3, in both countries, the dominant religious tradition is closely intertwined with their respective national identity. But there is a difference. In Poland, the radical wing of Catholicism, or national Catholicism, most notably the network led by Radio Maryja, operated independently of, and at times in opposition to, the Church (see Kasprowicz 2015; also Pankowski 2010). In Romania, the Church itself assumed a leading role in furthering key elements of the radical right agenda (see Andreescu 2015). Second, the other version of continuity in the face of disappearing or absent radical right parties has been the adoption of their agenda by other political parties, most notably but not exclusively the mainstream right, with Hungary being the most extreme case of such agenda co-optation (see Krekó and Mayer 2015; Pytlas 2016; see also Chapter 5). The analysis will now be completed by a closer look at the movement sector in the region.

3 Beyond Political Parties: The Movement Sector and Violence

If research on the radical right parties in Eastern Europe is lagging behind compared with research on Western Europe, this is even truer for social movement research in and on Eastern Europe. A follow-up to the first comprehensive volume by Petr Kopecký and Cas Mudde (2003); also Mudde 2005b) is long overdue, but so far only case studies with a limited scope have appeared (see e.g. Karl 2016; Mareš 2015; Mayer and Odehnal 2010; Vejvodová 2014). This is even more astounding considering the politico-systemic context in Eastern Europe, which provides ample opportunities for movement mobilization in the face of the under-institutionalization of the party systems, even though East Europeans tend to be very reluctant to engage in voluntary organizations and civil society participation (see Howard 2011). A tentative update of right-wing movement mobilization is provided by the various contributions to a recent study (see Minkenberg 2015a; in particular Minkenberg and Kossack 2015).

In his inventory of radical right movement organization in Eastern Europe on the eve of the EU's Eastern enlargement, Cas Mudde cautiously summarized the findings of various authors in his study (Mudde 2005b). He found no relevance or even a virtual absence of radical right mobilization in a first group of countries including Bulgaria, the Czech Republic, the Baltic States, and Slovenia. Second, in Hungary, there were some organizations with ties to MIÉP that operated within their own racist circles and without much resonance in the wider society. The third group encompassed countries with strong radical right movements, which either operated on their own or provided support to radical right parties or subcultures. These included Poland, with Radio Maryja and a large ultra-Catholic subculture, Slovakia with a number of ultranationalist movements such as Slovak Motherland (Matica Slovenská), and Romania (Mudde 2005a, 269–270; see also Tables 4.1–4.3). Mudde provides no reasons for this variation but it is safe to assume that the comparatively advanced state of democratic consolidation and state action against challengers in the first group depressed the building up of such networks to some degree (see Table 3.5; Mareš 2012).

However, in the wake of these countries' accession to the EU and political and economic changes, the picture looks different in the 2010s. The findings in the comparative study (Minkenberg 2015a) suggest more continuity in the movement sector than in the party sector, but also a disconcerting growth of movement activities, especially in countries where radical right parties have disappeared from the parliamentary and electoral arenas and left a void which could not be entirely filled by the mainstream parties (see Table 4.7).

Table 4.7 Strength of radical right-wing movements in Europe, pre-2004 and 2014

	pre-2004	2014
Strong	Poland Romania Slovakia	Czech Republic Hungary Latvia Poland Romania
Moderately strong	Hungary	Bulgaria Lithuania Slovakia
Weak	Bulgaria Czech Republic Estonia Latvia Lithuania	Estonia

Sources: Mudde (2005a, 269–270); Minkenberg and Kossack (2015, Table 15.2).

In Poland, the movement sector has always been rather strong (see Minkenberg 2002a; Mudde 2005b; Pankowski 2010; Pankowski and Kornak 2013), and it became even stronger after the demise of the LPR following the 2007 elections, when Radio Maryja continuously mobilized for its anti-liberal agenda and the National Movement absorbed the resources of two older right-wing movements, the All-Polish Youth and ONR (see Kasprowicz 2015). The Czech Republic and Romania bear witness to a wealth of movements and movement activities furthering neo-Nazi, racist, and revisionist goals. These goals are most fiercely propagated by the Hungarian Guard and its successor organizations which at times act as right-wing terrorist groups by inflicting violence against and terror on minorities, in particular the sizable group of Roma in the country (see Mayer and Krekó 2015). They are also the major "target group" of the most radical and violent spectrum of the radical right in other countries, such as the Czech Republic and Slovakia (see Gyárfášová and Mesežnikov 2015; Mareš 2015). These movement acitivities in the region are increasingly accompanied and reinforced by radical right Web activities. As in Western Europe (see Caiani and Parenti 2013), East European groups use the Internet and social networks for recruitment and communication. In some respects, they surpass Western groups in the intensity of Web-based communication, as a case study of the Hungarian Jobbik, its Internet activities, and mobilization efforts shows (see Karl 2016). In its approach to the various publics beyond the electoral arena, Jobbik appears more like a "movement party" in the above definition (see Kitschelt 2006) than a regular party because it is particularly intertwined with segments of the Hungarian far right ("identitarian") music scene and other non-party groups. It also shows an above-average presence in all major social networks, such as Facebook, YouTube, and Twitter, thereby surpassing the much larger Hungarian mainstream parties as well as West European parties and movements of the radical right (Karl 2016, 156–206).

Finally, racist violence has increased in a number of countries where radical right movements or parties have established themselves, especially in countries with strong movement activities (see contributions to Minkenberg 2015a). However, data on racist or right-wing extremist violence or crime need to be read with caution since sources are fragmentary and official statistics are not always reliable. For example, the European Union Agency for Fundamental Rights lists only four East European countries with reliable data recording (the criteria being "a range of bias motivations recorded; data generally published"; FRA 2015, 57), as compared to Sweden, Finland, the Netherlands, the UK, and Spain which provide comprehensive data ("a range of bias motivations, types of crimes, and characteristics recorded; data always published"; ibid.). Interestingly Germany and Austria with their annual government issued data books on extremism and violence (Verfassungsschutzbericht, or Report by the Office for the Protection of the Constitution) belong to the middle group with the East European countries. With these caveats in mind, Table 4.8 provides a glimpse of the development of racist offenses and crime from 2000 until 2013.

Due to different collection and counting methods, these data cannot be compared across countries, only within countries and periods when the same methods were applied. The Czech Republic exhibits some notable fluctuations: with EU accession, the numbers dropped somewhat; but by the end of the 2000s there was a rise with a peak in

Table 4.8 Trends in officially recorded racist crime, 2000–2013

	2000	2001	2002	2003	2004	2005	2006	2007	2008	2009	2010	2011	2012	2013
Czech Rep.	364	452	473	335	364	253	217	155	192	178	288	268	190	75
Lithuania	n.d.	n.d.	n.d.	n.d.	n.d.	n.d.	n.d.	n.d.	n.d.	n.d.	16	62	n.d.	10
Poland	215	103	94	111	113	172	48	41	98	124	146	272	390	835
Slovakia	35	40	109	119	79	121	143	129	218	79	53	97	n.d.	159

Notes: Data from 2000 until 2005 based on different recording methods; data from 2006 onwards result from the following modes: Czech Republic: recorded crimes motivated by racism based on court statistics; Lithuania: government statistics of discrimination based on ethnicity, incitement to hatred motivated by race, and incitement to hatred motivated by ethnicity; Poland: cases of racist and/or xenophobic crime registered by the General Prosecutor; Slovakia: number of prosecuted and investigated persons in relation to racially motivated crime.

Sources: FRA—European Union Agency for Fundamental Rights (2011, 37, 2012, 161, 2013, 183–184, 2015, 59–61).

2010 and 2011 which corresponds with the increasing movement mobilization (see Table 4.7). However, more recent data are necessary to assess whether the decline of the numbers after 2011 are a temporary reduction, possibly due to increasing state vigilance or changes in the movement sector. In contrast, the Polish case shows a linear trend up since 2006 with a doubling of the numbers between 2012 and 2013. As shown elsewhere, movement activities on the street level have increased significantly since the end of the 2000s, in particular the annual "Independence March" events in Warsaw since 2011, organized by the All-Polish Youth which even triggered riots in the streets and took right-wing violence in Poland to a new—and with increased media attention—visible level (see Pankowski and Kormak 2013, 162–167).

Another indicator for the potential of right-wing violence can be found in a recent study conducted in Hungary and the United Kingdom which asked respondents, among other questions, whether violence is justified (completely or somewhat) against particular groups. In the UK, the share of respondents was 6% against Gypsies, 6% against immigrants, 5% against Muslims, and 3% against Jews; the numbers for the Hungarian sample were 29% against Gypsies and 16% against Jews (the other groups were not included in the Hungarian questionnaire) (Political Capital 2015, 52, 82). Also, when other groups (left-wing radicals, homosexuals, politicians, or bankers) were mentioned, the readiness for political violence was higher in Hungary, often twice as high as in the UK. Only with regard to terrorists was the level the same (approximately 60%).

In his pre-EU accession overview, Cas Mudde identified Bulgaria, the Czech Republic, Hungary, Poland, and Slovakia as a group of countries with high levels of racist violence which he considered "a structural and long-term problem" and on a higher average level than in Western Europe (Mudde 2005a, 274–275). The developments outlined here do not contradict his prognosis, despite the enormously higher numbers of officially recorded racist crimes in Great Britain, Germany, the Netherlands, and Sweden which is probably related to better recording methods than to the occurrence of actual events (see FRA 2013). Moreover, Hungary, which Mudde saw on the move into the second group of countries with moderate levels of violence, has not arrived there, especially after the establishment of the Hungarian Guard and the terror wave against the Roma minority which included multiple murders (see Mayer and Odehnal 2010, 91–101).

Overall, the mapping of organizations and ideologies, along with that of voter motivations and movement activities, suggests profound and lasting differences between the East and West European radical right. Some signs of convergence exist in the religious outlook of the parties, with both discovering Islam as a new enemy, and the growing concern about immigration also in Eastern Europe. But the differences in other out-group hostilities, the weight of history on the agenda of the East European radical right, and organizational fissures outweigh these commonalities. This is finally underscored by the fact that the newly constituted radical right group in the European Parliament, the "Europe of Nations and Freedom," founded in 2015 after one year of negotiations between the French, Dutch, and other leaders of their countries' respective radical right parties, features a Who's Who of all successful radical right parties in Western Europe (the French FN, the Dutch PVV, the Italian LN, the Austrian FPÖ, the Belgian VB, even a UKIP and an AfD representative). But with the exception of two Polish KNP delegates, there is not a single radical right party from Eastern Europe in this group because of unbridgeable ideological differences between the West European parties and their parliamentarians and those in the East.

Notes

1. The classification of the National Alliance and its predecessors remains controversial. Against Bustikova and Kitschelt (2009), Auers and Kasekamp classify TB/LNNK as an "ethnocentrist" version of the radical right, rather than "extremist" (2015, 139). In another publication, they point out that the dictatorial "Ulmanis regime remains central to the National Alliance's ideology" (Auers and Kasekapm 2013, 243) which, according to the criteria developed in Chapter 1, puts the NA into the extremist category.
2. Keno Verseck, "Milliardär George Soros: Halb Europa hasst diesen Mann." *Der Spiegel* 26, February 2016. (http://www.spiegel.de/politik/ausland/george-soros-diesen-mann-hasst-halb-osteuropa-a-1078614.html; accessed November 30, 2016).

3. The recent refugee flow from Syria and Turkey into Central Europe on the so-called "Balkan route" might change far right mobilization patterns in some countries affected by this migration; but it is too early to analyze the electoral mechanisms.

CHAPTER 5

Configurations: Mobilization and Performance

Abstract The chapter points out a high degree of volatility of the radical right over time, in particular in the party sector. With a few exceptions and in stark contrast to Western Europe, radical right parties have relatively short lives, and their electoral results fluctuate enormously. But weak party organization and inconstancy at the polls do not translate into political irrelevancy, once the radical right's interaction with its political environment is taken into account. The chapter shows that conventional context factors are weak predictors of radical right successes; yet it is helped by slow but noticeable processes of ethnic pluralization. Finally, interaction between parties and movements is persistent, as is the competition between the radical right and its main competitors in the party system with programmatic spillover effects into the mainstream.

Keywords Electoral volatility · Party competition · Pluralization · Interaction patterns · State response

As the previous chapter showed on a general level, the East European countries' democratic consolidation and their integration into the European Union did not lead to a withering away of ultranationalism. Neither did the first outbreaks of racist extremism and the emergence of radical right actors after the collapse of communist regimes in 1989 coagulate into permanent features of the political order, as has happened with the radical right in most West European countries since the societal and political shifts of the 1970s and 1980s. Yet, while in some postcommunist countries radical right-wing parties experienced a decline or completely faded away, most notably in the Czech Republic and Romania, in other countries a resurgence occurred, which many experts had not foreseen when Eastern enlargement of the EU was accomplished. The most prominent summary of the situation on the eve of the countries' EU membership was supplied by Cas Mudde when he concluded that the radical right in Eastern Europe was not a major political force and looked "pathetic" in comparison to their Western counterparts by being more extremist and less successful (Mudde 2005a, 269; see Chapter 1). However, as has been outlined in the previous chapter, the picture has changed significantly since then. In this chapter I will take a closer look at the development of the radical right over time, suggest an explanation for the mobilization successes, and consider the interaction of radical right parties and movements with each other and with their environment.

1   Parties and Elections—Consistency in Fluidity

The electoral fortune of the East European radical right-wing parties since the onset of democracy in 1990 is shown in Table 5.1 and contrasted with that of their West European counterparts. As I have stated earlier (Minkenberg 2002a, 361), and as the fluctuations in Table 5.1 confirm, the radical right in the region has been and still is a moving target.

Only Estonia and the Czech Republic show some continuity in that the radical right has not emerged as a major player in the party system (yet). In the Czech case, the early rise of the Republicans (SPR-RSČ) was quelled by the other parties' strategy of demarcation and marginalization. Moreover the Workers' Party (DS) was banned in 2010 but returned as the Workers' Party Social Justice, though it has not posted an electoral threat so far (see Mareš 2015). In Estonia, on the other hand, a radical right party never surfaced despite a pronounced ethnic cleavage, again due to the other parties' strategies which in this case meant their own politicization of the minority issue (see Auers and Kasekamp 2015). In Lithuania, the radical right emerged only in 2008 as an electoral force, though this was due to the merger of the Lithuanian Nationalist Union (LTS) with other parties into the Homeland Union alliance which they left again in 2011. Romania appears to follow suit: the mainstream parties' strategy of containment toward the Party for Greater Romania (PRM)

Table 5.1 Radical right election results (%) in national parliamentary elections in Eastern Europe in comparison to Western Europe, from 1990 (average per five years, chambers of deputies)

	1990–1994	1995–1999	2000–2004	2005–2009	2010–2014
Eastern Europe					
Bulgaria	–	–	–	8.7	5.9
Czech Republic	6.8*	6.0	1.1	–	1.0
Estonia	–	–	0.5	0.2	0.4
Hungary	0.8	5.5	4.5	2.2	16.7
Latvia	–	–	–	1.5	18.5
Lithuania	2.0	2.2	0.9	19.7***	0.9
Poland	14.1	8.0**	18.1	10.4	0.0
Romania	5.8	9.2	20.9	3.1	1.2
Slovak Republic	6.7*	9.1	7.0	11.7	4.5
Western Europe					
Austria	19.6	24.4	10.0	28.3	24.0
Belgium	6.6	10.9	13.8	14.0	5.8
Denmark	6.4	9.8	12.6	13.9	12.3
France	12.7	14.9	12.4	4.7	13.6
Germany (Fed. Rep.)	2.3	3.3	1.0	2.1	1.7
Great Britain	0.9	–	0.2	0.7	1.8
Italy	18.0	25.8	4.3****	8.3****	4.1****
Netherlands	2.9	0.6	11.4	5.9	12.7
Norway	6.0	15.3	14.7	22.5	16.3
Sweden	4.0	–	1.5	3.0	9.3
Switzerland	11.9	18.7	26.6	30.0	26.6

The following parties are included: *Eastern Europe:* Bulgaria: Ataka; Czech Rep.: SPR-RSČ, DS; Estonia: EI; Hungary: MIÉP, Jobbik; Latvia: All for Latvia! (2006), National Alliance (VL + TB/LNNK, in 2010: 7.8%, 2011: 13.9%); Lithuania: LTS; Poland: KPN, ZChN, LPR, Samoobrona; Romania: PUNR, PRM; Slovak Republic: SNS; *Western Europe:* Austria: FPÖ, BZÖ; Belgium: VB, Front national; Denmark: FrP, DF; France: FN, MNR; Germany: Republikaner, DVU, NPD, Pro Deutschland; Great Britain: BNP, NF, Democratic Unionist Party; Italy: MSI, AN, MS-FT, LN; Netherlands: Center Party, CD, LPF List Pim Fortuyn, PVV; Norway: FrP; Sweden: Ny Demokrati, Sverigedemokraterna, Nationaldemokraterna; Switzerland: SVP; Autopartei, Schweizer Demokraten, Lega dei Ticinesi.
*Czech and Slovak National Council elections 1992, respectively
**Estimated proportion of ZChN and KPN, which ran on a common ticket with electoral alliance Solidarnosc AWS in 1997 (vote share 33.8%)
***As part of the electoral alliance Homeland Union (2008–2011)
****Excluding AN, but including Lega Nord, Movimento Sociale Fiamma Tricolore, Mussolini, Rauti
Sources: Minkenberg (2015b) and Nordsieck (2016).

after 2000 resulted in its gradual decline. No other party took its place; instead, mainstream parties have embraced former radical right politicians in their own ranks, granting them continuing access to power (see

Cinpoeş 2015). In all countries, the parties of the radical right underwent several ups and downs (as in Slovakia), or one party was replaced by another (as in Poland and Hungary), or such parties appeared where there were none before (Bulgaria, Latvia, Lithuania).

The ideological peculiarities of the East European radical right parties (as outlined in Chapter 4) are matched by their electoral patterns. While those parties in the region exhibit a generally higher degree of ideological extremism than their Western counterparts, their average electoral support, as shown in Table 5.1, is lower than that of Western parties. At the same time, there is more fluctuation than in Western Europe, where the radical right continuously achieves a relatively high and stable level of support at the polls in a sizable number of countries (Austria, Belgium, Denmark, France, Italy, Norway, and Switzerland). Not a single East European country can be found where this is the case as well. Moreover, while in Western Europe the electorally successful radical right parties have mostly remained the same over the entire time span since their breakthrough, the parties in the East, even those with strong electoral support, often do not last more than one or two legislative periods and then fragment or are replaced by or merge with others—with the notable exception of Slovakia (and Slovenia which is not discussed here; see Chapter 1).

To be more specific, the average life span of a radical right party in Eastern Europe (counting those with at least 1% in a national parliamentary election, i.e. 15 cases) is 9.5 years, with a large fluctuation between 3 years (in Estonia) and 26 years (in Slovakia). Table 5.2 compares the life span of West European with that of East European radical right parties.

The pattern reveals a significant difference, with twice as many long-living radical right parties in Western European compared to Eastern European countries, with the bulk of the latter lasting a maximum of 10 years only. Moreover, the overall number of parties which received at least 1% in national parliamentary elections is almost equal in East and West (15 vs. 14), although the overall time span for the possible existence of such parties is shorter in the East (27 years, or 1990–2016) than in the West (1980s–2016). These figures fit squarely into the general findings of under-institutionalized party systems in Eastern Europe, with higher levels of volatility, a larger number of new parties, and a weaker rootedness of parties in society (see Chapter 3). As outlined before, this under-institutionalization of the party systems can be attributed to the legacies of the old regime and common patterns of the subsequent transition

Table 5.2 Life span of radical right parties in Western and Eastern Europe (1990–2016)

	Life Span Based on Parliamentary Election Results (at least 1%)			
	< 6 years	6–10 years	11–15 years	> 15 years
Western Europe	AfD (DE) LPF (NL) SD (SE)	BZÖ (AT) MSI/AN (IT) PVV (NL)	DF (DK)	FPÖ (AT) VB (BE) SVP (CH) FN (FR) LN (IT) FrP (DK) FrP (NO)
Eastern Europe	DS (CZ) RN (PL)	Ataka (BG) SPR-RSČ (CZ) EI (EE) Jobbik (HU) VL (LV) LTS (LT) LPR (PL) PUNR (RO) Kotleba (SK)	MIÉP (HU) TB/LNNK (LV)	PRM (RO) SNS (SK)

Note: Life span is counted as the number of years between the first and the last time a party received at least 1% in national parliamentary elections. If a party got at least 1% in one election but not in the ones preceding and succeeding it, it is counted as one year (for a more sophisticated approach see Pedersen 1982). MSI/AN is counted only from 1990–1999 because of the party's conversion into a conservative party by the end of the decade.

Sources: Nordsieck (2016); www.electionresources.org (accessed July 30, 2016)

(Elster et al., Chapters 1 and 4; also Bunce 1999, Chapter 2; Minkenberg 2009a; Bunce and Wolchik 2010a).

Overall then, the East European radical right is still much less structured than that in Western Europe (see Ramet 1999; Minkenberg 2002a), as is true with most political parties in the region. The radical right's electoral fluctuations, and its tendency to reconstitute itself from one election to the next, make it disconcertingly fluid. This also contributes to the permeable border between radical right movements and radical right parties, as well as between the radical right and the mainstream right (see Chapter 6).

Under these circumstances, explanations for the electoral performance of radical right parties are a particular challenge. Numerous researchers emphasize the importance of the supply side of the electoral market, in particular the "internal supply side," that is ideology, leadership, and organization, as an important set of explanatory variables (see e.g. Mudde 2007, 257–273; Rydgren 2007). However, an East European equivalent to David Art's study (2011) has yet to be written. Recent research points at the particular dynamics of party competition in the region, and in particular the role of "issue ownership" and framing, which helps explain the success and failure of radical right parties (see contributions to Minkenberg 2015a; also Pirro 2015; Pytlas 2016). If radical right parties manage, by virtue of their leadership and resources or other parties' failures, to introduce new topics or convincingly claim new issues, nearby competitors adjust and thereby provide legitimacy to these claims or issues, which enhances the salience of the issue and generates a narrative shift in the radical right's favor. The Hungarian case illustrates this mechanism vividly. While Jobbik shared the Trianon and ultranationalist frame in an intense "frame competition" with Fidesz (Pytlas 2016, 178–180), Jobbik succeeded in establishing sole frame ownership of the alleged "Gypsy crimes" and remained the agenda setter on Roma issues. Fidesz's counter-frame "crime by Gypsies" contributed to the salience of the Roma issue without undermining Jobbik's distinctive place in this regard. In Poland, however, the narrative shift in favor of the LPR was short-lived. In the early 2000s, the party introduced an anti-Western, ultra-Catholic frame, which resonated widely in the public but was taken over by Law and Justice, the senior government partner, soon after the 2005 elections; this loss of frame ownership contributed to the electoral marginalization of the LPR in 2007 and afterwards (see Pytlas 2016, 115–121, 178–183, 115–121; 203–207; also Pytlas 2013). Party and frame competition in Bulgaria centered on the Turkish minority and their entitlements (dual citizenship, Turkish radio and TV programs) and resulted in the mainstream and populist right-wing party GERB and other parties partially adopting Ataka positions without the radical right party losing its frame ownership (see Pirro 2015, 126–129).

However, these mechanisms have been established on the basis of a small number of country cases only and may be hard to verify in a more general way for the entire region, in particular considering the volatility of the East European party systems and the many comings and goings of radical right parties since 1990. Therefore, it may be useful to take a step back and include more of the context as outlined in Chapter 3, even though Cas Mudde's caveat that the demand side is a necessary but not sufficient condition for electoral success of radical right parties, and that political opportunity structures are more facilitating than determining factors for success or failure, will not be disputed (see Mudde 2007, 230, 253). As before, this will be done against the backdrop of the West European situation.

2 Patterns of Change—The Role of Differentiation

Numerous studies have shown that the cases of the most significant upswing of radical right voting support and consolidation of these parties in the countries' party systems include those of a new radical right, newly formed or reformed parties, which belong to the ethnocentrist rather than the extremist or fascist variant (see Carter 2005; Ignazi 2003; Kitschelt 1995). As argued elsewhere (Minkenberg 1998, 2000, 2013a), an ideological and strategic renewal—along with the changing cleavage patterns in party competition and the rise of the immigration issue—has opened the electoral gates for these parties. None of the more successful parties in the West advocates the return to a pre-democratic, dictatorial regime (as presented in Table 4.4) or cherishes anti-democratic political leaders of the past; all accept more or less the liberal-democratic order and the rules of the game. This is a significant difference to interwar fascism and also to the immediate post-war radical right in Western democracies. Or, when looking at Germany, Britain, and Sweden up until recently (see Table 5.1), it becomes evident that, where the radical right has remained more traditional, that is extremist and more or less true to a fascist-autocratic agenda, it has not fared well in elections, at least at the national level (see also Art 2011). By the same token, these are the countries in Western Europe where the movement and subcultural sector is livelier, where levels of racist or right-wing extremist violence are higher (see Minkenberg 2003, 2008; also Nwabuzo 2014, 12–13). Already in the 1990s, scholars had suggested that there appears to be a dynamic link between various organizational manifestations, that is more right-wing radical mobilization in the electoral arena tends to go along with less mobilization in the ideologically more extreme movement sector and vice versa (Koopmans 1996; Rucht and Koopmans 1996).

The model has been developed further and applied to Western Europe at the turn of the century. The main point is that a country's opportunity structures, including institutional and cultural variables as well as the structure of party competition, largely determine the organizational manifestations as well as ideological variations which dominate the radical right sector and hence influence the parties' relevance for other parties and their strength vis-à-vis that of right-wing movements. Following these considerations and based on the voting trends shown in Table 5.1 as well as circumstantial data on movement activities, a map of radical right mobilization can be constructed, including the major independent variables in the cultural and structural context (see Minkenberg 1998; idem 2003; also Kitschelt 1995; Rydgren 2007). Cultural context is conceptualized in terms of the dominant understanding of national identity, whether in ethnic, cultural, or political terms, the share of foreign born population, the level of resistance to multiculturalism, the religious traditions according to the predominant confessional patterns, and the strength of Islam. Structural variables include: the degree of polarization or convergence between the major parties; the level of voting along a value-based, New Politics cleavage; the states' and major parties' response to the radical right; and the type of electoral system (for details, see Minkenberg 2008). Table 5.3 presents an overview of these factors as a foil for the East European situation.

The message of this table consists of a particular pattern: countries with strong radical right-wing parties exhibit a weak movement sector and vice versa. For an analysis of this pattern, it is important to evaluate the role of certain contextual factors. The usual factors such as the voting system, the presence of foreigners, or the resistance to multicultural society do not account for much of the variation (see also Mudde 2007, 210–220). The major mobilizing factors in Western Europe appear to lie in the New Politics cleavage (see Chapter 2 and Bornschier 2010; Kitschelt 1995) and in the cultural and religious sphere. Regarding the party sector, Table 5.3 and the modernization theoretical argument above suggest that large non-Christian immigrant communities and an accelerated process of religious and cultural differentiation drive the success and consolidation of radical right parties more than do structural factors (see Minkenberg 2003, 2013a, 2017 forthcoming).

Turning to Eastern Europe, the processes of regime transformation and implementation of the EU's *acquis communautaire* have introduced the same basic constitutional structures as in Western Europe, but they were accompanied by more profound changes and another set of context factors (see Table 3.5).

In some of the literature, the role of sizable ethnic minorities has been singled out as an important independent variable for the success of radical right parties (see Chapter 3 and Beichelt and Minkenberg 2002). However, since almost all countries under consideration have a significant share of national minorities (i.e. more than 3%; see Chapter 3, endnote 2), this factor

Table 5.3 Party strength and movement strength of the radical right and context factors in Western Europe (c.2000)

	Culture					Structure				Actor	
	1a	1b	1c	1d	1e	2a	2b	2c	2d	Party Strength	Movement Strength
Austria	0.5	1	0.5	1	0.5	1	1	1	1	High	Low
France	0.5	1	0	1	1	0	0	0.5	0	High	Low
Italy	0.5	0	0.5	1	0.5	0	1	1	1	High	Low
Denmark	1	0	0.5	0	1	0.5	1	1	1	High	Medium
Norway	1	0	n.d.	0	1	0.5	0.5	1	1	High	Medium
Switzerland	0	1	n.d.	0	1	0.5	0.5	1	1	High	Medium
Belgium	0	0	1	1	1	1	1	0	1	High–medium	Medium
Netherlands	0	1	0	0	0	0.5	1	1	1	Low	Medium
Germany (West)	0.5	1	1	0.5	0	1	1	0	1	Low	Medium
Germany (East)	1	0	1	0	0	1	0	0	1	Low	High
United Kingdom	1	0.5	0	0	0	0	0	0	0	Low	High
Sweden	1	1	0	0	0.5	0.5	0.5	0	1	Low	High

Note: Shading highlights groups of countries with either strong party and weak movement sectors or vice versa.
Context Factor 1: Culture
1a nation type: ethno-cultural nation 1, political nation 0
1b share of foreign-born population: 1 high, 0 low
1c level of resistance to multicultural society: 1 above EU level, 0 below EU level
1d predominant religious tradition: Catholic 1, Protestant 0
1e Islam: second largest religion 1, other 0
Context Factor 2: Structure
2a cleavages: convergence 1, polarization 0
2b cleavages: strong New Politics voting 1, weak 0
2c political opportunity structures: state and parties' latitude 1, exclusion/repression 0
2d political opportunity structures: PR electoral system 1, majority 0
Sources: Minkenberg (2003, 2008)

alone cannot account for the variety of electoral success or movement mobilization (see also Mudde 2007, 214). In combination with the level of xenophobia in these countries (see Table 3.3), however, this factor provides a breeding ground which can be politically exploited by the radical right (see Pirro 2015; Pytlas 2016). Yet, as Table 5.4 suggests, in contrast to the West European scenario, there is another pattern which connects the context conditions with party and movement strength: (i) there are more countries with congruent rather than divergent strength of party and movement sectors (Hungary, Estonia, Bulgaria, Romania, and to some extent Poland); and (ii) the countries with medium to strong radical right parties in the 2000s differ in many of the contextual factors. The connection seems stronger with regard to movement strength: the three countries with a strong movement sector (Poland, Slovakia, and Romania) share a high fusion of national and religious identity, medium-to-high levels of ethnic homogeneity, and a lack of a clear distinction between political camps. In other words, high cultural homogeneity and diffuse party competition can be seen as facilitating right-wing movement mobilization. But the connection to the radical right party sector shows a weak correlation between party strength and movement strength in Eastern Europe in the early 2000s, in contrast to Western Europe. If at all, the tendency is congruence rather than an inverse relationship.

Ten years into the countries' EU membership, the party–movement relationship has changed but it does not look more similar to that in Western Europe, as Table 5.5 illustrates.

In two countries, Hungary and Latvia, both movement and party sectors can be considered strong, whereas in Estonia and Slovakia, the two sectors exhibit medium strength. Only in the Czech Republic and Poland and in Bulgaria and Romania does the strength of one sector correspond with the weakness of the other. Moreover, while between 2000 and 2010 the number of divergent country cases (strong party sector and weak movement sector, or vice versa) has doubled, this does not mean an approximation between the West and the East European situation, because what has not changed is the ideological extremism of most of these parties in the East, in addition to the different context factors. The context factors which were held constant do not explain these changes; among the structural factors, state repression seemed to have some impact on radical right parties in the Czech Republic, Estonia, and, to some extent, Romania, and in the absence of strong radical right parties, cultural homogeneity appeared to have facilitated medium to high movement mobilization.

CONFIGURATIONS: MOBILIZATION AND PERFORMANCE   109

Table 5.4 Context factors and radical right actors in Eastern Europe (2000–2004)

	Historical and cultural conditions				Opportunity structures			Actor type		
	Nation type (Main mode of reference)	Fusion of religious and national identity (a)	Existence of external national homelands	Ethnic homogeneity in the early 1990s (b)	Regime conflict: Regime contested by major political forces in 1990s	Party competition (Clear distinction between political camps)	State repression or containment of radical right	Party strength (c)	Dominant party type (d)	Strength of movement sector
Czech Rep.	Ethnic	Low	No	Medium	No	Yes	Yes	Medium	Extremist	Low
Hungary	Ethnic	Medium	Yes	High	No	Yes	No	Medium	Ethnocentrist	Medium
Estonia	Ethnic	Low	No	Low	No	Yes	Yes	Low	–	Low
Latvia	Ethnic	Low	No	Low	No	Yes	No	High	Ethnocentrist	Low
Lithuania	Ethnic	High	No	Medium	No	Yes	No	Low	Extremist	Low
Poland	Culture	High	No	High	No	No	No	Medium	Ethnocentrist, fundamenalist	High
Slovakia	Ethnic	High	No	High	Yes	No	Yes	Low	Extremist	High
Bulgaria	Culture	High	No	High	Yes	No	No	Low	–	Low
Romania	Ethnic	High	Yes	High	Yes	No	No	High	Extremist	High

(a) + (b) see Table 3.5
(c) High party strength is measured by 5% or more of the national vote in at least two elections in the 2000s (see also Tables 4.2 and 5.1)
(d) Ideological type according to Chapter 2 and Table 4.1
Sources: Table 3.5 and Beichelt and Minkenberg (2002); Minkenberg (2002a), (2015b), Minkenberg and Kossack (2015), Mudde (2005a)

Table 5.5 Context factors and radical right actors in Eastern Europe (2010–2014)

	Historical and cultural conditions				Opportunity structures			Actor type	
	Nation type (Main mode of reference)	Fusion of religions and national identity (a)	Existence of external national homelands	Ethnic homogeneity in the 2000s (b)	Regime conflict: Regime contested by major political forces in 2010s	Party competition (Clear distinction between political camps)	State repression or containment of radical right	Party strength (c)	Dominant party type (d)	Strength of movement sector
Czech Rep.	Ethnic	Low	No	High	No	Yes	Yes	Low	Extremist	High
Hungary	Ethnic	Medium	Yes	Medium	Yes	Yes	No	High	Ethnocentrist	High
Estonia	Ethnic	Low	No	Low	No	Yes	Yes	Low	Ethnocentrist	Low
Latvia	Ethnic	Low	No	Low	No	Yes	No	High	Extremist	High
Lithuania	Ethnic	High	No	High	No	Yes	No	Low	Extremist	Medium
Poland	Culture	High	No	High	Yes	Yes	No	Low	Ethnocentrist, fundamentalist	High
Slovakia	Ethnic	High	No	Medium	No	No	Yes	Medium*	Extremist	Medium
Bulgaria	Culture	High	No	Medium	No	No	No	High	Extremist	Low
Romania	Ethnic	High	Yes	High	No	No	No	Low	Extremist	High

* Reflects situation before the 2016 parliamentary elections
(a)–(d) see Table 5.4
Sources: Tables 3.5 and 5.4

These relatively inconclusive findings should not come as a surprise to those familiar with Mudde's comparative study (2007). He forcefully refutes the so-called "ethnic backlash" argument by showing that there is no clear relationship between the number or percentage of immigrants, asylums seekers, or national minorities on the one hand, and the electoral success of the radical right on the other, and he sees no East–West difference in this regard (see Mudde 2007, 201–216). This is also borne out by the data in Tables 5.4 and 5.5, although for Western Europe, the pattern is somewhat clearer (Table 5.3). Clearly, the juxtaposition of favorable conditions and electoral performance alone does not suffice to explain the possible relationship, and more dynamic approaches are required. The following provides a first step in that direction by using the modernization-theoretical argument (Chapter 2) and looking at rates of cultural pluralization and electoral success of the radical right, first in Western Europe and then in Eastern Europe, bearing in mind the different sets of context factors which matter in the two regions.

For Western Europe, the focus will be on religious pluralization as the most salient of these processes. As shown earlier in a comparative overview of the religious composition of Western societies (Minkenberg 2007, Table 2, 898–899), already in 2000 Islam was the third or even second largest religious community in 14 out of 15 West European countries. The countries where Islam was second are among those which were traditionally very homogeneous in denominational terms, two Lutheran cases (Denmark, Norway) and five Catholic cases (Austria, Belgium, France, Italy, Spain; see also Pew 2010). Moreover, from around 1980 until around 2000, religious diversity increased in all of Western Europe, except for Sweden. According to the modernization-theoretical argument outlined in Chapter 2, these processes and the growing presence of (non-Christian) immigrants provide opportunities for radical right parties. This dynamic is depicted in Table 5.6 which measures "religious diversity" as the degree of religious fragmentation and "pluralization" as an increase in such diversity over time (for details, see Minkenberg 2017, [?] forthcoming).

One group of countries exhibits low levels of diversity, that is pronounced religious homogeneity, and a low degree of pluralization (Ireland, Portugal); here the monopoly of Catholicism by and large persists, and the pressure for change is limited. In these countries, no radical right party has emerged. The situation changes in the other countries with low levels of religious diversity as a starting point and a medium-to-high degree of pluralization. In all of them but Finland, by 2000 Islam occupies the second place among the

Table 5.6 Religious diversity, pluralization, and the radical right in Western Europe (1980–2000)

	Weak pluralization (d < 0.10)	Moderate pluralization (0.10–0.20)	Strong pluralization (d > 0.20)
Low level diversity (< 0.20)	Ireland Portugal (Sweden: d = negative)	**Belgium** **Denmark** Finland **Norway**	**France** *Italy* **Austria** *Spain*
Moderate diversity (0.20–0.50)			
High level diversity (> 0.50)	**Switzerland**	Germany Great Britain Netherlands	

Notes: Countries in **bold** have a strong radical right-wing party in their party system (at least 5% in every national election in the past 20 years). Religious diversity is measured by 1–H (value of the Herfindahl Index: the smaller the value H, the higher the degree of diversity. H is defined as the probability that two randomly drawn persons belong to the same religious denomination)
The base of categorization is the diversity value of 1980 (0: completely homogeneous, 1.00: completely diverse); d = difference of diversity value between 1980 and 2000 (trend; in countries in italics, Islam is the second largest religious community
Source: Minkenberg (2007, 898–899, 2013a)

religious communities, broadly defined. With the exception of Finland and Spain, it is in these countries of high homogeneity in the 1970s and an accelerated differentiation in the 1980s and 1990s where a radical right party has become a permanent fixture in the party system.

The other exception here is Switzerland, where a radical right party has existed as a firm element of the party system while only limited religious pluralization took place; some authors point at the particular regional context of Switzerland which feeds what has been termed "Alpine populism" (see Chapter 2, and Betz 2005; Skenderovic 2009).

Regarding Eastern Europe, it should be remembered that religious pluralization proceeds at another speed which stems from the fact that mass immigration has been largely absent in the region until very recently, at least when compared to the West European experience. Cas Mudde observes correctly: "here, it makes more sense to study the ethnic backlash thesis by focusing on the majority mobilization against large groups of [domestic] ethnic minorities" (Mudde 2007, 214). With the admittedly limited data at hand (see Table 3.2), one can distinguish nonetheless different processes of *ethnic* pluralization. East European countries can

Table 5.7 Ethnic pluralization and the radical right in Eastern Europe (1990–2015)

	Radical Right Success (2000–2015)	
	No	Yes
Ethnic homogeneity (1990–2015)		
Decline		Bulgaria Hungary Slovakia
Equal	Romania	Poland
Increase	Czech Republic Estonia Lithuania	Latvia

Notes: Decline: ethnic homogeneity is more than 3% down from the 1990s census. Increase: ethnic homogeneity is more than 3% up from the 1990s census. Equal: ethnic homogeneity stays within the range of plus/minus 3% between the two data points. Shaded areas indicate countries in which ethnic composition has changed between the early 1990s and the 2000s. Radical right success is measured here by a radical right party obtaining at least 5% of the vote in at least three national parliamentary elections between 1995 and 2015.
Sources: Tables 3.2 and 5.1.

be classified according to whether there has been a reduction or increase in ethnic homogeneity, as measured in the censuses immediately after the end of the communist era and the data for a later point in time, and whether they display a strong or weak performance of radical right parties. Table 5.7 provides such an estimate, bearing in mind that such processes do not translate into political shifts immediately, hence the different sequence for the radical right.

Similar to Western Europe but in a less pronounced way, Table 5.7 reveals a relationship between a growing ethnic diversity and the success of the radical right. The three countries which experienced such a pluralization process also witness repeated—albeit not continuous—successes of radical right parties. The country which stands out in this regard is Latvia. Here it is not the ethnic difference itself (which changes in the direction of more rather than less homogeneity) but the politicization of this difference by the mainstream parties and the pro-Russian-speaking parties (see Auers and Kasekamp 2015, 139).

In sum, although it is not the sole causal factor, ethnic differentiation fuels the electoral success of the radical right in Eastern Europe while, in the West, a mix of ethnic and increasingly important religious ingredients feeds the radical right. In the East so far, religion is a constant rather than a variable. There is very little immigration and concomitantly little change in the religious field except for the ongoing process of secularization (see Norris and Inglehart 2011; Kilp 2009). However, the absence of large Muslim minorities does not mean the absence of Islamophobia which, like "anti-Semitism without Jews," exists throughout the region and in some countries exceeds the levels in Western Europe (see Mudde 2007, 84–86 Pew 2016; Zick et al. 2011, 69–72). It remains to be seen to what extent the current migration and refugee movements into the EU and across parts of Eastern Europe represent an episodic concern or contribute to a consolidation of the radical right in the region.

3   Patterns of Interaction

Clearly, radical right parties are still "at the margin" in European party systems, that is on the far right of the political spectrum; and even while many of them have joined the mainstream as well—to the point where, in a number of states, these parties are or have been part of coalition governments or crucial supporters of minority governments—in Eastern Europe they have not become stable and mainstream parties. Next to the behavior of other key actors (parties, elites), it is the following factors which matter in determining how the parties affect the political system: national context (as outlined in Chapter 3 and summarized in Tables 5.4 and 5.5) along with the ideological nature of these parties and the structure of the political space surrounding them. As pointed out in Chapter 3, a particular region-specific factor structures the relationship between the radical right and its political environment in Eastern Europe, that is the rehabilitation of the nation-state and nationalism brought about by the anti-communist pressures in 1989. That is why nationalist and ethnocentric rhetoric is not marginal there, but an axis that structures public and political life, especially in a post-communist context, which grants civil society only a minor role. In this context, interaction patterns can be detected along the lines outlined in the process model above (see Figure 2.1; for the following, see Minkenberg and Kossack 2015).

To begin with, parties and movements have different strategies and repertoires to advance their goals. But as is evident so far, many actors in the region mobilize support along an ethno-cultural or ethno-nationalist conflict axis (see contributions to Minkenberg 2015a; Pytlas 2016). In the electoral arena, the radical right parties push their ultranationalist agenda, often centered on the attempted restriction of minority rights (see Bustikova 2015) along with an anti-Brussels and anti-(post)communist thrust in competition with other parties. Thereby they seek alliances with nearby competitors against the political left—except where parties of the political left themselves (sometimes labeled "social populists") collaborate with the radical right to combat their adversaries (e.g. in Slovakia and Bulgaria; see Gyárfásová and Mseznikov 2015; Avramov 2015;). On the party level, the interaction patterns between the radical right and other parties is still informed by the lack of a cordon sanitaire among the mainstream, except in the Czech Republic, as has been shown already (see Mudde 2005a, 277). EU membership, despite the manifold implementations of the *acquis communautaire* prior to 2004, has not affected the room for maneuver of the radical right in these countries.

Nationalism pervades the platforms of the mainstream parties, especially on the right. This can be seen when studying the parties' position on particular issues such as ethnic minorities or the entire ideological dimension between a Green-Alternative-Libertarian (GAL) pole and the Traditionalist-Authoritarian-Nationalist (TAN) pole of the socioeconomic conflict axis (see Bustikova and Kitschelt 2009, 469–472; Kossack and Pytlas 2016, 111–121; Pirro 2015, 126–135; for the GAL-TAN cleavage and its measurement based on expert surveys, see Hooghe et al. 2002; Pytlas 2016, 226–236). These positions collide, or at least co-exist unpeacefully, with the supranational logic of EU membership, human rights principles, and the values of democracy.

In the public arena, the radical right has frequently pursued a populist strategy portraying their adversaries and in particular the countries' elites as the enemies of the people. They have attacked the alleged continuation of communism in disguise, for example in the respective campaigns by the radical right *and* the mainstream right in Poland and Hungary or by exposing and exploiting corruption, scandals, and failures (see Mayer and Odehnal 2010, 33–40; Pankowski 2010, 158–165; Pirro 2015, 135–145). Cas Mudde's elaboration of the populist strategies of radical right parties in West and East (2007, Chapter 6) has not lost any of its validity today. Seen in the light of the process model outlined in Chapter 2, the radical right's politics of populist ultranationalism, by following strategies of framing the core issues (minorities, elites, Europe) and appropriating their collective identity as the true spokesperson for "the people," has emerged as an integral part of the sustained confrontation over these and related issues, even if the organizational resources have withered (see Pytlas and Kossack 2015). Against this backdrop, radical right movement politics has not been an alternative to party politics but rather, as demonstrated most clearly by the Hungarian case, a complement to it. The trend towards congruence on the medium-to-high end of party *and* movement strength, as expressed in Table 5.5, underscores this complementarity. Sometimes, as the case of Slovakia shows (Gyárfásová and Mseznikov 2015), new populist organizations emerge which capture seats in parliament but defy the characteristics of a political party and resemble more the movement type of organization and mobilization. And in the Polish case, an extremist movement, Ruch Narodowy, joined the electoral game and, despite limited electoral appeal but due to an effective strategy of coalition building, ended up with seats in parliament (see Chapter 4).

Table 5.8 presents a summary of the modes and patterns of interaction between the radical right and various key actors, based on the evidence in the contributions to an earlier volume (Minkenberg 2015a) and related research; the summary follows the logic of distinguishing arenas of interaction as outlined in Chapter 2.

Three groups of countries can be distinguished. (i) In the first group which includes the Czech Republic and Estonia, to some extent also Lithuania, the weakness or absence of radical right parties leaves room for independent movements and violent activities. These movements and actions are met with isolation and sometimes repression by the state and the establishment. (ii) The second group encompasses Bulgaria, Poland, Slovakia and Latvia. Here, the mainstream parties are or were willing to cooperate with the radical right instead of demarcating them—the opposite of a cordon sanitaire. (iii) To the third group belong Hungary and Romania where the mainstream right pursues co-optation strategies (which in Romania shifted towards cooperation in the 1990s). As a result, the agenda of the radical right enters the top level of government while, formally, a demarcation is proclaimed (see Cinpoeş 2013, 2015).

It is important to remember that the fluidity of the radical right party sector in the region does not allow more than snapshots but, even so, a difference between West and East emerges in that Western radical right parties stay clear of such movements, not the least because the movements' extremism and uncontrollability is more often than not a liability instead of a resource. In the East, however, margin and mainstream are not as clearly divided, and movements are often accepted as resources rather than

Table 5.8 The radical right in Eastern Europe: Patterns of interaction in selected arenas (post-2000)

Country	Party–movement relationship	Evolution of relationship between party (P) and movement (M)	Right-wing violence	Counter-mobilization (Strength)	Mainstream parties' strategy towards radical right party	The state
Poland	Complementary	M replacing P	+	Medium	Cooperation	Lenient
Slovakia	Antagonistic	P dominant	+/−	Weak	Cooperation	Containment
Czech Rep.	Complementary	M dominant	+	Medium	Demarcation	Repression
Hungary	Complementary	P guiding M	+	Medium-strong	Co-optation	Lenient
Lithuania	Complementary	P dominant	−	Weak	Cooperation	Lenient
Latvia	Complementary	P dominant	−	Medium-strong	Cooperation	Containment
Estonia	Complementary	M dominant	−	Weak	Co-optation	Containment
Romania	Complementary/Church as ally	M replacing P	+/−	Weak	Co-optation	Lenient
Bulgaria	Complementary	P dominant	+	Weak	Cooperation	Lenient

Source: Minkenberg and Kossack (2015), Tables 15.4 and 15.5

feared as liabilities. The relationship between the Hungarian party Jobbik and the Magyar Garda is a case in point. First created by Jobbik in 2007, then banned by the government in 2009, the Hungarian Guard turned into a liability for Jobbik (see Chapter 4; Karácsony and Róna 2011; Krekó and Mayer 2015). The newly formed successor organizations, such as the New Hungarian Guard (Új Magyar Gárda) and the For a Better Future Hungarian Self-Defense (Szebb Jövőért Magyar Önvédelem), were kept at a distance by the party—but only officially. Informally, they continue to cooperate on their common anti-Roma agenda, and Jobbik even invited a New Hungarian Guard member to run for a Jobbik seat in the parliamentary elections in 2014 (see The Orange Files 2014).

In Poland, Ruch Narodowy has replaced the vanished LPR as the most important radical right actor. It started as a movement but, by the 2014 European elections, had become a party as well, and is now present in the Polish parliament in the Kukiz'15 group (see Chapter 4 and Kasprowicz 2015). A similar but more impressive development took place with the neo-fascist movement Slovak Togetherness (Slovenská Pospolitost'), founded in 1995 and led by Marián Kotleba since 2003. After he turned this movement into a party in 2005, the party was banned by the Slovak Supreme Court one year later, and Kotleba withdrew from the party while Slovak Togetherness then continued political activities as a movement. When Kotleba finally created his own party, the People's Party—Our Slovakia, in 2009, the movement decided to support it in the upcoming elections (see Mrázová 2016; Vyhlásenie SP 2016).

In sum, in this chapter I have demonstrated a high degree of volatility in the radical right sector over time, in particular the political parties. With a few exceptions, radical right parties have relatively short life spans, and their electoral results fluctuate enormously. In this regard the East European radical right stands out compared to the Western European situation. But weak party organization and inconstancy at the polls do not translate into political irrelevancy, once the radical right's interaction with its political environment is taken into account. The scenario of volatility does not apply to the far right ideology; instead, a remarkable persistence can be observed. Two factors can be emphasized. First, in the absence of relevant parties, the radical right agenda is carried on by a plethora of movements and other organizations against the backdrop of generally high levels of xenophobia in all these countries. In many countries these movements stage racist protest events, often directed at the Roma and other minorities, and impact on local politics in extreme ways, as the Hungarian Guard's anti-Roma activities show. Second, even if individual parties disappear, new parties arise, or movements transform into parties and play the electoral game. This is helped by the slow but noticeable processes of ethnic pluralization, the magnitude of which, however, trails comparable West European processes by a large margin. Under these conditions, the political effectiveness of the East European radical right might still range significantly below that of Western Europe. To answer this question, Chapter 6 turns to the subject matter of impact.

CHAPTER 6

Consequences: Interaction and Impact

Abstract In the final chapter the author addresses the effects of the radical right and makes the point that the East European radical right has lasting effects not only on its nearby competitors but also on the larger political system. The analysis of government participation and policy making in coalition government (as in Poland, Slovakia, Romania, and more recently Latvia and Bulgaria) is complemented by a study of interaction patterns between the radical right and mainstream actors, including the state. The most important effect is not the implementation of a distinct set of radical right policies but rather the radicalization of (parts of) the mainstream (instead of mainstreaming the radical right). This poses severe challenges to the democratic quality of the political systems in question.

Keywords Impact · Cordon sanitaire · Mainstreaming · Radicalization · Policy shifts · Governmental participation

The final chapter continues the discussion of the radical right's interaction with its political environment but shifts the focus to the question of impact. The discussion applies the model outlined in Chapter 2 (see Fig. 2.1) and the socio-cultural issue area which has been identified as the major structuring conflict dimension along which the radical right in post-communist democracies mobilizes and tries to exert influence (see Chapter 3 and Pytlas 2016). Several aspects can be distinguished.

First, the radical right can cause a rightward shift on the policy level, for example in the areas of minority rights, law and order, and the politics of memory; here other parties' strategies are important because they affect the chances of the radical right being effective. Second, on the level of political actors, the question arises to what extent other parties' strategies toward the radical right, such as the effort to marginalize it by co-opting its agenda, will result in a rightward shift, not only of policies but of other parties as well. Third, it should be considered, as before, whether these interactions and their effects play out differently in the East European context than in Western Europe. A quick glance at the literature shows that there is no consensus on this issue, with some arguing that the influence of the Western radical right on other parties' strategies or at the policy level has been overstated (see Akkerman 2012; Alonso and Fonseca 2012; Mudde 2007, Chapter 12), while others try to demonstrate an effect, either directly or indirectly (see Bale 2003; Minkenberg 2001; Schain et al. 2002; Schain 2006; Williams 2006).

These questions cannot be answered here in any comprehensive way, considering both the infancy of comparative research in this area and the patchy data situation concerning Eastern Europe; such a task must be left to a larger project. Instead, the following remarks provide an overview on which future research can build, concerning the radical right in government, the interaction effects on the larger political environment, and the policy effects—on the basis of the process model outlined in Chapter 2, the findings in the preceding chapters, and recent work by me and my collaborators (Minkenberg 2015a).

1   At the Top: Government Participation

In general, governmental coalitions between mainstream parties and the radical right, informal or formal, evince a basic fact: they mark the absence of a cordon sanitaire between the radical right and the mainstream parties involved. Additionally, in Western Europe they challenge all notions to interpret the radical right as a populist catch-all party which cuts across the political spectrum by gathering voters from all segments of the electorate and remaining programmatically ambivalent (see Mény and Surel 2000, 306f.; Reynié 2013, 25; Wilson and Hainsworth 2012, 9). Neither is their electorate a cross-section of "the people," nor do these parties render obsolete the established distinctions between left and right. This becomes particularly pronounced whenever the radical right has been invited into a coalition government in Western Europe, the invitation being extended by the major conservative or center-right party (e.g. the Austrian or Dutch Christian Democrats) or a right-wing populist party (the Italian Forza Italia) (see Table 6.1). Except for Switzerland, where there are no coalitions but the requirement to represent all major parties in the executive in the logic of the proportional system (*Proporz*), the radical right expands the availability of coalition parties to the right of the center. In the words of Tim Bale: "the centre-right, by including the far right either as a coalition partner or as a support party, has removed what was essentially an artificial constraint on the size of any right bloc in parliament" (Bale 2003, 69; see also Mudde 2007, 280–281). Efforts by various radical right parties to appear "respectable" have changed their outsider status and turned them into being more acceptable, without having transformed them into "normalized" conservative or right-wing parties in the vein of the Italian MSI/AN (see Minkenberg 2013a). The key factor in coalition building usually lies in the ideological proximity between the radical right and the formateur party, most likely in the issue areas dear to the radical right, that is in matters of socio-cultural values and identities and of law and order; such closeness reduces bargaining costs (see De Lange 2008, 2012; Laver and Schofield 1998). However, there are variations across countries, which are tied to the particular set of context factors (see Tables 5.3–5.5) and call for a closer look at some of the country cases, in particular with regard to the importance of the cordon sanitaire and its role in preventing or facilitating such coalition governments.

The 1994 government of Silvio Berlusconi with his Forza Italia and coalition partners MSI/AN and Lega Lord is the first post-war coalition government involving a radical right party in Europe. The neo-fascist MSI, due to a strong cordon sanitaire imposed by all parties in parliament in response to the MSI's hostility to the institutions and values of Italian democracy, was, for a long time, one of the most isolated parties in any West European parliament. This secured their niche in the Italian electorate but condemned them to the status of a pariah which could only hope for the downfall of the system. Only with the end of the Cold War, the collapse of the post-war Italian party system, and the reorganization and rebranding of the party as Alleanza Nazionale under Fini's leadership did the political legitimacy of the party increase. But in the 1990s, this was more a result of the other parties' behavior than of a true democratization of the party from within (see Ignazi 1994; Merkel 1996). With the breakdown of the *partitocrazia*, the post-war cordon sanitaire vanished as well,

Table 6.1   The radical right in European national government, 1990–2016

Country	Party	Period	Coalition partners
West			
Austria	FPÖ	2000–2005	ÖVP (CD/conservative)
	BZÖ	2005–2006	ÖVP
Denmark	DF*	2001–2011	Support for minority government of Venstre (liberal) and Conservative People' Party (cons.)
Italy	LN, AN	1994	FI (neoliberal populist)
	LN	2001–2005	FI, AN (conservative), UDC (Christian Democrat)
	LN	2008–2011	People of Freedom (FI, AN and 2 CD parties)
Netherlands	LPF	2002–2003	Christian Democrats and Liberals
	PVV*	2010–2012	Christian Democrats and Liberals
Norway	FrP	2013 – ?	Høyre (conservative)
Switzerland	SVP	2004 – ?	SPS (socialist), FDP (liberal), CVP (CD)
East			
Bulgaria	Ataka*	2009–2013	Support of minority government of GERB (center-right/nationalist)
	Ataka*	2013–2014	Support of minority coalition government of BSP (socialist) and DPS (Turkish minority party)
Latvia	NA	2011–2014	Unity (center-right), RP (center-right)
	NA	2014 – ?	Unity, ZZS (green-agrarian)
Hungary	*Fidesz***	1998–2002	MDF, FKGP (agrarian, bourgeois) – MIÉP in opposition
	*Fidesz***	2005–2006	KDNP (Christian Democrat)
	*Fidesz***	2010– 2014	no coalition partner – Jobbik in opposition
	*Fidesz***	2014 – ?	KDNP (CD) – Jobbik in opposition
Poland	LPR	2005–2006	PiS (ultraconservative and populist), SO (agrarian populist)
	*PiS***	2015 – ?	
Romania	PUNR, PRM	1992–1996	PDSR (diffuse) and PSM (social populist)
Slovakia	SNS	1992–1998	HZDS (populist) and ZRS (communist)
	SNS	2006–2010	HZDS (populist) and Smer-SD (social democrat)
	SNS	2016 – ?	Smer-SD, Most-Híd, Network

*Not part of a coalition but supporting a minority government.
**Not a radical right party but right-wing populist with programmatic elements of radical right.
Sources: Akkerman (2012), Mudde (2007: 280, 2011: 14), amended and updated.

and the new major party on the right, the FI, was sufficiently right wing and populist to accept the former pariah into the coalition. Yet, still in 1994, after having joined Berlusconi's coalition government, the AN introduced—as it has in every year since 1978—a proposal to the Italian parliament to revoke the constitutional ban on the revival of the Fascist Party (see Gallagher 2000, 75).

In the case of the Austrian Freedom Party FPÖ, the story follows a slightly different logic. As in Italy (and Germany), the main right-wing radical party must look back on a fascist history. But unlike Italy (and Germany), and very much like Denmark, another case of collaboration between the radical and the mainstream right, this party had no formal connection to the fascist past. Instead, it evolved from an emphasis on a neo-liberal critique of the welfare state towards a greater emphasis on a comparatively moderate ethnocentrism that facilitated its move into or close to the centers of political power (see Minkenberg 2013a). As shown in Chapter 5, Austria experienced a particularly sharp increase in religious pluralization and exhibited an above average proportion of xenophobes (see Fig. 3.3 and Tables 5.3 and 5.6). Against this backdrop, in the 1999 elections the FPÖ, which had taken a sharp right turn since Jörg Haider assumed its leadership in 1986, achieved the highest electoral result so far in the 1999 elections (see Carter 2005, 86–88). But it was not the electoral success as such which mattered for the FPÖ joining the ÖVP in a coalition government in 2000. Already in previous years, the cordon sanitaire had eroded when the governing ÖVP (in a coalition with the Social Democrats) collaborated selectively with the FPÖ on particular issues (see Minkenberg 2001). For its part, the ÖVP embraced the FPÖ as a coalition partner to win over former FPÖ voters, as ÖVP Interior Minister Strasser admitted: "there must be no room to the right of the ÖVP for a right-wing populist party" (Luther 2003, 148).[1] As it turned out, this strategy was successful in fragmenting the FPÖ temporarily but not in marginalizing it effectively. The Italian and Austrian cases of government coalitions with a radical right illustrate different versions of "change through rapprochement" between the mainstream right and the radical right and two types of breakdown of the cordon sanitaire: evolutionary in Austria, and revolutionary in Italy. They prepared the stage for further such coalitions in other countries, and altogether these developments constituted a considerable step in the process of mainstreaming the radical right.

In contrast, the East European characteristics of government formation including the radical right followed a different logic. Two early cases occurred in Slovakia and Romania only a few years after the end of the communist regimes. The first such coalition was formed in Slovakia shortly after the "velvet divorce" of Czechoslovakia in 1992. The first national elections after Slovak independence in June 1992 resulted in a coalition, first informal (1992), then formal (1993), between the SNS and Permier Mečiar's party, HZDS. However, at the time, the SNS was internally divided between moderate and radical wings, and these rivalries contributed to the breakup of the coalition in 1994. Unter Slota's leadership, the SNS took a sharp right turn and reentered a coalition with the "national-populist" HZDS after the early elections of 1994 (see Cibulka 1999, 117–118; Gyárfášová and Mesežnikov 2015, 242–243), a coalition that lasted the entire legislative period until 1998. An in-depth analysis shows a large ideological overlap between the HZDS and the SNS, especially in the areas of nationalism, Euroscepticism, anti-minority politics, and welfare chauvinism (see Kossack 2012, 50–53). As a consequence, the government as a whole entered a political path which entailed illiberal and anti-democratic activities and temporarily reversed the processes of democratic consolidation and rapprochement with the European Union (see Bunce and Wolchik 2010b, 136–140). The second coalition lasted from 2006 until 2010 and came to pass under entirely different circumstances. Slovakia had completed its regime transfer, was considered a consolidated democracy, and had become a member of the EU two years earlier. The SNS's major coalition partner was a newly established party, Smer-SD (founded in 1999), which functioned as the counterpole to the HZDS, considered itself social democratic, and was invited into the Party of European Socialists in 2006. On the ground, however, both parties had more in common than their labels and official histories suggest, because they shared a dose of nationalism, xenophobia, and a strong welfare chauvinism, though they differed on economic and social issues (see Kossack 2012, 52–53; Mesežnikov 2008, 13–19). Moreover, "as a major SNS coalition partner, Smer-SD...adopted and implemented (in a more moderate form) several initial legislative proposals made by the SNS, such as a law on patriotism, an amendment to education law, and a law on the merits of the pre-war Slovak politician Andrej Hlinka" (Gyárfášová and Mesežnikov 2015, 243). In the most recent coalition formed after the March 2016 elections between

Smer-SD, the SNS, and two smaller parties, SNS adopted a less radical tone under its new leader Danko (see Chapter 4)—a strategic necessity in light of the participation of the predominantly ethnic-Hungarian party Most-Híd in the coalition government. The latter's position in the cabinet strengthened as the Network party left the coalition in September 2016 and some of its deputies joined Most-Híd afterwards, thereby increasing the latter's number of cabinet posts.

The second early case of a government coalition which included the radical right took place in Romania in 1992 where the post-communist PDSR invited the radical right parties PUNR and PRM into a coalition. All parties shared a communist legacy or "radical continuity" (Shafir 2000; see Chapter 4) and an illiberal nationalism, at the expense of national minorities such as the Hungarians (see Kossack 2012, 48). During the four years of coalition government, no taming of the parties' ultranationalism could be observed; instead some experts argue that "the co-opting of the two extreme right parties into a coalition government reflected a process of 'acclimatization' of Romanian society to right-wing extremism" (Cinpoeş 2015, 285). Both countries, Slovakia and Romania (as well as Bulgaria), have been considered cases of backsliding in the democratization processes in the 1990s and laggards in EU accession, entering a nationalist-authoritarian or national communist phase, and in both cases radical right parties in government contributed to this turn of events (see Elster et al. 1998, 267; Mungiu-Pippidi 2010, 66–67).

Like Slovakia and Romania, Bulgaria was also falling behind the Visegrád group (Hungary, Czech Republic, Poland) in the pace of democratization and Europeanization—in part explained by the relatively large policy distances between government and opposition parties—as well as in keeping ethnic conflict within a peaceful framework (Mungiu-Pippidi 2010, 66). Shortly after the country's accession to the EU, the radical right party Ataka assumed the role of kingmaker by supporting two minority coalition governments, the first one (2009–2013) led by the social-populist GERB, the second one (2013–2014) led by the BSP and its Coalition for Bulgaria, a leftist electoral alliance, and its government coalition partner, the ethnic Turkish party DPS. While the first informal coalition rested on an ideological overlap in nationalism and welfare issues (see Avramov 2015, 303–305; Kossak 2012, 40) and lasted four years, the following one was an uneasy alliance which included socialist and communist parties, the Turkish minority party, and the radical right. This government was immediately challenged by an unprecedented cycle of protest reacting to the new prime minister appointing compromised individuals as cabinet members and heads of state agencies (see Ganev 2014). The protests succeeded in bringing down the BSP–DPS–Ataka cabinet, and new elections were held in October 2014. These events cost Ataka popularity and led to its return to the opposition after being reduced to about half of its voting support; with 4.5% of the votes, Ataka barely crossed the 4% electoral threshold. The new GERB-led coalition also formed a minority government—again short-lived and resigning by November 2016. Unlike its predecessors, this government did not rely on Ataka but, due to GERB's rightward shift, carried on Ataka's politics.

The coalition building in Poland in 2005–2006 followed a similar logic as the GERB–Ataka alliance in Bulgaria. A large ideological affinity between Law and Order (Pis) and LPR in 2005, except for their position on the EU, resulted in first an informal coalition, together with Lepper's agrarian-populist Samoobrona, and then, in a step by step approach carefully contrived by PiS leader Jarosław Kaczyński, in a full-fledged government coalition in May 2006 (see Kasprowicz 2015, 168; Kossack 2012, 46, Pankowski 2010, 170–172). Compared to the other countries, however, this coalition was one of the most short-lived in Eastern Europe; it broke apart in 2007, only one year after it was formally concluded, due to internal conflicts, scandals, and inconsistencies. Yet, there was an emergence of a right-wing ideological bloc in this coalition: "by 2006, the PiS-LPR-Self-Defence coalition could be seen as a natural reflection of a convergence of ideologies. It was, arguably, no longer an issue of two extremist parties entering a coalition with a mainstream democratic party, but rather of three parties of different shades of nationalist populism joining forces for a shared vision of radical anti-liberal transformation" (Pankowski 2010, 172). In fact, both PiS and LPR had the highest level of ideological affinity between a coalition formateur and the radical right across all cases in the region (see Kossack 2012, 47).

The Latvian case of a government coalition involving a radical right party can be considered the least spectacular in that the National Alliance joining a three-party coalition following the September 2011 election occurred in a rather routine way (see Auers and Kasekamp 2015, 141). Given that the National Alliance emerged from the fusion of the radical— and electorally unimpressive—All for Latvia! with the more established nationalist TB/LNNK and coalesced with several center-right parties, this constellation did not promise a departure into political spectacle, as in the other cases discussed here. The recent reshuffling of the coalition government in February 2016 has resulted in Latvia's first green prime minister but kept the three-party constellation of 2014 and the National Alliance's participation in it intact.

Overall, the role of the radical right in East European coalition governments can be summarized as follows. (i) In all cases, the radical right entered the government only a few years after the party had been formed or shortly after the onset of democratization (Romania, Slovakia); there was little time for a "change through rapprochement." In the West European cases, with the notable exception of Italy, there was a time span of about 20 years between the electoral breakthrough of the radical right and its inclusion in a national government. (ii) The radical right parties in Eastern Europe which joined a governmental coalition or supported a minority government are ideologically more extreme than those in Western Europe (see Chapter 4). In fact, those West European parties of the radical right which were invited into a coalition government belong to the ideologically most moderate type of this party family, such as the Austrian Freedom Party, the Swiss People's Party, the Italian Lega Nord, the Dutch List Pim Fortuyn, and its successor, the Party of Freedom (see Akkerman 2012; also Minkenberg 2013a). (iii) There is not a single case in Western Europe where a government with the radical right was formed with a left-wing coalition partner, though there are several such cases in the East (Bulgaria, Romania, and Slovakia). (iv) All three observations lead to a fourth point: while in Western Europe there is a cordon sanitaire between many mainstream parties and the radical right, and between *all* left-wing mainstream parties and the radical right, no such cordon sanitaire exists in Eastern Europe, with the exception of the Czech Republic, where a legacy—or memory—of the interwar experience of democracy may have survived (see Capoccia 2005; also Mareš 2012, 2015).

Hence, the mechanism of coalition building in Eastern Europe and the role of ideological proximity, as far as the radical right is concerned, is comparable to but unfolds in a different way from that in Western Europe. This is due to the divergent contexts of the party systems and the pervasive ultranationalism in East European societies in the triadic dynamism suggested by Brubaker which also informs the programmatic positions of mainstream parties (see Chapter 3). More specifically, the lack of clear cut cleavages in the economic dimension and the almost inverse relationship between the political left and right in this regard (see Tavits and Letki 2009) provide more opportunities for the inclusion of the radical right in coalition governments than in the West by adding left-wing parties as potential partners, especially since the voters of radical right parties do not hold particular pro- or anti-market positions in a strict sense (see Allen 2015; also Bustikova and Kitschelt 2009).

2 INTERACTION EFFECTS

The interaction of the radical right with mainstream parties and their impact on these and on policy making in Central and Eastern Europe do not diverge much from the Western European cases in their mechanisms—yet the outcome looks more radical. As noted above, the first cases of government participation of radical right parties occurred in Slovakia and in Romania, in 1992. While the Romanian coalition government lasted four years, the Slovak experience ended after one-and-a-half full terms, if the internally divided SNS from 1992 to 1994 is added. Moreover, as in Italy, the SNS returned to government status in 2006 for another full term—in both cases allied to the right-wing populist HZDS of Vladimir Meciar. Meciar's style of government in the 1990s has already been criticized as populist and autocratic (see Thanei 2002; see also Mesežnikov 2008, 13–19), and the contribution of the SNS to the government's policies is hard to disentangle. Among the major accomplishments of the first Meciar–Slota coalition were restrictions on self-administration and language use of the Hungarian minority in local affairs and public schools. Moreover, an ethno-national history policy was introduced for the national school curriculum, along with other measures to foster a Slovak sense of identity and to marginalize, if not suppress, the Hungarian minority (see Deegan-Krause 2004; Mihailescu 2008; also Chapter 4 on the SNS and its platform). Jan Slota's SNS returned to the government table in 2006 when the Social Democrat Robert Fico asked both the SNS and Meciar's HZDS to join him in a coalition. Under this coalition, state support for ultranationalist organizations and associations, for example the cultural institute "Matica slovenská", increased. As outlined above, Smer initiated several legislative proposals generated by the SNS, but with limited effects; for example, the effort to rehabilitate Andrej Hlinka, Slovakia's proto-fascist leader of the interwar era, and elevate him to the status of "Father of all Slovaks," for the parliamentary vote failed in 2007 (see Mayer and Odehnal 2010, 185). On the other hand, during the entire period, the prime minster failed to distance himself from the occasional anti-Hungarian and racist statements by

Slota, Smer's vice prime minister Čaplovič attacked the Hungarian minority party for its allegedly extremist and revisionist goals, and social democratic ministers and representatives attempted to discredit Hungarian Slovak's complaints about discrimination and the historical record about the forced resettlement of Hungarians in the Slovak part of the CSSR after World War II (see Mesežnikov 2008, 19–27; Petöcz 2009, 71–74). The newly formed coalition government after the March 2016 elections renewed the collaboration between the Social Democrat Fico as prime minister and the SNS, now led by Andrej Danko, the party's number two under former leader Slota. They were joined by two other parties, Most-Híd, which promotes civic rights for the Hungarian minority, and the pro-business Network (see Virostkova 2016). This constellation, which was only one of several options for coalition building, signals the moderation of the SNS under the new chairman but also the openness of the Slovak left for cross-cutting alliances. It ended in 2016 with the Network party leaving and Most-Híd increasing its share of seats in the cabinet.

As in Slovakia, Bulgarian politics saw the emergence of a government collaboration which included both left-wing and radical right parties, albeit in an informal coalition with Ataka supporting the governments, first led by a GERB prime minister, then by a socialist. In both instances, Ataka supported government initiatives on a case by case basis with the result that Ataka's "mainstreaming" went along with other parties' move to the right, in particular GERB and the minority party DPS. Whether as a supporter of minority governments perceived as corruptible or in opposition, Ataka contributed to a new salience of "identity politics" and populist anger in the country (see Avramov 2015, 308–312; Ganev 2014, 40; Pirro 2015, 126–129). So even after Ataka was electorally marginalized in the 2014 elections and discontinued supporting the new GERB-led minority government under prime minister Borisov, it had noticeable effects on the latter and on Bulgarian politics: "the interplay dynamics between 'generic' and radical right populists have produced negative effects for the suppliers of radical populism (Ataka)... However, the general impact of the process of mainstreaming Ataka was GERB's adoption of some of the most abrasive standards, resulting in a growth of hate speech and intolerance in public life" (Avramov 2015, 315).

In contrast to Slovakia and Bulgaria, the government experience of radical right-wing parties in Poland was rather short lived. From 2005 until 2007, the League of Polish Families joined the populist Samoobrona and the ultra-conservative Law and Justice (PiS), first as a supporter of a minority government of PiS (from October 2005), then in a coalition government (May 2006–August 2007) which was united by a strong nationalist and anti-liberal outlook, disregard for civil liberties and the rule of law, and a populist style in government (see Kucharcyzk and Wysocka 2008; Pankowski 2010, 169–189). The short life of the coalition was not the result of ideological differences, which were modest both on the party and voter level when compared to other parties and their voters (see De Lange and Guerra 2009, 542; Pytlas 2016, 96). Rather, a series of scandals which rocked both Samoobrona and the LPR during 2006 and 2007, and the personalities of Samoobrona's leader Lepper and some PiS ministers, including the prime minister, proved fatal for the coalition (see Kopka 2014, 327–331; Pankowski 2010, 173). Moreover, the ultra-Catholic radio network Radio Maryja, which was not only instrumental in the founding of the LPR but also in bringing the coalition together, switched its support to PiS in 2006 after the prime minister courted Radio Maryja publicly (see Pankowski 2010, 174), thereby signaling where it saw the future of its own agenda.

An analysis of the interaction of radical right parties with other parties in five East European countries shows significant shifts in the party systems of the region between 2002 and 2010. Bartek Pytlas and Oliver Kossack (2015) studied the position of all parties in Bulgaria, Hungary, Poland, Romania, and Slovakia based on the expert survey location along the so-called GAL-TAN continuum which captures socio-cultural positions between a Green-Alternative-Libertarian and a Traditionalist-Authoritarian-Nationalist pole (see Hooghe et al. 2002). Instead of a polarization, the authors could demonstrate a right-wing shift in all party systems (see Fig. 6.1).

In Bulgaria, the Turkish minority party DPS and later GERB reacted to the appearance of Ataka by moving to the right, followed by the socialist BSP (not covered in Fig. 6.1; see Avramov 2015, 306), while parties which remained in the left range of the GAL/TAN dimension suffered electoral losses. In Hungary, Fidesz was already on the far right in this dimension, pulled earlier by MIÉP until the latter's demise from parliament in 2002. Fidesz moved away from that position but ended up moving back somewhat (or at least did not continue the shift away) when Jobbik appeared. The Polish case shows the most dramatic shifts in the period during which LPR governed in a coalition with PiS. Here, the Law and Justice Party approached LPR positions during the short

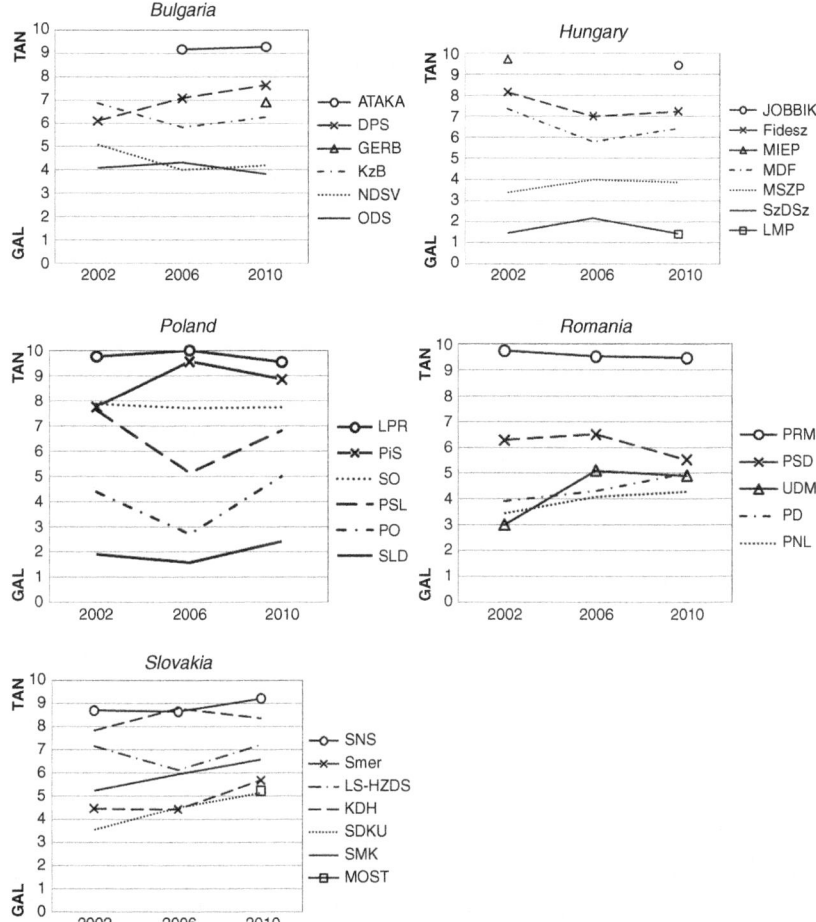

Fig. 6.1 Spatial shifts in East European party systems, 2002–2010 (*Source*: Pytlas and Kossack (2015, 111–121, Figs. 5.1–5.5), based on data from the Chapel Hill Expert Survey, 2002–2010.)

period of joint government but stayed on the right position after the breakup of the coalition and its role as opposition party. As has been shown elsewhere, PiS has absorbed by and large the LPR agenda since 2006, along with the support of Radio Maryja (see Pankowski 2010, 174), and continued the ideological trajectory of the LPR long after it had disappeared. As Fig. 6.1 illustrates, all other parties followed the rightward shift of PiS with a little delay in the GAL/TAN dimension. A similar rightward drift across the party spectrum can be observed in Slovakia. With the social democratic party Smer moving towards the center, there was no vigorous left-wing representation in sociocultural terms left by 2010. The only country with a limited rightward shift is Romania where an electorally weak radical right party did not exert a pull to the right; instead the party system seemed to coalesce in the center. Overall, a striking pattern emerged in these countries: "facing a viable threat from a radical right party, nearby competitors tend to react with an accommodative strategy" (Pytlas and Kossack 2015, 120).

Hence, electoral strategies by the established right which attempts to co-opt the radical right agenda but demarcates the party opened up new opportunities for the radical right by adding legitimacy to their concerns. Another scenario is the strategy of government parties to co-opt the radical right agenda and positions. A recent study (Kossack 2012) has confirmed with new data and in a qualitative comparative analysis that in the cases of Poland and Slovakia the strategy of co-optation in the 2000s resulted in the electoral marginalization of the radical right. In Poland, the radical right party LPR never recovered; in Slovakia, the SNS was forced out of parliament, but only temporarily. Hungary provides the odd case: while marginalization through co-optation worked between Fidesz and MIÉP, this strategy did not prevent the rise of Jobbik (see Chapter 5 and also Pytlas 2016).

A summary overview of the radical right's impact in the countries under consideration is given in Table 6.2. Based on the premise that the radical right's impact cannot be measured by its electoral strength or organizational persistence alone—for reasons discussed earlier in Eastern Europe even more so than in Western Europe—the evidence suggests that the radical right's effects occurred primarily in shifting the overall political agenda to the right in the dimension of identity politics. For such an impact, government participation was not necessary: the shift happened in conjunction with the parliamentary presence—or threat thereof, if the radical right parties were large enough to reach "blackmail potential" (Sartori 1976)—rather than being part of the executive (see also Pytlas and Kossack 2015). This finding is analogous to research on Western Europe where the

Table 6.2 Radical right parties in Eastern Europe: Impact in selected arenas (post-2000)

Country	Right-wing radicalism in public discourse*	Mainstream parties	Policy making
Poland	Expansion	Radicalization of mainstream right	Marginal shift**
Slovakia	Expansion	Selective radicalization of the coalition partners	Shift to right
Czech Republic	Radicalization	Insignificant	Insignificant
Hungary	Expansion and radicalization	Radicalization of mainstream right	Shift to right
Lithuania	Expansion	Insignificant	Marginal shift
Latvia	Radicalization	Indeterminate	Shift to right
Estonia	Insignificant	Insignificant	Insignificant
Romania	Expansion	Indeterminate	Shift to right
Bulgaria	Expansion and radicalization	Radicalization of the mainstream right	Shift to right

*Expansion: increase in the amount of radical right framing in public discourse toward new or existing policy fields; radicalization: ideological radicalization of framing in existing policy fields.
**Only during the government period 2006–2007. From 2015, the shift became strong.
Source: Minkenberg and Kossack (2015, 356).

presence of the radical right in parliament, in combination with a mainstream right government, accounted more for a right-wing shift in immigration policies than the radical right's government participation (see e.g. Akkermann 2012; Schain 2006). However, in contrast to Western Europe, government participation in the East often meant the end of the radical right's parliamentary presence, as the cases of Poland (2006–2007) and Slovakia (2006–2010) most vividly illustrate (see also Table 6.1). In the Polish case the mainstream right party Law and Justice co-opted the LPR's agenda while in a coalition government with it; this and the support by Radio Maryja made the LPR superfluous at the end of the government term. In contrast, the Hungarian mainstream right, Fidesz, never openly cooperated with the parties of the radical right and had already shifted to the right before the rise of Jobbik when it co-opted the agenda of Jobbik's predecessor, the Hungarian Life and Justice Party (MIÉP). As shown above, it was the "Gypsy crime" issue which helped Jobbik find its niche on the right of Fidesz; Jobbik's interpretive frames of minority issues were not adopted in whole (see Pytlas 2016; also Bíró Nagy et al. 2013). In sum, the radical right in government did not result in a mainstreaming of the radical right but instead in a radicalization of the mainstream. An exception can be seen in the Slovak case after 2010 where the mainstream coalition partner applied a populist strategy and a right-wing shift but reverted from it once the radical right was marginalized (see Pytlas and Kossack 2015).

The interaction effects of the movement sector are harder to assess because of the sparse evidence of right-wing movement research so far, but a number of recent studies suggest a significant impact as well (see e.g. contributions to Minkenberg 2015a). In general, policy impact by movement activities occurs, if at all, in a very indirect fashion (see Rucht 1994; Tilly and Tarrow 2006); the arenas of the public, of the mass media, and of particular institutions such as the education system provide opportunities for political effects by radical right movements. The Polish and Romanian cases demonstrate that religious actors who carry a radical right agenda command powerful means to disseminate the message, provided they enjoy moral or other authority in society (see Grzymała-Busse 2015): on the one hand, the right-wing media can count on dedicated listeners, which in the Polish case encompasses several million; on the other hand, they can use state–church relations, if organized favorably for religious interests, to affect society. In both countries, the educational realm was directly targeted by radical right actors (see Andreescu 2015; Kasprowicz 2015).

3   Policy Shifts: Toward Regime Change?

As mentioned before, the radical right's political and policy effects remain a matter of controversy. With regard to the West European experience, some argue that the effects are limited because these parties are typically junior partners in government and restrained by the judicial system; they matter mainly as opposition parties rather than government parties (see Heinisch 2003; Mudde 2007, 277–292; also idem 2011). Others point out significant effects on relevant policy areas, such as immigration and law and order, and on other parties, even the party system as a whole (see Albertazzi 2009; Bale 2003). Finally, these parties can be seen under the influence of a "taming effect" by joining or collaborating with others, especially when doing so over an extended period of time (Minkenberg 2001, 2009b). The final step of our examination takes a closer look at right-wing policy shifts with lasting and corrosive effects in Eastern Europe. Here the focus is on Hungary and Poland, which have been identified as the most important cases or even "worst case scenarios" for a decline of democracy in the region (Ágh 2016; Pappas 2014; Rupnik 2016); this development cannot be fully understood without assessing the role of the radical right in it.

Hungary in the three periods of Fidesz in government (1998–2002, 2010–2014, and 2014–present) is a case of radical right governmental politics without such a party in government. Here, the radical right parties were neither coalition partners nor supporters of a right-wing minority government, yet their very presence and articulation of ultranationalist issues, in particular their questioning the legitimacy of the Treaty of Trianon and their pan-Hungarian agenda, coupled with their racism and anti-Semitism, contributed to the major mainstream right party Fidesz's continued shift to the right on these issues. As the party in government from 1998 to 2002, Fidesz under its prime minister Viktor Orbán introduced the controversial Status Law of 2001 which granted access to a "national citizen certificate" providing health and education benefits to all three million Hungarians living in neighboring countries (Slovenia, Slovakia, Croatia, Serbia, Ukraine, Romania). This law was meant to heal the effects the Trianon Treaty and also to be a step toward the unity of the Hungarian nation. As such, it was in line with the platform of MIÉP, then an opposition party in Budapest. The protest coming from Romania and Slovakia was countered by a number of amendments to the law after the 2002 elections when Fidesz had lost and a new government had taken over. But this did not mean Fidesz retreated from its overall positions (see Pytlas 2016, Chapters 6 and 7). Moreover, Prime Minister Orbán's Fidesz and MIÉP cooperated in manipulating the boards of public radio and television in order to grant Fidesz control of the media (see Mayer and Odehnal 2010, 35; also Uitz 2008). This political strategy continued and intensified after 2010, without any substantial parliamentary opposition. Viktor Orbán and his party are today considered the most prominent and powerful right-wing populist party in Central and Eastern Europe which, after the 2010 election and reelection in 2014, has governed the country with large majorities and begun a process to rebuild the Hungarian state according to its own ideas. As a result of the ongoing competition between Fidesz and the radical right, first MIÉP and then Jobbik, Fidesz's agenda includes large parts of the radical right ideology, most notably its anti-liberalism and anti-pluralism, along with a pronounced nationalism and the quest for a strong state. In this, the Fidesz government since 2010 is but the latest incarnation of what has been described as "populism from above" in the region, that is mainstream parties which try to be elitist and populist at the same time (see Ágh 2016, 279).

An analysis of the major party platform planks of Jobbik and the policies enacted by Fidesz after 2010 concludes that the latter carried out many of the Jobbik propositions, such as: special taxes on multinational telecommunication corporations; the nationalization of savings in private pension funds; the incorporation of the reference to the Crown of Saint Stephen in the Fundamental Law, that is Hungary's new constitution; a new law and constitutional change to place all Hungarian media under the control of officials assigned by the government; the renaming of Roosevelt Square in Budapest to Széchenyi Square, and similar acts of revisionist politics of history and a return to the nineteenth century and nationalism, to name only a few examples (see Ágh 2016, 280–281; Bíró Nagy et al. 2013, 244– 249). While Fidesz and the radical right-wing opposition party Jobbik fight each other in the public sphere, their main ideas exhibit a number of similarities in their ethnic nationalism—which may also be attributed to the fact that Orbán and Jobbik leader Gábor Vona started their career together in Fidesz and differ more in style than in substance (see Mayer and Odenahl 2010, 77; Uitz 2008, 64).

Hence, from 2010 onwards, the Fidesz government began to transform the Hungarian system into an "elected autocracy" based on the new constitution's damage to the institutional checks and balances, the marginalization of other political and social actors, and the revival of legal traditionalism. After the government's reelection in 2014, Viktor Orbán continued the process to strengthen the state under his party's dominance by concentrating power in the executive and expanding the reach of central government into the municipalities, churches (i.e. by withdrawing legal status from churches not loyal to Fidesz), and the cultural sector (see Ágh 2016, 281–282). This new regime which Orbán himself declared an "illiberal democracy" in a speech in July 2014[2] resembles in many aspects the political vision of the radical right in the region (see Chapter 4): an authoritarian state with a strong executive and weak institutional obstacles, a renationalization of politics in the vein of the nineteenth and early twentieth century, that is an illiberal or "Potemkin democracy" (Ágh 2015) or "Frankenstate" which means putting together the worst practices of major areas of governance (Rupnik 2016, 78). An assessment of conventional democratic indicators reaches a similar conclusion, namely "that the 'procedural minimum' of democracy—as defined in Dahl's conception of polyarchy—was eroded by these [i.e. the Fidesz government's] reforms" (Herman 2016, 259). The Hungarian system under the third Orbán government may not be a dictatorship resembling its interwar predecessors, and hence not the complete fulfillment of right-wing radical dreams; but it can be considered a regime in transition, with a serious input by the radical right, and the process is not yet completed. In light of recent protests and the loss of by-elections after 2014, "the Fidesz regime, having come under this pressure, has begun a radicalization, appropriating the extreme topics represented so far by Jobbik, in order to regain supporters; but this is in vain, since Jobbik has greater credibility on the issues of national-social populism" (Ágh 2016, 283).

The current developments in Poland under the PiS government since 2016 are often likened to the Hungarian "master case": "the PiS government seems to use to some extent the Hungarian roadmap for its reforms, as references to Hungary's prime minister Viktor Orbán in particular and Hungary in general abound in the Polish public sphere" (Karolewski and Benedikter 2016, 3; see also Hanley and Dawson 2016; Rupnik 2016). This relating of the Polish to the Hungarian scenario overlooks two things: first, the current PiS government has a predecessor in 2005 with no external reference but a homegrown program to rebuild the Polish system into a "IV Republic"; second, this program was carried out in a coalition with a radical right party, the LPR. Among the building blocks on the way to this more authoritarian and ultranationalist version of the Polish state were efforts to concentrate power in the executive at the expense of civil liberties, for example by establishing a central anti-corruption office outside of parliamentary control, and a new media law which aimed at putting all public broadcasting under the control of the government, thereby incidentally privileging Radio Maryja over other private broadcasters (the law was annulled by the Constitutional Tribunal; see Kopka 2014, 338–368; Pankowski 2010, 175–179). More specifically, with LPR leader Roman Giertych as minister of education, the PiS-led coalition pressed for the introduction of a conservative Catholicism as the basis for Polish politics and the state. The school curriculum began to reflect this ultranationalism and Catholic fundamentalism, introducing "patriotic education" as a course of study, while the government banned "homosexual propaganda" from school grounds in 2007 (see Golebiowska 2009; also Zubrzycki 2006). In foreign affairs, the government reevaluated Polish–German relations and took a hardened position on its Western neighbor which introduced a sense of suspicion and aggressiveness unknown since the fall of the Berlin Wall. Coupled with the government's anti-EU rhetoric, this led to a growing isolation of Poland in the EU (see Kucharczyk and Wysocka 2008, 91–92). Overall, while this government lasted less than two years and its successor undid many of its decisions, it can be considered the most rightwing coalition government in Eastern Europe at the time.

The effects by the radical right's participation in the first PiS government include in particular the enduring positioning of Law and Justice on the far right of the Polish political spectrum. In the political space defined by the two axes of secularism vs. religiosity and state interventionism vs. free market economy, PiS occupies the same spot in 2011 which had been taken by LPR in 2001 (see Kopka 2014, 594). A radical right party in Poland seems futile in this light, and election results in 2015 confirm that voters did not see a special need for such a party—some of them rather preferred new and idiosyncratic formations such as Kukiz'15 which carried a new wave of right-wing radicals into parliament without much public notice.

More importantly, PiS carried on the legacy of its radical right coalition partner: it absorbed LPR's political agenda, the alliance with Radio Maryja, former LPR voters, and some of its leading personnel. Among the latter are Jacek Kurski who had organized xenophobic campaigns for the LPR and assumed in 2016, with the support of PiS, the post of director of the TV station TVP; or Antoni Macierewicz who in his LPR days edited the right-wing magazine *Głos*, allegedly expressed sympathy for the anti-Semitic pamphlet *Protocols of the Elders of Zion*, and became Poland's minister of defense in the PiS cabinet after the 2015 elections (see Kublik 2016, 154; Maszkowki 2004; Pankowski 2010, 121, 159; also Vetter 2016).

The policies carried out by the current PiS government with Prime Minister Beata Szydło in the proscenium and party leader Jarosław Kaczyński in the background resumed the earlier efforts but pushed them further. While avoiding the rhetoric of the "IV Republic," the government passed a new media law and purged government critics from public broadcasting services, abolished the neutrality of the civil service, and because it did not have the parliamentary votes to change the constitution, amended the law on the Constitutional Tribunal so it could staff it with loyal judges (see Fomina and Kucharczyk 2016, 62–63; Rupnik 2016, 79). The law on the Constitutional Court was disregarded by the Court itself and ruled unconstitutional—a ruling that the government refused to publish, thereby paving the way for an ongoing constitutional crisis (see Fomina and Kucharczyk 2016, 63). These reforms were accompanied by a costly welfare program (additional child support, subsidized medicine for seniors) to be financed by taxes from the banking sector and multinational corporations. While this program may look leftist to some (see Karolewski and Benedikter 2016, 12), it can also be subsumed under the typical welfare chauvinism of the radical right in East and West (see Chapter 4 and Mudde 2007, Chapter 5), particularly when considering the return of identity politics with the PiS party in power: the favoritism towards ultra-Catholics, the culture war against the "gender ideology," the fight against refugees and the EU's approach to the refugee crisis, and the denunciation of government critics as "Poles of the worst sort" by Kaczyński (see Fomina and Kucharczyk 2016, 61–63). Taken together, these changes may not amount to the level of regime change as in the Hungarian case, in particular since public protest has risen and the Catholic Church has taken a critical stance. But the pace with which the PiS government enacted them and the public display of the closing of ranks between Kaczyński and Orbán in their fight against liberalism at their meeting in the Tatra Mountains (see Rupnik 2016, 79) points at a larger dimension than a simple assemblage of policy shifts. The Polish and Hungarian governments are busy reconstructing the liberal-democratic regimes in a fashion which approximates to the enactment of radical right visions of an ethno-nationalist and authoritarian state (see Lang 2016). In line with this, both governments belong to the fiercest critics of the German chancellor's refugee policy and efforts to move the EU towards a humanitarian solution in the handling of the African and Near Eastern refugees' escape to Europe.

Overall, the radical right in most cases examined here has significantly contributed to political changes which have undercut the liberalization processes since 1989, in particular the resistance to the opening of society and further European integration. The most obvious example of a backlash is the politicization of minority issues after 1989 and the subsequent polarization in the political spectrum (see Bustikova 2015; Pytlas 2016). Advances in human rights and minority issues are fundamentally challenged by the radical right, and often thwarted by the co-optation of radical right platforms by mainstream parties. The quality of democracy is immediately affected where such rights are violated—not to mention the more direct attacks on liberal institutions in Hungary and Poland, by parties which have largely absorbed the agenda and even some of the personnel and networks of the radical right.

Notes

1. This echoes Bavarian leader Franz Josef Strauß's famous dictum in the 1980s that there must not be a democratically legitimized party to the right of the CSU (the Bavarian sister party of the Christian Democratic Union) (see Minkenberg 1998, 243–245, 2002b, 259–261; also Stöss 1989, 181–183).
2. The speech was held on July 26, 2014 (see Ágh 2016, 282; Rupnik 2016, 79; also Keno Verseck, "Orbáns Verbündete blasen zum Kampf gegen liberales Europa." *Der Spiegel* 7, January 2016 http://www.spiegel.de/politik/ausland/viktor-orban-und-der-aufstand-gegen-das-system-eu-a-1070728.html; accessed November 21, 2016).

CHAPTER 7

Conclusions

Abstract A summary view of the radical right in Eastern Europe reveals that despite its organizational and electoral volatility it has not remained on the political margins; major parties as well as governments have adopted parts of their agenda, as Hungary and Poland illustrate most vividly. While in general the same can be said about Western Europe, the evidence shows that the radical right in Eastern Europe adds a particularly pervasive challenge to the democratic order in a number of countries and to the region's politics. This can be read off the radical right's ideological extremism, its electoral volatility in the context of under-institutionalized party systems, and the easy contagion of the mainstream discourse by the radical right's message, which resonates more widely in Eastern societies than in the West.

Keywords Anti-democratic challenge · Ideological extremism · Radicalization · Contagion effects

With the EU's enlargement in 2004/2007, the process of political transformation in Eastern Europe seems to have reached a conclusion; systemic opposition was marginalized and the radical right was far from being a serious political force. To many, it looked quite "pathetic" (Mudde 2005a). Today, the picture has changed: the radical right has not remained on the sidelines and major parties in the region as well as governments have adopted parts of their agenda, as Hungary and Poland illustrate. While in general the same can be said about Western Europe, this book has shown that the radical right in Eastern Europe adds a particularly pervasive challenge to the democratic order in a number of countries and to the region's politics. This can be inferred from the radical right's ideological extremism, its electoral volatility in the context of under-institutionalized party systems, and the easy contagion of the mainstream discourse by the radical right's message, which resonates more widely in Eastern societies than in the West.

On the conceptual level, the radical right is understood as a collective actor with an ideology, the core element of which consists in a myth of a homogeneous nation, a romantic and populist ultranationalism. This ideology challenges the idea and reality of liberal and pluralistic democracy by radicalizing the inclusionary and exclusionary criteria of a primary "we group" (typically the nation), such as ethnicity, religion, and/or gender. This definition does not include an explicitly anti-democratic stance, such as the fascist view of the desired political order, but it places the radical right at the ideological margin of the political spectrum in liberal democracies.

However, the radical right is not a homogeneous block itself. This political family can be differentiated into ideological variants, which range from outright anti-democratic or fascist-autocratic (here: extremist) to ethno-centrist but not explicitly anti-democratic, to religious-fundamentalist versions, and from parties to movements to often violent subcultures.

Ideologically, the East European radical right challenges the new liberal-democratic order, including the EU, and the state socialist system that preceded it. Typically, these parties' as well as these movements' ideologies are characterized by a troubled or antithetical relationship to democracy. They proclaim nostalgia for the old despotic regimes and the ethnic and territorial conception of national identity that prevailed under them, following the nation-building struggles before and after World War I. Many of these groups adopt symbols of the fascist movements and regimes of the 1930s and 1940s such as Hungary's Arrow Cross movement, Romania's Iron Guard and the Romanian Legion, or the revival of Roman Dmowski's anti-liberal, anti-Western ultra-Catholicism in Poland. Moreover, territorial revisionism is high on the agenda of many of these parties and movements. In Romania, the Party of Greater Romania promotes interwar borders as a way of demanding the annexation of Moldova, in the meantime the Orthodox Church has taken over some of the PRM's agenda. While the party has largely disappeared from the electoral map, movements such as Noua Dreaptă continue to mobilize for territorial revisions.

The desire for change is particularly pronounced in Hungary. The now defunct Hungarian Justice and Life Party (MIÉP) and the Movement for a Better Hungary (Jobbik) both have attacked the Treaty of Trianon and publicly imagined Hungary within its Habsburg-era borders. The Slovak radical right attempts to mobilize its support by arousing fears of the alleged Hungarian expansionism, which it portrays as the line of the Hungarian official policies rather than of the radical right, thereby intimidating the Hungarian minority in Slovakia. At the same time, its leaders celebrate fascist politicians of the interwar and World War II period, particular the newly established Kotleba party. In Poland, the radical right has been heavily influenced by religious fundamentalism. By the end of the 1990s, Radio Maryja and its political outlet, the League of Polish Families (LPR), picked up the anti-liberal and ultra-Catholic message of interwar ideologue Roman Dmowski. In the meantime, Radio Maryja switched its support to the Law and Justice Party (PiS), which also absorbed LPR ideas, members, and voting support. In many countries, the Roma minority serves as a scapegoat for all kinds of social and political ills and is subject to acts of terrorism by radical right movements such as the Hungarian Guard in Hungary.

The current situation is shaped by the history and legacies of diverging nation-building processes in East and West. Almost all of Eastern Europe was subject to multinational empires, that is the Habsburg, the Russian, and the Ottoman empires. The dominant pattern was the emergence of a national identity without the nation-state, that is an ethno-cultural nationhood, and the establishment of a nation-state along with rapid democratization after World War I, soon to be replaced by authoritarian dictatorships in the interwar period and communist regimes after World War II. These are region-specific legacies shared by most countries in Eastern Europe and with relevance to the radical right. Moreover, while in Western Europe immigrants take the role of scapegoats, these are not readily available in Eastern Europe; instead, national minorities and neighboring countries take this position. As Rogers Brubaker (1997) pointed out, many post-socialist nations could be characterized by a "triadic" configuration of nations between nationalizing states, the existence of national minorities within the new states, and the existence of "external homelands'." It is in this arena where ongoing efforts of nation-building tend to override other issues; they, more than other factors, help explain the mobilization of the radical right.

The ideological extremism corresponds with limited and highly volatile electoral appeals and frequent opportunities for radical right parties when voter dissatisfaction spreads. Here, another set of historical legacies comes into play. Compared to Lipset and Rokkan's idea of "frozen" party alternatives in the West (1967), a very different kind of "freezing" occurred in the East with the disappearance of democracy and party competition in the interwar and postwar eras. The party systems in the entire region today are characterized by a low alignment of voters and unstable cleavage patterns, as well as low levels of party membership. These factors point at the general feature of East European party systems as significantly under-institutionalized, thus providing more opportunities for new and radical parties. In addition the mainstream, both right and left, differs from that in Western Europe in that outright nationalism is not confined to the far right sector of the political spectrum but constitutes part of the mainstream itself, including major left-wing parties. Moreover, numerous survey data show a level of xenophobia in the East which is markedly higher than that in the West. Consequently, the overall support for radical right parties in national elections in the region is generally lower than in Western Europe. Finally, while in nearly all West European countries the same parties have run in each national election since the 1980s, Eastern Europe is characterized by a frequent coming and going of such parties. The average life span of an East European radical right party, measured by at least 1% of the vote in national parliamentary elections, is just under 10 years. The only party in the entire region which consistently received more than 3% in all national elections since 1990 is the Slovak SNS.

The inconstancy at the polls does not translate into political irrelevancy, once the radical right's interaction with its political environment is taken into account. The scenario of volatility does not apply to the radical right ideology; instead, a remarkable persistence can be observed in two ways. First, in the absence of relevant parties, the radical right agenda is carried on by a plethora of movements and other organizations against the backdrop of generally high levels of xenophobia in all these countries. In many countries radical right movements stage racist protest events, often directed at the Roma minority, and affect local politics in extreme ways, as the Hungarian Guard's activities show. An analysis of movement activities across the entire region revealed an increase rather than decrease after the countries' accession to the EU (see Minkenberg and Kossack 2015).

Moreover, in Poland and Romania, religious actors emerged as the torchbearers of radical right thinking; in both countries, the dominant religious tradition is closely intertwined with their respective national identity.

Second, another and more consequential version of continuity in the face of volatile radical right parties has been the adoption of their agenda by other political parties, most notably but not exclusively the mainstream right. As is evident from research, most radical right parties in the region mobilize support in the arena of "identity politics," along an ethno-cultural or ethno-nationalist cleavage, and are helped by a wholesale lack of a cordon sanitaire among the mainstream, except in the Czech Republic. Consequently, in a number of countries the radical right was invited to join national governments in a coalition relatively soon after the introduction of democracy: Romania (1992–1996), Slovakia (1992–1998, 2006–2010, and again in 2016), Poland (2006–2007), and Latvia (since 2011). In Bulgaria, the radical right has supported two different minority governments (2009–2014). In most countries the impact of the radical right occurred primarily in shifting the political agenda to the right along the ethno-cultural cleavage. But as the cases of Hungary and of Poland show, government participation in itself was unnecessary for such effects: the shift happened as a result of strategic adjustments of the mainstream right, if the radical right was large enough to reach "blackmail potential" (Sartori 1976). This finding is in line with research on Western Europe where the presence of the radical right in government is not a necessary condition for a right-wing shift in immigration policies. But unlike in Western Europe, the evidence suggests that the East European radical right in government or in cooperation with other parties did not result in its mainstreaming but instead in a radicalization of the mainstream. In other words: the primary effects of the radical right do not consist in the passing of particular laws or policies but in the radicalization of public discourse on minority and related issues and in lasting programmatic shifts of mainstream parties, such as the Law and Justice Party (PiS) in Poland, Smer in Slovakia, GERB in Bulgaria, the center-right parties in Latvia (Unity, ZRP), and Fidesz in Hungary.

In sum, in Eastern Europe, the agenda of the radical right has reached the mainstream. In the course of the transformation process, the radical right's ultranationalist agenda initially appeared rather marginal, but the constant calls for a strong nation did not subside with democratic consolidation. Rather, they traveled across the political board. Instead of a convergence of the radical right across Europe, this book has shown that almost 30 years after the end of the Cold War there are distinct differences between East and West when it comes to the politics of the radical right and that the roots of recent developments in the East precede the various all-European crises, such as the "refugee crisis" of 2015 or the "financial crisis of 2008."

Due to a region-specific confluence of factors, the radical right in Eastern Europe has profound effects on the workings of democracy despite it being electorally weaker and more volatile than in Western Europe. The changes outlined above may not amount to the return of "Weimar" and the imminent transition of the region's democratic regimes to autocracies. But the rebuilding of the political orders in Hungary and Poland, along with the recurring government crises, radical right revivals, and the prevalent identity politics in other countries (Bulgaria, Romania, Slovakia) amounts to more than a "post-democratic" syndrome (Crouch 2004). Democracy in Eastern more than in Western Europe is under siege by illiberal and ultranationalist forces which carry images of national greatness that are inspired by their countries' pre-communist and dictatorial pasts rather than by liberal and democratic traditions (see Krastev 2016; Pappas 2016). As Attila Ágh summarizes:

> After a quarter-century, these ECE [East-Central European] countries have to be assessed as (semi-) authoritarian systems; they developed reform fatigue and were not ready for further political transformations. Consequently, they became vulnerable first to a populist turn and then to an authoritarian turn with the elitist, oligarchy-prone parties in their over-centralized states. (Ágh 2016, 278)

My argument in this book is that the East European radical right has had a significant role in this populist-authoritarian turn and the backsliding of democracy—changes which refute the assumed linearity of the post-1989 transformation processes, most notably the deepening of ethno-cultural conflicts and the politicization of national and minority issues. Advances in human and minority rights are frequently challenged by the radical right and —where these challenges translate into mainstream politics—undermined, and the quality of democracy is immediately affected where such rights are violated. Pressure and help from Western Europe may have extinguished the most obvious perils of "Leninist legacies" in Eastern Europe, as Kenneth Jowitt presaged right after the end of the Cold War (1992). But EU membership and the institutions of liberal democracy prove insufficient to quell the anti-liberal and anti-minority effects of the radical right. In whatever organizational form and independent of high election results, the radical right's anti-systemic course in connection with the relatively young age of the democratic regimes, their under-institutionalized party systems, and unresolved ethnic cleavages make for continuous challenges to the new political order.

BIBLIOGRAPHY

Ágh, Attila. 2009. *The Politics of Central Europe*. London: Sage.
Ágh, Attila. 2015. "De-Europeanization and De-Democratization Trends in ECE: From the Potemkin Democracy to the Elected Autocracy in Hungary." *Journal of Comparative Politics* 8(2): 4–26.
Ágh, Attila. 2016. "The Decline of Democracy in East-Central Europe: Hungary as the Worst Case Scenario." *Problems of Post-Communism* 63(5–6): 277–287.
Akkerman, Tjitske. 2012. "Comparing Radical Right Parties in Government: Immigration and Integration Policies in Nine Countries." *West European Politics* 35(3): 511–529.
Akkerman, Tjitske, and Sarah de Lange. 2012. "Radical Right Parties in Office: Incumbency Records and the Electoral Cost of Governing." *Government and Opposition* 47(4): 574–596.
Albertazzi, Daniele. 2009. "Reconciling 'Voice' and 'Exit': Swiss and Italian Populists in Power." *Politics* 29(1): 1–10.
Albrecht, Holger, and Rolf Frankenberger. 2010a. "Autoritarismus Reloaded: Konzeptionelle Anmerkungen zur vergleichende Analyse politischer Systeme." In *Autoritarismus Reloaded. Neuere Ansätze und Erkenntnisse der Autokratieforschung*, edited by Holger Albrecht and Rolf Frankenberger, 37–60. Baden-Baden: Nomos.
Albrecht, Holger, and Rolf Frankenberger, eds. 2010b. *Autoritarismus Reloaded. Neuere Ansätze und Erkenntnisse der Autokratieforschung*. Baden-Baden: Nomos.
Allen, Trevor J. 2015. "All in the Party Family? Comparing Far Right Voters in Western and Eastern Europe." *Party Politics* July 2015: 1–12. Accessed August 19, 2016. doi: 10.1177/1354068815593457.

Almond, Gabriel, and G. Bingham Powell Jr. 1966. *Comparative Politics. System, Process, and Policy.* Boston: Little, Brown.

Almond, Gabriel, Russell J. Dalton, G. Bingham Powell Jr, and Kaare Strøm, eds. 2009. *European Politics Today.* 4th edition New York: Longman.

Alonso, Sonia, and Sara Claro Fonseca. 2012. "Immigration, Left and Right." *Party Politics* 18(6): 865–884.

Alter, Peter. 1985. *Nationalism.* London: Edward Arnold.

Anderson, Benedict. 1983. *Imagined Communities.* London: Verso.

Anderson, John. 2003. *Religious Liberty in Transitional Societies. The Politics of Religion.* Cambridge: Cambridge University Press.

Anderson, John. 2009. *Christianity and Democratization.* Manchester: Manchester University Press.

Andor, László. 2000. *Hungary on the Road to the European Union: Transition in Blue.* Westport: Praeger.

Andreescu, Gabriel. 2005. "Romania." In *Racist Extremism in Central and Eastern Europe*, edited by Cas Mudde, 184–209. London/New York: Routledge.

Andreescu, Gabriel. 2015. "The emergence of a new radical right power: The Romanian Orthodox Church." In *Transforming the Transformation? The East European Radical Right in the Political Process*, edited by Michael Minkenberg, 251–277. London/New York: Routledge.

Art, David. 2011. *Inside the Radical Right. The Development of Anti-Immigration Parties in Western Europe.* Cambridge: Cambridge University Press.

Arzheimer, Kai. 2008. *Die Wähler der extremen Rechten 1980-2002.* Wiesbaden: VS Verlag für Sozialwissenschaften.

Auer, Stefan. 2000. "Nationalism in Central Europe—a Chance or a Threat for the Emerging Liberal Democratic Order?" *East European Politics and Societies* 14(2): 213–245.

Auers, Daunis. 2013. "Lativa." In *The Handbook of Political Change in Eastern Europe*, edited by Sten Berglund, Joakim Ekman, Kevin Deegan-Krause, and Terje Knutsen, 85–124. 3rd edition. Cheltenham: Edward Elgar.

Auers, Daunis, and Andres Kasekamp. 2013. "Radical-Right Populism in Estonia and Latvia." In *Right-Wing Populism in Europe. Politics and Discourse*, edited by Ruth Wodak, Majid KhosraviNik, and Brigitte Mral, 235–248. London et al.: Bloomsbury.

Auers, Daunis, and Andres Kasekamp. 2015. "The Impact of Radical Right Parties in the Baltic States." In *Transforming the Transformation? The East European Radical Right in the Political Process*, edited by Michael Minkenberg, 137–153. London/New York: Routledge.

Avramov, Kiril. 2015. "The Bulgarian Radical Right. Marching Up from the Margins." In *Transforming the Transformation? The East European Radical Right in the Political Process*, edited by Michael Minkenberg, 299–318. London/New York: Routledge.

Bachrynowski, Szymon. 2015. "Between Europe and Russia: The Foreign Policy of Janusz Korwin-Mikke's New Right in Poland." *The Polish Quarterly of International Affairs* 24(2): 135–144.

Backes, Uwe, and Eckhard Jesse. 1989. *Politischer Extremismus in Deutschland*. Bonn: Bundeszentrale für politische Bildung.

Bale, Tim. 2003. "Cinderella and Her Ugly Sisters. The Mainstream and the Extreme Right in Bipolarising Party Systems." *West European Politics* 26(3): 67–90.

Bale, Tim, Christoffer Green-Pedersen, Andre Krouwel, Kurt Richard Luther, and Nick Sitter. 2010. "If You Can't Beat Them, Join Them? Explaining Social Democratic Responses to the Challenge from the Populist Radical Right in Western Europe." *Political Studies* 58(3): 410–426.

Bank, André. 2010. "Die neue Autoritarismusforschung: Ansätze, Erkenntnisse und konzeptionelle Fallstricke." In *Autoritarismus Reloaded. Neuere Ansätze und Erkenntnisse der Autokratieforschung*, edited by Holger Albrecht and Rolf Frankenberger, 21–36. Baden-Baden: Nomos.

Barnickel, Christiane, and Timm Beichelt. 2013. "Shifting Patterns and Reactions— Migration Policy in the New EU Member States." *East European Politics and Society* 27(3): 466–492.

Bayer, József. 2009. "Country Report Hungary." In *Strategies for Combating Right-Wing Extremism in Europe*, edited by Bertelsmann-Stiftung, 285–326. Gütersloh: Verlag Bertelsmann Stiftung.

Beck, Ulrich. 1992. *Risk Society. Towards a New Modernity*. London and New York: Sage.

Beichelt, Timm. 2001. *Demokratische Konsolidierung im postsozialistischen Europa. Die Rolle der politischen Institutionen*. Opladen: Leske + Budrich.

Beichelt, Timm. 2012. "Prinzip 'Worst Practice'? Demokratiedefiziente Regimeelemente und die Wechselwirkungen mit der EU-Ebene." FIT Paper No. 01/12. Frankfurt (Oder): Frankfurt Institute for Transformation Studies.

Beichelt, Timm, and Michael Minkenberg. 2002. "Explaining the Radical Right in Transition: Theories of Right-wing Radicalism and Opportunity Structures in Post-socialist Europe." *FIT Paper* 3/2002. Frankfurt (Oder): Frankfurt Institute of Transformation Studies.

Benford, Robert D., and David A. Snow. 2000. "Framing Processes and Social Movements: An Overview and Assessment." *Annual Review of Sociology* 26: 611–639.

Berglund, Sten, Joakim Ekman, Terje Knutsen, and Frank Aarebrot. 2013. "The Resilience of History." In *The Handbook of Political Change in Eastern Europe*, edited by Sten Berglund, Joakim Ekman, Kevin Deegan-Krause, and Terje Knutsen, 15–34. 3rd edition. Cheltenham: Edward Elgar.

Bergmann, Werner. 1994. "Ein Versuch, die extreme Rechte als soziale Bewegung zu beschreiben." In *Neonazismus und rechte Subkultur*, edited by Werner Bergmann and Rainer Erb, 183–207. Berlin: Metropol Verlag.

Berg-Schlosser, Dirk, and Jeremy Mitchell, eds. 2002. *Authoritarianism and Democracy in Europe, 1919–39. Comparative Analyses*. Basingstoke/New York: Palgrave.

Berlet, Chip, and Matthew N. Lyons. 2000. *Right-wing Populism in America. Too Close for Comfort*. New York/London: Guilford Press.

Bernhard, Michael, ed. 2015. "Whither Eastern Europe? Changing Approaches and Perspectives on the Region in Political Science." *Special Issue East European Politics & Societies and Cultures* 29(2): 311–540.

Bernhard, Michael, and Krzysztof Jasiewicz. 2015. "Whither Eastern Europe? Changing Approaches and Perspectives on the Region in Political Science." *East European Politics & Societies and Cultures* 29(2): 311–322.

Betz, Hans-Georg. 1994. *Radical Right-wing Populism in Western Europe*. New York: Macmillan.

Betz, Hans-Georg. 2005. "Mobilising Resentment in the Alps: The Swiss SVP, the Italian Lega Nord, the Austrian FPÖ." In *Challenges to Consensual Politics. Democracy, Identity, and Populist Protest in the Alpine Region*, edited by Daniele Caramani and Yves Mény, 147–166. New York et al.: Peter Lang.

Bielasiak, Jack. 2002. "The Institutionalization of Electoral and Party Systems in Postcommunist States." *Comparative Politics* 34(2): 189–210.

Bíró Nagy, András, Tamás Boros, and Zoltán Vasali. 2013. "More Radical than the Radicals. The Jobbik Party in International Comparison." In *Right-wing Extremism in Europe. Country Analyses, Counter-Strategies and Labor-Market Oriented Exit Strategies*, edited by Ralf Melzer and Sebastian Serafim, 229–253. Berlin: Friedrich Ebert Stiftung.

Bíró Nagy, András, and Tamás Boros. 2016. "Jobbik Going Mainstream. Strategy Shift of the Far-Right in Hungary." In *Extreme Right in Europe*, edited by Jerôme Jamin, 243–263. Brussels: Bruylant.

Bleich, Erik. 2011. *The Freedom to Be Racist? Ho the United States and Europe Struggle to Preserve Freedom and Combat Racism*. Oxford: Oxford University Press.

Blokker, Paul. 2005. "Post-communist Modernization, Transition Studies, and Diversity in Europe." *European Journal of Social Theory* 8(4): 503–525.

Blühdorn, Ingolfur. 2013. *Simulative Demokratie. Neue Politik nach der postdemokratischen Wende*. Berlin: Suhrkamp.

Bochsler, Daniel, and Edina Szöcsik. 2013. "The Forbidden Fruit of Federalism: Evidence from Romania and Slovakia." *West European Politics* 36(2): 426–446.

Bornschier, Simon. 2010. *Cleavage Politics and the Populist Right. The New Cultural Conflict in Western Europe*. Philadelphia: Temple University Press.

Brendgens, Guido. 1998. "Demokratische Konsolidierung in der Tschechischen Republik." M.A. diss. Heidelberg: University of Heidelberg.
Brubaker, Rogers. 1992. *Citizenship and Nationhood in France and Germany*. Cambridge/London: Harvard University Press.
Brubaker, Rogers. 1997. *Nationalism Reframed. Nationhood and the National Question in the New Europe*. Cambridge: Cambridge University Press.
Brubaker, Rogers. 2012. "Religion and Nationalism: Four Approaches." *Nations and Nationalism* 18(1): 2–20.
Bruce, Steve. 2003. *Politics and Religion*. Oxford: Polity Press.
Bunce, Valerie. 1999. *Subversive Institutions. The Design and the Destruction of Socialism and the State*. Cambridge: Cambridge University Press.
Bunce, Valerie, and Sharon Wolchik. 2010a. "A Regional Tradition. The Diffusion of Democratic Change under Communism and Postcommunism." In *Democracy and Authoritarianism in the Postcommunist World*, edited by Valerie Bunce, Michael McFaul, and Kathryn Stoner-Weiss, 30–56. Cambridge: Cambridge University Press.
Bunce, Valerie, and Sharon Wolchik. 2010b. "Defining and Domesticating the Electoral Model: A Comparison of Slovakia and Serbia." In *Democracy and Authoritarianism in the Postcommunist World*, edited by Valerie Bunce, Michael McFaul, and Kathryn Stoner-Weiss, 134–154. Cambridge: Cambridge University Press.
Bunce, Valerie, Michael McFaul, and Kathryn Stoner-Weiss, eds. 2010. *Democracy and Authoritarianism in the Postcommunist World*. Cambridge: Cambridge University Press.
Bustikova, Lenka. 2014. "The Revenge of the Radical Right." *Comparative Political Studies* 47(12): 1738–1765.
Bustikova, Lenka. 2015. "The Democratization of Hostility. Minorities and Radical Right Actors after the Fall of Communism." In *Transforming the Transformation? The East European Radical Right in the Political Process*, edited by Michael Minkenberg, 59–79. London: Routledge.
Bustikova, Lenka, and Herbert Kitschelt. 2009. "The Radical Right in Post-Communist Europe. Comparative Perspectives on Legacies and Party Competition." *Communist and Post-Communist Studies* 42(4): 459–483.
Caiani, Manuela, and Linda Parenti. 2013. *European and American Extreme Right Groups and the Internet*. Aldershot: Ashgate.
Camus, Jean-Yves. 2011. "The European Extreme Right and Religious Extremism." *Central European Political Studies Review* 9(4): 263–279.
Canovan, Margaret. 1981. *Populism*. New York/London: Harcourt, Brace, Jovanovich.
Capoccia, Giovanni. 2005. *Defending Democracy. Reactions to Extremism in Interwar Europe*. Baltimore: Johns Hopkins University Press.

Capoccia, Giovanni. 2013. "Militant Democracy: The Institutional Bases of Democratic Self-Preservation." *Annual Review of Law and Social Science* 9 (November): 207–226.
Carothers, Thomas. 2002. "The End of the Transition Paradigm." *Journal of Democracy* 13(1): 5–21.
Carter, Elizabeth. 2005. *The Extreme Right in Western Europe. Success or failure?* Manchester: Manchester University Press.
Casal Bértoa, Fernando. 2012. "Parties, Regimes and Cleavages: Explaining Party System Institutionalization in East Central Europe." *East European Politics and Societies* 28(4): 452–472.
Cibulka, Frank. 1999. "The Radical Right in Slovakia." In *The Radical Right in Central and Eastern Europe since 1989*, edited by Sabrina Ramet, 109–131. University Park, P.A: The Pennsylvania State University Press.
Cinpoeş, Radu. 2013. "Right-wing Extremism in Romania." In *Right-wing extremism in Europe. Country Analyses, Counter-Strategies and Labor-Market Oriented Exit Strategies*, edited by Ralf Melzer and Sebastian Serafim, 169–197. Berlin: Friedrich Ebert Stiftung.
Cinpoeş, Radu. 2015. "'Righting It Up'. An Interplay-Based Model for Analyzing Extreme Right Dynamics in Romania." In *Transforming the Transformation? The East European Radical Right in the Political Process*, edited by Michael Minkenberg, 278–298. London/New York: Routledge.
Crouch, Colin. 2004. *Post-Democracy*. Cambridge: Polity Press.
Dalton, Russell J. 2008. *Citizen Politics. Public Opinion and Political Parties in Advanced Industrial Democracies*. 5th edition. Washington DC: CQ Press.
Davies, Norman. 1986. *Heart of Europe. A Short History of Poland*. Oxford: Oxford University Press.
Dawson, James, and Séan Hanley. 2016. "The Fading Mirage of the 'Liberal Consensus'." *Journal of Democracy* 27(1): 20–34.
De Lange, Sarah. 2008. "From Pariah to Power: The Government Participation of Radical Right-wing Populist Parties in West European Democracies." Ph.D. diss. Antwerp: University of Antwerp.
De Lange, Sarah. 2012. "New Alliances: Why Mainstream Parties Govern with Radical Right-Wing Populist Parties." *Political Studies* 60(4): 899–918.
De Lange, Sarah, and Simona Guerra. 2009. "The League of Polish Families between East and West, Past and Present." *Communist and Post-Communist Studies* 42(4): 527–550.
Decker, Frank, ed. 2006. *Populismus—Gefahr für die Demokratie oder nützliches Korrektiv?* Wiesbaden: VS Verlag für Sozialwissenschaften.
Deegan-Krause, Kevin. 2004. "Uniting the Enemy: Politics and the Convergence of Nationalisms in Slovakia." *East European Politics and Societies* 18(4): 651–696.

Deegan-Krause, Kevin. 2013. "Full and Partial Cleavages." In *The Handbook of Political Change in Eastern Europe*, edited by Sten Berglund, Joakim Ekman, Kevin Deegan-Krause, and Terje Knutsen, 35–50. 3rd edition. Cheltenham: Edward Elgar.

Diamond, Larry. 2002. "Thinking about Hybrid Regimes." *Journal of Democracy* 13(2): 21–35.

Douglas, Mary, and Aaron Wildavsky. 1982. *Risk and Culture. An Essay on the Selection of Technological and Environmental Dangers*. Berkeley: University of California Press.

Downs, William. 2001. "Pariahs in their Midst: Belgian and Norwegian Parties React to Extremist Threats." *West European Politics* 24(3): 23–42.

Downs, William. 2012. *Political Extremism in Democracies. Combating Intolerance*. New York: Palgrave.

Eatwell, Roger, and Cas Mudde, eds. 2004. *Western Democracies and the New Extreme Right*. London: Routledge.

Eckstein, Harry. 1988. "A Culturalist Theory of Political Change." *American Political Science Review* 82(3): 787–804.

Eisenstadt, S.N. 2000. "Multiple Modernities." *Daedalus* 129(1): 1–29.

Ekiert, Grzegorz. 2015. "Three Generations of Research on Post-Communist Politics—A Sketch." *East European Politics and Societies and Cultures* 29(2): 323–337.

Ekiert, Grzegorz, and Stephen Hanson. 2003. "Time, Space, and Institutional Change in Central and Eastern Europe." In *Capitalism and Democracy in Central and Eastern Europe*, edited by Grzegorz Ekiert and Stephen Hanson, 15–48. Cambridge: Cambridge University Press.

Ekiert, Grzegorz, and Jan Kubik. 2014. "Myths and Realities of Civil Society." *Journal of Democracy* 25(1): 46–58.

Elster, Jon, Claus Offe, and Ulrich K. Preuss. 1998. *Institutional Design in Post-communist Societies. Rebuilding the Ship at Sea*. Cambridge: Cambridge University Press.

Engler, Sarah. 2016. "Corruption and Electoral Support for New Political Parties in Central and Eastern Europe." *West European Politics* 39(2): 278–304.

Evans, Geoffrey. 1999. "Class Voting: From Premature Obituary to Reasoned Appraisal." In *The End of Class Politics? Class Voting in Comparative Context*, edited by Geoffrey Evans, 1–22. Oxford: Oxford Univ. Press.

Evans, Geoffrey, and Stephen Whitefeld. 2000. "Explaining the Formation of Electoral Cleavages in Post-Communist Democracies." In *Elections in Central and Eastern Europe. The First Wave*, edited by Hans-Dieter Klingemann, 36–70. Berlin: Ed. Sigma.

Falter, Jürgen. 1991. *Hitlers Wähler*. München: Beck.

Fennema, Meindert. 2000. "Legal Repression of Extreme Right Parties and Racial Discrimination." In *Challenging Immigration and Ethnic Relations Politics*.

Comparative European Perspectives, edited by Ruud Koopmans and Paul Statham, 119–144. Oxford: Oxford University Press.

Fischer, Holger. 1999. *Eine kleine Geschichte Ungarns.* Frankfurt/Main: Suhrkamp.

Fomina, Joanna, and Jacek Kucharczyk. 2016. "Populism and Protest in Poland." *Journal of Democracy* 27(4): 58–68.

FRA—European Union Agency for Fundamental Rights. 2011. *Annual Report 2010.* Luxembourg: Publications Office of the European Union.

FRA—European Union Agency for Fundamental Rights. 2012. *Annual Report 2011.* Luxembourg: Publications Office of the European Union.

FRA—European Union Agency for Fundamental Rights. 2013. *Annual Report 2012.* Luxembourg: Publications Office of the European Union.

FRA—European Union Agency for Fundamental Rights. 2015. *Annual Report 2014.* Luxembourg: Publications Office of the European Union

Frusetta, James, and Anica Glont. 2009. "Interwar Fascism and the post-1989 Radical Right: Ideology, Opportunism and Historical Legacy in Bulgaria and Romania." *Communist and Post-Communist Studies* 42(4): 551–571.

Fuchs, Dieter, and Edeltraud Roller. 2006. "Learned Democracy? Support of Democracy in Central and Eastern Europe." *International Journal of Sociology* 36(3): 70–96.

Gallagher, Tom. 1995. *Romania after Ceauşescu: The Politics of Intolerance.* Edinburgh: University of Edinburgh Press.

Gallagher, Tom. 2000. "Exit from the ghetto: The Italian far right in the 1990s." In *The Politics of the Extreme Right: From the Margins to the Mainstream*, edited by Paul Hainsworth, 64–86. London: Pinter.

Gamson, William. 1988. "Political Discourse and Collective Action." In *International Social Movement Research: From Structure to Action*, edited by Bert Klandermans, Hanspeter Kriesi, and Sidney Tarrow, 219–246. Greenwich: JAI Press.

Ganev, Venelin I. 2014. "Bulgaria's Year of Civic Anger." *Journal of Democracy* 25(1): 33–45.

Golebiowska, Ewa. 2009. "Ethnic and Religious Tolerance in Poland." *East European Politics and Societies* 23(3): 371–391.

Goodwin, Matthew. 2011. *New British Fascism. Rise of the British National Party.* London: Routledge.

Greenfeld, Liah. 1992. *Nationalism. Five Roads to Modernity.* Cambridge, MA/London, UK: Harvard University Press.

Grescovits, Béla, and Dorothee Bohle. 2001. "Development Paths on Europe's Periphery: Hungary's and Poland's Return to Europe Compared." *Polish Sociological Review* 133: 3–27.

Grienig, Gregor. 2010. "Roma in Europa." Accessed October 31, 2013. http://www.berlin-institut.org/online-handbuchdemografie/bevoelkerungsdynamik/regionale-dynamik/roma-in-europa.html.

Griffin, Roger. 1991. *The Nature of Fascism*. New York: St. Martin's Press.
Griffin, Roger. 1999. "Afterword. Last Rights?" In *The Radical Right in Central and Eastern Europe since 1989*, edited by Sabrina Ramet, 297–321. University Park, P.A: The Pennsylvania State University Press.
Grün, Michaela. 2002. "Rechtsradikale Massenmobilisierung und 'radikale Kontinuität' in Rumänien." *Osteuropa* 52(2): 293–304.
Grzymała-Busse, Anna. 2015. *Nations under God: How Churches Use Moral Authority to Influence Policy*. Oxford: Oxford University Press.
Gusy, Christoph, ed. 2008. *Demokratie in der Krise: Europa in der Zwischenkriegszeit*. Baden-Baden: Nomos Verlag.
Gyárfášová, Ol'ga, and Grigorij Mesežnikov. 2015. "Actors, Agenda, and Appeal of the Radical Nationalist Right in Slovakia." In *Transforming the Transformation? The East European Radical Right in the Political Process*, edited by Michael Minkenberg, 224–248. London/New York: Routledge.
Hadenius, Axel, and Jan Teorell. 2007. "Pathways from Authoritarianism." *Journal of Democracy* 18(1): 143–156.
Hainsworth, Paul. 2008. *The Extreme Right in Western Europe*. New York and London: Routledge.
Heinisch, Reinhard. 2003. "Success in Opposition—Failure in Government: Explaining the Performance of Right-Wing Populist Parties in Public Office." *West European Politics* 26(3): 91–130.
Heitmeyer, Wilhelm. 2005. "Gruppenbezogene Menschenfeindlichkeit." In *Deutsche Zustände*. Vol. 3, edited by Wilhelm Heitmeyer, 13–36. Berlin: Suhrkamp.
Heitmeyer, Wilhelm. 2012. "Gruppenbezogene Menschenfeindlichkeit (GMF) in einem entsicherten Jahrzehnt." In *Deutsche Zustände*. Vol. 10, edited by Wilhelm Heitmeyer, 15–41. Frankfurt/Main: Suhrkamp.
Herman, Lise Esther. 2016. "Re-evaluationg the post-communist success story: Party elite loyalty, citizen mobilization and the erosion of Hungarian democracy." *European Political Science Review* 8(2): 251–284.
Hirsch, Marianne, and Nancy K. Miller, eds. 2011. *Rites of Return. Diaspora Poetics and the Politics of Memory*. New York: Columbia University Press.
Hobsbawm, Eric. 1990. *Nations and Nationalism since 1780. Programme, Myth, Reality*. Cambridge: Cambridge University Press.
Hobsbawm, Eric. 1996. *The Age of Extremes. A History of the World, 1914–1991*. New York: Vintage Books.
Hooghe, Liesbet, Gary Marks, and Carole J. Wilson. 2002. "Does Left/Right Structure Party Positions on European Integration?" *Comparative Political Studies* 35(8): 965–989.
Horowitz, Donald. 1985. *Ethnic Groups in Conflict*. Berkeley: University of California Press.

Howard, Marc M. 2003. *The Weakness of Civil Society in Post-Communist Europe.* Cambridge: Cambridge University Press.
Howard, Marc M. 2006. "The Leninist legacy revisited." In *World Order After Leninism*, edited by Vladimir Tismaneanu, Marc M. Howard, and Rudra Sil, 34–46. Seattle and London: University of Washington Press.
Howard, Marc M. 2011. "Civil Society in Post-Communist Europe." In *The Oxford Handbook of Civil Society*, edited by Michael Edwards, 134–145. New York: Oxford University Press.
Hroch, Miroslav. 2005. *Das Europa der Nationen. Die moderne Nationsbildung im europäischen Vergleich.* Göttingen: Vandenhoeck & Ruprecht.
Huber, John, and Ronald Inglehart. 1995. "Expert Interpretations of Party Space and and Party Locations in 42 Societies." *Party Politics* 1(1): 73–111.
Huntington, Samuel P. 1991. *The Third Wave. Democratization in the Late Twentieth Century.* Norman: University of Oklahoma Press.
Ignazi, Piero. 1992. "The silent counter-revolution: Hypotheses on the emergence of right-wing parties in Europe." *European Journal of Political Research* 22(1): 3–34.
Ignazi, Piero. 1994. *Postfascisti? Dal Movimento sociale italiano ad Alleanza nazionale.* Bologna: Il Mulino.
Ignazi, Piero. 2003. *Extreme Right Parties in Western Europe.* Oxford: Oxford University Press.
Inglehart, Ronald. 1977. *The Silent Revolution. Changing Values and Political Styles Among Western Publics.* Princeton: Princeton University Press.
Inglehart, Ronald. 1997. *Modernization and Postmodernization. Cultural, Economic and Political Change in 43 Societies.* Princeton: Princeton University Press.
Ishiyama, John. 2009. "Historical Legacies and the Size of the Red-Brown Vote in Post-communist Politics." *Communist and Post-Communist Studies* 42(4): 485–504.
Ivarsflaten, Christine. 2008. "What Unites Right-wing Populists in Western Europe? Re-examining Grievance Mobilization Models in Seven Successful Cases." *Comparative Political Studies* 41(1): 3–23.
Jaffrelot, Christophe. 2009. "Religion and Nationalism." In *The Oxford Handbook of the Sociology of Religion*, edited by Peter Clarke, 406–417. Oxford: Oxford University Press.
Janos, Andrew. 2000. *East Central Europe in the Modern World. The Politics of the Borderlands from Pre- to Postcommunism.* Stanford: Stanford University Press.
Jaschke, Hans-Gerd. 1994. *Rechtsextremismus und Fremdenfeindlichkeit.* Wiesbaden: Westdeutscher Verlag.
Jenne, Erin. 2000. "The Roma of Central and Eastern Europe: Constructing a Stateless Nation." In *The Politics of National Minority Participation in Post-Communist Europe*, edited by Jonathan Stein, 189–212. Armonk/London: M.E. Sharpe.

Jesse, Eckhard, and Tom Thieme. 2011. "Extremismus in den EU-Staaten im Vergleich." In *Extremismus in den EU-Staaten*, edited by Eckard Jesse and Tom Thieme, 431–482. Wiesbaden: VS Verlag für Sozialwissenschaften.
Jowitt, Kenneth. 1992. "The Leninist legacy." In *New World Disorder. The Leninist Extinction*, by Kenneth Jowitt, 284–305. Berkeley: The University of California Press.
Judt, Tony. 2005. *Postwar. A History of Europe Since 1945*. New York: Penguin.
Juhasz, Attila. 2010. "Anti-Immigrant Prejudice in Central and Eastern Europe." Accessed March 15, 2014. http://riskandforecast.com/post/in-depth-analysis/anti-immigrant-prejudice-in-central-andeastern-europe_581.html.
Kalina, Tomasz. 2000. "Polskie Partie Narodowe." M.A. diss. Warsaw: Institute of Political Science, Warsaw University.
Kántor, Zsoltán, Balázs Majtényi, Ieda Osamu, and Balázs Vizi, and Iván Halász, eds. 2004. *The Hungarian Status Law: Nation Building and/or Minority Protection*. Sapporo: Hokkaido University - Slavic Research Center.
Kaplan, Jeffrey, and Heléne Lööw, eds. 2002. *The Cultic Milieu. Oppositional Subcultures in the Age of Globalization*. Walnut Creek, CA: AltaMira Press.
Karácsony, Gergely, and Dániel Róna. 2011. "The Secret of Jobbik. Reasons behind the Rise of the Hungarian Radical Right." *Journal of East-European and Asian Studies* 2(1): 61–92.
Karl, Philipp. 2016. "Die Etablierung Jobbiks in Ungarn nach 2010. Zwischen Bewegung und Partei des Internetzeitalters." Ph.D. diss., Andrássy Universität Budapest.
Karolewski, Paweł, and Roland Benedikter. 2016. "Poland's Conservative Turn and the Role of the European Union." *European Political Science*: 1–20. doi: 10.1057/s41304-016-0002-x.
Karsai, László. 1999. "The Radical Right in Hungary." In *The Radical Right in Central and Eastern Europe since 1989*, edited by Sabrina Ramet, 133–146. University Park, P.A: The Pennsylvania State University Press.
Kasprowicz, Dominika. 2015. "The Radical Right in Poland—From the Mainstream to the Margins: A Case of Interconnectivity." In *Transforming the Transformation? The East European Radical Right in the Political Process*, edited by Michael Minkenberg, 157–182. London: Routledge.
Kazin, Michael. 1995. *The Populist Persuasion. An American History*. New York: Basic Books.
Kilp, Alar. 2009. "Secularization of Society After Communism: Ten Catholic-Protestant Societies." *KVÜÕA Toimetised* 12: 194–231.
Kis, Janós. 2004. "The Status Law: Hungary at the Crossroads." In *The Hungarian Status Law: Nation Building and/or Minority Protection*, edited by Zoltán Kántor, Balázs Majtényi, Ieda Osamu, Balázs Vizi, and Iván Halász, 152–177. Sapporo: Hokkaido University - Slavic Research Center.

Kitschelt, Herbert. 1995. *The Radical Right in Western Europe. A Comparative Analysis.* With Anthony McGann. Ann Arbor, MI: University of Michigan Press.
Kitschelt, Herbert. 2003. "Accounting for Postcommunist Regime Diversity. What Counts as a Good Cause?" In *Capitalism and Democracy in Central and Eastern Europe*, edited by Grzegorz Ekiert and Stephen Hanson, 49–86. Cambridge: Cambridge University Press.
Kitschelt, Herbert. 2006. "Movement Parties." In *Handbook of Party Politics*, edited by Richard Katz and William Crotty, 278–290. London: Sage.
Kitschelt, Herbert. 2007. "Growth and Persistence of the Radical Right in Postindustrial Democracies: Advances and Challenges in Comparative Research." *West European Politics* 30(5): 1176–1206.
Kitschelt, Herbert, Zdenka Mansfeldowa, Radoslaw Markowski, and Tóka. Gábor. 1999. *Post-Communist Party Systems. Competition, Representation, and Inter-Party Cooperation.* Cambridge: Cambridge University Press.
Klingemann, Hans-Dieter. 2014. "Dissatisfied Democrats: Democratic Maturation in Old and New Democracies." In *The Civic Culture Transformed: From Allegiant to Assertive Citizens*, edited by Russell J. Dalton and Christian Welzel, 116–157. New York: Cambridge University Press.
Knöbl, Wolfgang. 2003. "Theories That Won't Pass Away: The Never-ending Story of Modernization Theory." In *Handbook of Historical Sociology*, edited by Gerard Delanty and Enger F. Isin, 96–109. London: Sage.
Koenen, Krisztina. 2015. "Orbánismus in Ungarn. Ursprünge und Elemente der 'Illiberalen Demokratie'." *Osteuropa* 65(11-12): 33–44.
Kohn, Hans. 1944. *The Idea of Nationalism: A Study in Its Origins and Background.* New York: The Macmillan Company.
Koopmans, Ruud. 1996. "Explaining the Rise of Racist and Extreme Right Violence in Western Europe: Grievances or Opportunities." *European Journal of Political Research* 30(2): 185–216.
Koopmans, Ruud, and Dieter Rucht. 1996. "Rechtsradikalismus als soziale Bewegung?" In *Rechtsextremismus*. Special Issue 27/1996 of *Politische Vierteljahresschrift*, edited by Jürgen Falter, Hans-Gerd Jaschke, and Jürgen Winkler, 423–442. Opladen: Westdeutscher Verlag.
Koopmans, Ruud, and Paul Statham, eds. 2000. *Challenging Immigration and Ethnic Relations Politics. Comparative European Perspectives.* Oxford: Oxford University Press.
Koopmans, Ruud, Paul Statham, Marco Giugni, and Florence Passy. 2005. *Contested Citizenship. Immigration and Cultural Diversity in Europe.* Minneapolis: University of Minnesota Press.
Kopecký, Petr, and Cas Mudde, eds. 2003. *Uncivil Society? Contentious politics in post-communst Europe.* London: Routledge.

Kopka, Artur. 2014. "Rechtspopulistische Politik in Polen im Kontext der Regierungsperiode 2005–2007: Ursachen, Ausprägungsformen, Effekte." Ph. D. diss. Frankfurt (Oder): European University Viadrina.

Kopstein, Jeffrey. 2003. "Postcommunist Democracy: Legacies and Outcomes." *Comparative Politics*, 35(2): 231–250.

Kornai, János. 2006. "The Great Transformation of Central and Eastern Europe: Success and Disappointment." *Economics of Transition* 14(2): 207–244.

Kossack, Oliver. 2012. "Von der Hinterbank ins Kabinett. Regierungsbeteiligung rechtsradikaler Parteien in Mittelosteuropa." M.A. diss. Frankfurt (Oder): European University Viadrina.

Kossack, Oliver, and Bartek Pytlas. 2015. "Lighting the Fuse. The Impact of Radical Right Parties on Party Competition in Central and Eastern Europe." In *Transforming the Transformation? The East European Radical Right in the Political Process*, edited by Michael Minkenberg, 105–113. London: Routledge.

Kovács, János Mátyás. 1998. "Frustration with Liberalism? `Sound` Interventionism in East European Economics." In *Reform of the Socialist System in Central and Eastern Europe*, edited by Martin Bull and Mike Ingham, 77–91. New York: St. Martin's Press.

Kovács, Zoltán. 2001. "The Geography of Post-Communist Parliamentary Elections in Hungary." In *Transformations in Hungary*, edited by Peter Meusburger and Heike Jöns, 249–272. Berlin and Heidelberg: Springer-Verlag.

Krastev, Ivan. 2016. "The Unraveling of the Post-1989 Order." *Journal of Democracy* 27(4): 88–98.

Krekó, Peter, and Gregor Mayer. 2015. "Transforming Hungary—Together? An Analysis of the Fidesz-Jobbik Relationship." In *Transforming the Transformation? The East European Radical Right in the Political Process*, edited by Michael Minkenberg, 183–205. London: Routledge.

Kriesi, Hanspeter, Ruud Koopmans, Jan Willem Dyvendak, and Marco G. Giugni. 1995. *New Social Movements in Western Europe*. Minneapolis, MN: University of Minnesota Press.

Kublik, Agnieszka. 2016. "Auf Linie gebracht—Polens öffentlich-rechtlicher Rundfunk unter PiS Kuratel." In *Gegen die Wand. Konservative Revolution in Polen*, edited by Deutsche Gesellschaft für Osteuropakunde. Special Issue of *Osteuropa* 66 (1–2): 153–160.

Kuczarchyk, Jacek, and Olga Wysocka. 2008. "Poland." In *Populist Politics in Liberal Democracy in Central and Eastern Europe*, edited by Grigorij Mesežnikov and Oľga Gyárfášová, 71–100. Bratislava: Institute for Public Affairs.

Lane, Jan-Erik, and Svante Ersson. 2007. "Party System Instability in Europe: Persistent Differences in Volatility between West and East?" *Democratization* 14(1): 92–110.
Lang, Kai-Olaf. 2016. "Zwischen Rückbesinnung und Erneuerung. Polens PiS und Ungarns Fidesz im Vergleich." In *Gegen die Wand. Konservative Revolution in Polen*, edited by Deutsche Gesellschaft für Osteuropakunde. Special Issue of *Osteuropa* 66 (1–2): 61–78.
Laver, Michael, and Norman Schofield. 1998. *Multiparty Government: The Politics of Coalition in Europe*. Ann Arbor: University of Michigan Press.
Lipset, Seymour M. 1963. *Political Man. The Social Bases of Politics*. Garden City N.Y.: Doubleday.
Lipset, Seymour M., and Stein Rokkan. 1967. "Cleavage Structures, Party Systems and Voter Alignments." In *Party Systems and Voter Alignments*, edited by Seymour M. Lipset and Stein Rokkan, 1–64. New York: Free Press.
Luther, Kurt Richard. 2003. "The Self-Destruction of a Right-Wing Populist Party? The Austrian Parliamentary Election of 2002." *West European Politics* 26(2): 136–152.
Mahoney, John, and Daniel Schensul. 2006. "Historical Context and Path Dependence." In *The Oxford Handbook of Contextual Political Analysis*, edited by Robert Goodin and Charles Tilly, 454–471. Oxford: Oxford University Press.
Mainwaring, Scott, and Timothy R. Scully. 1995. "Introduction: Party Systems in Latin America." In *Building Democratic Institutions: Party Systems in Latin America*, edited by Scott Mainwaring and Timothy R. Scully, 1–34. Stanford: Stanford University Press.
Mainwaring, Scott, and Euren Zoco. 2007. "Political Sequences and the Stabilization of Interparty Competition. Electoral Volatility in Old and New Democracies." *Party Politics* 13(2): 155–178.
Mair, Peter, and Cas Mudde. 1998. "The Party Family and Its Study." *Annual Review of Political Science* 1: 211–229.
Mareš, Miroslav. 2011. "Czech Extreme Right Parties an Unsuccessful Story." *Communist and Post-Communist Studies* 44(4): 283–298.
Mareš, Miroslav. 2012. "Czech Militant Democracy in Action: Dissolution of the Workers' Party and the Wider Context of This Act." *East European Politics and Societies* 26(1): 33–55.
Mareš, Miroslav. 2014. "The Extreme Right's Relationship with Islam and Islamism in East-Central Europe: From Allies to Enemies." *East European Politics and Societies and Cultures* 28(1): 205–224.
Mareš, Miroslav. 2015. "The impact of the Czech radical right on transformation and (de-) consolidation of democracy after 1989." In *Transforming the Transformation? The East European Radical Right in the Political Process*, edited by Michael Minkenberg, 206–223. London: Routledge.

Marx, Anthony. 2003. *Faith in Nation: Exclusionary Origins of Nationalism.* Oxford: Oxford University Press.
Maszkovski, Rafał. 2004. "Otwarte społeczeństwo i jego radio." ("Open Society and Its Radio Station") *Nigdy Więcej* 14: 38–42.
Mayer, Gregor, and Bernd Odehnal. 2010. *Aufmarsch. Die rechte Gefahr aus Osteuropa.* St. Pölten/Salzburg: Residenz Verlag.
McAdam, Doug. 1994. "Culture and Social Movements." In *New Social Movements. From Ideology to Identity,* edited by Enrique Laraña, Hank Johnston, und Joseoph R. Gusfield, 36–57. Philadelphia: Temple University Press.
McAdam, Doug. 1999. *Political Process and the Development of Black Insurgency.* 2nd edition. Chicago, IL: University of Chicago Press.
Meguid, Bonnie. 2008. *Party Competition between Unequals: Strategies and Electoral Fortunes in Western Europe.* Cambridge: Cambridge University Press.
Meguid, Bonnie M. 2005. "Competition between Unequals: The Role of Mainstream Party Strategy in Niche Party Success." *American Political Science Review* 99(3): 347–359.
Meinecke, Friedrich. 1908. *Weltbürgertum und Nationalstaat. Studien zur Genesis des deutschen Nationalstaats.* München and Berlin: R. Oldenbourg.
Melvin, Neil J. 2000. "Post-Imperial Ethnocracy and the Russophone Minorities of Estonia and Latvia." In *The Politics of National Minority Participation in Post-Communist Europe,* edited by Jonathan Stein, 129–166. Armonk/London: M.E. Sharpe.
Mény, Yves, and Yves Surel. 2000. *Par le peuple, pour le peuple. Le populisme et les démocraties.* Paris: Fayard.
Merkel, Wolfgang. 1996. "Rechtsextremismus in Italien: Von der neofaschistischen Systemopposition zur postfaschistischen Regierungspartei: Der Aufstieg der Alleanza Nazionale." In *Rechtsextremismus.* Special Issue of *Politische Vierteljahresschrift* 27, edited by Jürgen Falter, Hans-Gerd Jaschke, and Jürgen Winkler, 406–422. Opladen: Westdeutscher Verlag.
Merkel, Wolfgang. 2004. "Embedded and defective democracies." *Democratization* 11(5): 33–58.
Merkel, Wolfgang. 2010. *Systemtransformation. Eine Einführung in die Theorie und Empirie der Transformationsforschung.* 2nd rev. edition. Wiesbaden: VS Verlag für Sozialwissenschaften.
Merkel, Wolfgang. 2014. "Is There a Crisis of Democracy?" *Democratic Theory* 1(2): 11–25.
Mesežnikov, Grigorij. 2008. "National Populism in Slovakia: Actors, Issues, Strategies." In *National Populism in Slovakia,* edited by Grigorij Mesežnikov and Oľga Gyárfášová, 7–34. Bratislava: Institute for Public Affairs.
Mesežnikov, Grigorij, and Oľga Gyárfášová, eds. 2008. *National Populism in Slovakia.* Bratislava: Institute for Public Affairs.

Mihailescu, Mihaela. 2008. "The Politics of Minimal 'Consensus'. Interethnic Opposition Coalitions in Post-Communist Romania and Slovakia." *East European Politics and Societies* 22(3): 553–594.
Mihálik, Jaroslav. 2014. "The Rise of Anti-Roma Positions in Slovakia and Hungary: A New Social and Political Dimension of Nationalism." *Baltic Journal of Law & Politics* 7(2): 179–208.
Minkenberg, Michael. 1993. *The New Right in Comparative Perspective. The USA and Germany.* Ithaca, N.Y.: Cornell University.
Minkenberg, Michael. 1998. *Die neue radikale Rechte im Vergleich. USA, Frankreich, Deutschland.* Opladen/Wiesbaden: Westdeutscher Verlag.
Minkenberg, Michael. 2000. "The Renewal of the Radical Right: Between Modernity and Anti-Modernity." *Government and Opposition* 35(2): 170–188.
Minkenberg, Michael. 2001. "The Radical Right in Public Office: Agenda-Setting and Policy Effects." *West European Politics* 24(4): 1–21.
Minkenberg, Michael. 2002a. "The Radical Right in Post-socialist Central and Eastern Europe: Comparative Observations and Interpretations." *East European Politics and Society* 16(2): 335–362.
Minkenberg, Michael. 2002b. "The New Radical Right in the Political Process: Interaction Effects in France and Germany." In *Shadows over Europe: The Development and Impact of the Extreme Right in Western Europe*, edited by Martin Schain, Aristide Zolberg, and Patrick Hossay, 245–268. New York: Palgrave Macmillan.
Minkenberg, Michael. 2003. "The West European Radical Right as a Collective Actor: Modeling the Impact of Cultural and Structural Variables on Party Formation and Movement Mobilization." *Comparative European Politics* 1(2): 149–170.
Minkenberg, Michael. 2006. "Repression and reaction: Militant democracy and the radical right in Germany and France." *Patterns of Prejudice* 40(2): 25–44.
Minkenberg, Michael. 2007. "Democracy and Religion—Theoretical and Empirical Observations on the Relationship between Christianity, Islam and Liberal Democracy." *Journal of Ethnic and Migration Studies* 33(6): 887–909.
Minkenberg, Michael. 2008. *The Radical Right in Europe: An Overview.* Gütersloh: Verlag Bertelsmann Stiftung.
Minkenberg, Michael. 2009a. "Leninist beneficiaries? Pre-1989 legacies and the radical right in post-1989 Central and Eastern Europe. Some introductory observations." *Communist and Post-Communist Studies* 42(4): 445–458.
Minkenberg, Michael. 2009b. "Anti-Immigrant Politics in Europe: The Radical Right, Xenophobic Tendencies, and Their Political Environment." In *Bringing Outsiders In. Transatlantic Perspectives on Immigrant Political Incorporation*, edited by Jennifer Hochschild and John Mollenkopf, 140–157. Ithaca, NY: Cornell University Press.

Minkenberg, Michael, ed. 2010. *Historical Legacies and the Radical Right in Post-Cold War Central and Eastern Europe.* Stuttgart: ibidem.

Minkenberg, Michael. 2013a. "From Pariah to Policy-Maker? The Radical Right in Europe, West and East: Between Margin and Mainstream." *Journal of Contemporary European Studies* 21(1): 5–24.

Minkenberg, Michael. 2013b. "Political Opportunity Structures and the Mobilization of Anti-Immigration Actors: Modeling Effects on Immigrant Political Incorporation." In *Outsiders No More? Models of Immigrant Political Incorporation*, edited by Jennifer Hochschild, Jacqueline Chattopadhyay, Claudine Gay, and Michael Jones-Correa, 241–253. Oxford: Oxford University Press.

Minkenberg, Michael, ed. 2015a. *Transforming the Transformation? The East European Radical Right in the Political Process.* London: Routledge.

Minkenberg, Michael. 2015b. "Profiles, Patterns, Process. Studying the East European Radical Right in Its Political Environment." In *Transforming the Transformation? The East European Radical Right in the Political Process*, edited by Michael Minkenberg, 27–56. London: Routledge.

Minkenberg, Michael. 2017. "Religion and the Radical Right." In *The Oxford Handbook of the Radical Right*, edited by Jens Rydgren. Oxford: Oxford University Press (forthcoming).

Minkenberg, Michael, and Ronald Inglehart. 1989. "Neoconservatism and Value Change in the USA: Tendencies in the Mass Public of a Post-industrial Society." In *Contemporary Political Culture. Politics in a Postmodern Age*, edited by John Gibbins, 81–109. London and New York: Sage.

Minkenberg, Michael, and Oliver Kossack. 2015. "Conclusions: Actors, Interaction, and Impact in Comparison." In *Transforming the Transformation? The East European Radical Right in the Political Process*, edited by Michael Minkenberg, 348–359. London: Routledge.

Minkenberg, Michael, and Bartek Pytlas. 2013. "The Radical Right in Central and Eastern Europe: Class Politics in Classless Societies?" In *Class Politics and the Radical Right*, edited by Jens Rydgren, 206–223. London: Routledge.

Mrázová, Martina. 2016. "Is Kotleba—People's Party Our Slovakia an Extreme Right Party?" Unpublished manuscript. Frankfurt (Oder): European University Viadrina.

Mudde, Cas. 1996. "The War of Words Defining the Extreme Right Party Family." *West European Politics* 19(2): 225–248.

Mudde, Cas. 2000a. *The Ideology of the Extreme Right.* Manchester: Manchester University Press.

Mudde, Cas. 2000b. "Extreme-right Parties in Eastern Europe." *Patterns of Prejudice* 34(1): 5–27.

Mudde, Cas. 2003. "Civil society in post-communist Europe. Lessons from the 'dark side'." In *Uncivil Society? Contentious politics in post-communst Europe*, edited by Petr Kopecký and Cas Mudde, 157–170. London: Routledge.
Mudde, Cas. 2005a. "Central and Eastern Europe." In *Racist Extremism in Central and Eastern Europe*, edited by Cas Mudde, 267–285. London: Routledge.
Mudde, Cas, ed. 2005b. *Racist Extremism in Central and Eastern Europe*. London: Routledge.
Mudde, Cas. 2007. *Populist Radical Right Parties in Europe*. Cambridge: Cambridge University Press.
Mudde, Cas. 2010. "The Populist Radical Right: A Pathological Normalcy." *West European Politics* 33(6): 1167–1186.
Mudde, Cas. 2011. "Radical Right Parties in Europe: What, Who. Why?" *Participation* 35(1): 12–15.
Müller, Jan-Werner. 2012. "Militant Democracy." In *The Oxford Handbook of Comparative Constitutional Law*, edited by Michel Rosenfeld and András Sajó, 1253–1269. Oxford: Oxford University Press.
Mungiu-Pippidi, Alina. 2010. "When Europeanization Meets Transformation. Lessons from the Unfinished Eastern European Revolutions." In *Democracy and Authoritarianism in the Postcommunist World*, eds. Valerie Bunce et al., 59–81. Cambridge: Cambridge University Press
Mungiu-Pippidi, Alina. 2015. *Public Integrity and Trust in Europe*. Berlin: Hertie School of Governance.
Nelson, Joan M. 1998. "Social Costs, Social-Sector Reforms, and Politics in Post-Communist Transformations." In *Transforming Post-Communist Political Economies*, edited by Joan M. Nelson, Charles Tilly, and Lee Walker, 247–271. Washington, DC: National Academy Press.
Nordsieck, Wolfram. 2016. *Parties and Elections in Europe*. Accessed July 11, 2016. http://www.parties-and-elections.eu.
Norris, Pippa. 2005. *The Radical Right. Voters and Parties in the Electoral Market*. Cambridge: Cambridge University Press.
Norris, Pippa, and Ronald Inglehart. 2011. *Sacred and Secular. Religion and Politics Worldwide*. 2nd edition. Cambridge: Cambridge University Press.
Nwabuzo, Ojeaku. 2014. *Racist Crime in Europe. ENAR Shadow Report 2013–2014*. Brussels: European Network Against Racism.
O'Donnell, Guillermo, Philippe C. Schmitter, and Laurence Whitehead, eds. 1986. *Transitions from Authoritarian Rule. Tentative Conclusions about Uncertain Democracies*. Baltimore: Johns Hopkins University Press.
Offe, Claus, ed. 2003. *Demokratisierung der Demokratie: Diagnosen und Reformvorschläge*. Frankfurt (Main): Campus.
Öhlén, Mats. 2014. "Towards Ideological East/West Convergence? European Party Families 1990-2013." Paper presented at the 23rd World Congress of Political Science, Montréal, Canada, July 19–24.

Olsen, Jonathan. 2000. "The European Radical Right: Back to the Future?" *East European Politics and Societies* 15(1): 195–200.

Ost, David. 1999. "The Radical Right of Poland: Rationality of the Irrational." In *The Radical Right in Central and Eastern Europe since 1989*, edited by Sabrina Ramet, 85–108. University Park, P.A: The Pennsylvania State University Press.

Ost, David. 2005. *The Defeat of Solidarity. Anger and Politics in Postcommunist Europe*. Ithaca: Cornell University Press.

Pan, Christoph, and Beate Sibylle Pfeil. 2000. *Die Volksgruppen in Europa. Ein Handbuch*. Wien: Braumüller.

Pankowski, Rafal. 2010. *The Populist Radical Right in Poland. The Patriots*. London: Routledge.

Pankowski, Rafal, and Marcin Kornak. 2013. "Radical Nationalism in Poland: From Theory to Practice." In *Right-wing extremism in Europe. Country Analyses, Counter-Strategies and Labor-Market Oriented Exit Strategies*, edited by Ralf Melzer and Sebastian Serafim, 157–168. Berlin: Friedrich Ebert Stiftung.

Pappas, Takis. 2014. "Populist Democracies: Post-Authoritarian Greece and Post-Communist Hungary." *Government and Opposition* 49(1): 1–25.

Pappas, Takis. 2016. "Distinguishing Liberal Democracy's Challengers." *Journal of Democracy* 28(4): 22–36.

Pedersen, Mogens. 1982. "Towards a New Typology of Party Lifespan and Minor Parties." *Scandinavian Political Studies* 5(1): 1–16.

Perrineau, Pascal. 2016. "Europeans and the Migratory Issue." *The Schuman Report on Europe, State of the Union 2016*, edited by Thierry Chopin and Michel Fourier, 185–192. Paris: Lignes de Repères.

Petková, Zuzana. 2016. „Ktorých neonacistov vytiahol Kotleba do parlamentu." Accessed August 11, 2016. http://www.etrend.sk/ekonomika/ktorych-neo nacistov-vytiahol-kotleba-do-parlamentu.html.

Petöcz, Kálmán. 2009. "Slovakia since 2004—National Populism and the Hungarian Issue." In *National Populism and the Hungarian-Slovak Relations in Slovakia*, edited by Kálmán Petöcz, 67–98. Šamorín: Forum Minority Research Institute.

Petr, Macek, and Ivana Marková. 2004. "Trust and Distrust in Old and New Democracies." In *Trust and Democratic Transition in Post-Communist Europe*, edited by Ivana Marková, 173–194. Oxford: Oxford University Press.

Pew. 2010. Global Religious Futures. Accessed June 10, 2016. http://www.globalreligiousfutures.org/countries.

Pew. 2015. The Continuing Decline of Europe's Jewish Population. Accessed August 30, 2016. http://www.pewresearch.org/fact-tank/2015/02/09/eur opes-jewish-population/.

Pew. 2016. 5 facts about the Muslim population in Europe. Accessed August 30, 2016. http://www.pewresearch.org/fact-tank/2016/07/19/5-facts-about-the-muslim-population-in-europe/.

Pirro, Andrea. 2015. *The Populist Radical Right in Central and Eastern Europe. Ideology, Impact and Electoral Performance.* London: Routledge.
Plasser, Fritz, Peter Ulram, and Harald Waldrauch. 1997. *Politischer Kulturwandel in Ost-Mitteleuropa. Theorie und Empirie demokratischer Konsolidierung.* Opladen: Leske+Budrich.
Political Capital. 2015. *Measuring Political Violence.* Budapest: Political Capital.
Pop-Eleches, Grigore. 2015. "Pre-Communist and Communist Developmental Legacies." *East European Politics and Societies* 29(2): 391–408.
Pop-Eleches, Grigore, and Joshua Tucker. 2013. "Associated with the Past? Communist Legacies and Civic Participation in Post-Communist Countries." *East European Politics and Societies and Cultures* 27(1): 45–68.
Porter-Szücs, Brian. 2011. *Faith and Fatherland. Catholicism, Modernity and Poland.* Oxford: Oxford University Press.
Powell, Eleanor Neff, and Joshua A. Tucker. 2014. "Revisiting Electoral Volatility in Post-Communist Countries: New Data, New Results and New Approaches." *British Journal of Political Science* 44(1): 123–147.
Pribar, Jiri, and Wojciech Sadurski. 2006. "The Role of Political Rights in the Democratization of Central and Eastern Europe." In *Political Rights under Stress in the 21st Century Europe*, edited by Wojciech Sadurski, 219–230. Oxford: Oxford University Press.
Prowe, Diethelm. 1998. "Fascism, Neo-Fascism, New Radical Right?" In *International Fascism: Theories, Causes, and the New Consensus*, edited by Roger Griffin, 305–324. London: Arnold and New York: Oxford University Press.
Przeworski, Adam, and Henry Teune. 1970. *The Logic of Comparative Social Inquiry.* New York: John Wiley & Sons.
Pytlas, Bartek. 2013. "Radical Right Narratives in Slovakia and Hungary: Historical Legacies, Mythic Overlaying and Contemporary Politics." *Patterns of Prejudice* 47(2): 162–183.
Pytlas, Bartek. 2016. *Radical Right Parties in Central and Eastern Europe: Mainstream Party Competition and Electoral Fortune.* London: Routledge.
Ramet, Sabrina, ed. 1999. *The Radical Right in Central and Eastern Europe since 1989.* University Park: The Pennsylvania State University Press.
Reynié, Dominique. 2013. *Les noveaux populismes.* Paris: Pluriel.
Rovny, Jan. 2013. "Where Do Radical Right Parties Stand? Position Blurring in Multidimensional Competition." *European Political Science Review* 5(1): 56–74.
Rucht, Dieter. 1994. *Modernisierung und neue soziale Bewegungen.* Frankfurt/Main: Campus.
Rudi, Tatjana. 2010. *Wahlentscheidungen in postsozialistischen Demokratien in Mittel- und Osteuropa. Eine vergleichende Untersuchung.* Baden-Baden: Nomos.
Rupnik, Jacques. 2016. "Surging Illiberalism in the East." *Journal of Democracy* 27(4): 77–87.

Rydgren, Jens. 2007. "The Sociology of the Radical Right." *Annual Review of Sociology* 33: 241–262.
Rydgren, Jens, ed. 2013. *Class Politics and the Radical Right.* London: Routledge.
Sajó, András, ed. 2004. *Militant Democracy.* Utrecht: Eleven International Publishing.
Sartori, Giovanni. 1976. *Parties and Party Systems.* Cambridge: Cambridge University Press.
Savage, Lee. 2016. "Party System Institutionalization and Government Formation in New Democracies." *World Politics* 68(3): 499–537.
Schain, Martin. 2006. "The Extreme-right and Immigration Policy-Making: Measuring Direct and Indirect Effects." *West European Politics* 29(2): 270–289.
Schain, Martin, Aristide Zolberg, and Patrick Hossay, eds. 2002. *Shadows over Europe. The Contemporary Radical Right, its Causes and Effects.* New York: Palgrave.
Schedler, Andreas, ed. 2006. *Electoral Authoritarianism: The Dynamics of Unfree Competition.* Boulder: Lynne Rienner.
Scheuch, Erwin, and Hans-Dieter Klingemann. 1967. "Theorie des Rechtsradikalismus in westlichen Industriegesellschaften." *Hamburger Jahrbuch Für Wirtschafts- und Gesellschaftspolitik* 12: 11–29.
Seefried, Elke. 2016. "Die Krise der Weimarer Demokratie—Analogien zur Gegenwart?" *Aus Politik und Zeitgeschichte* 66(40-42): 18–23.
Shafir, Michael. 2000. "Marginalization or Mainstream? The Extreme Right in Post-Communist Romania." In *The Politics of the Extreme Right. From the Margins to the Mainstream*, edited by Paul Hainsworth, 247–267. London and New York: Pinter.
Shapiro, Ian. 2003. *The State of Democratic Theory.* Princeton: Princeton University Press.
Shulman, Stephen. 2002. "Challenging the Civic/Ethnic and the West/East Dichotomies in the Study of Nationalism." *Comparative Political Studies* 35(5): 554–585.
Sikk, Allan. 2005. "How Unstable? Volatility and the Genuinely New Parties in Eastern Europe." *European Journal of Political Research* 44: 391–412.
Skenderovic, Damir. 2009. *The Radical Right in Switzerland. Continuity and Change, 1945-2000.* New York: Berghahn Books.
Smith, Anthony. 1995. *The Ethnic Origins of Nations.* Oxford: Blackwell.
Smith, Anthony. 2001. *Nationalism. Theory, Ideology, History.* Cambridge: Polity Press.
Spáč, Peter, and Petr Voda. 2014. "Slovak Extreme Right and its Support based on Local Roma Incidence." Paper presented at ECPR General Conference, Glasgow, September.

Spohn, Willfried. 2003a. "Multiple Modernity, Nationalism and Religion: A Global Perspective." *Current Sociology* 51(3–4): 265–286.
Spohn, Willfried. 2003b. "Nationalismus und Religion. Ein historisch-soziologischer Vergleich West –und Osteuropas." In *Politik und Religion*. special issue of *Politische Vierteljahresschrift* 33/2002, edited by Michael Minkenberg and Ulrich Willems, 323–345. Wiesbaden: Westdeutscher Verlag.
Stankiewicz, Katharina. 2002. "Die 'neuen Dmowskis' - eine alte Ideologie im neuen Gewand?" *Osteuropa* 52(3): 263–279.
Stein, Jonathan P., ed. 2000. *The Politics of National Minority Participation n Post-Communist Europe. State-Building, Democracy, and Ethnic Mobilization*. Armonk and London: M.E. Sharpe.
Stepan, Alfred, and Juan Linz. 1996. *Problems of Democratic Transition and Consolidation: Southern Europe, South America, and Post-Communist Europe*. Baltimore, MD: Johns Hopkins Univ. Press.
Stöss, Richard. 1989. *Die extreme Rechte in der Bundesrepublik*. Opladen: Westdeutscher Verlag.
Stöss, Richard. 2010. *Rechtsextremismus im Wandel*. 3rd edition. Berlin: Friedrich-Ebert Stiftung.
Stöss, Richard, and Dieter Segert. 1997. "Entstehung, Struktur und Entwicklung von Parteiensystemen in Osteuropa nach 1989—eine Bilanz." In *Parteiensysteme in postkommunistischen Gesellschaftten Osteuropas*, edited by Dieter Segert, Richard Stöss, and Oskar Niedermayer, 379–428. Opladen: Leske+Budrich.
Sum, Paul E. 2010. "The radical right in Romania: Political party evolution and the distancing of Romania from Europe." *Communist and Post-Communist Studies* 43(1): 19–29.
Szayna, Thomas. 1997. "The Extreme Right Political Movements in Post-Communist Central Europe." In *The Revival of Right-wing Extremism in the Nineties*, edited by Peter Merkl and Lenoard Weinberg, 111–148. London: Frank Cass.
Sztompka, Piotr. 1992. "Dilemmas of the Great Transition." *Sisyphus* 8(2): 9–28.
Sztompka, Piotr. 1993. "Civilizational Incompetence: The Trap of Post-Communist Societies." *Zeitschrift Für Soziologie* 22: 85–95.
Szücs, Jenö. 1990. *Die drei historischen Regionen Europas*. Frankfurt: Verlag Neue Kritik.
Taggart, Paul. 2000. *Populism*. Buckingham: Open University Press.
Tarrow, Sidney. 1994. *Power in Movement*. Cambridge: Cambridge University Press.
Tarrow, Sidney. 2012. *Strangers at the Gate. Movements and States in Contentious Politics*. Cambridge: Cambridge University Press.
Tavits, Margit. 2008. "Party Systems in the Making: The Emergence and Success of New Parties in New Democracies." *British Journal of Political Science* 49(2): 283–298.

Tavits, Margit. 2013. *Post-Communist Democracies and Party Organization*. Cambridge: Cambridge University Press.

Tavits, Margit, and Natalia Letki. 2009. "When Left is Right: Party Ideology and Policy in Post-Communist Europe." *American Political Science Review* 103: 444–469.

Thanei, Christoph. 2002. "Vladimír Mečiar: Ein Mythos polarisiert (Slowakei)." In *Haider, Le Pen & Co: Europas Rechtspopulisten*, edited by Michael Jungwirth, 218–237. Graz: Styria Verlag.

The Orange Files. 2014. "Notes on the End of Liberal Democracy in Hungary: The New Hungarian Guard/For a Better Future Hungarian Self Defense." Last updated 23 June 2014. https://theorangefiles.hu/the-new-hungarian-guardfor-a-better-future-self-defense/.

Thieme, Tom. 2007. *Hammer, Sichel, Hakenkreuz. Parteipolitischer Extremismus in Osteuropa: Entstehungsbedingungen und Erscheinungsformen*. Baden-Baden: Nomos.

Thompson, Mark. 2002. "Building Nations and Crafting Democracies—Competing Legitimacies in Interwar Eastern Europe." In *Authoritarianism and Democracy in Europe, 1919–39. Comparative Analyses*, edited by Dirk Berg-Schlosser and Jeremy Mitchell, 20–38. Basingstoke and New York: Palgrave Macmillan.

Tilly, Charles. 2006. "Why and How History Matters." In *The Oxford Handbook of Contextual Political Analysis*, edited by Robert Goodin and Charles Tilly, 417–437. Oxford: Oxford University Press.

Tilly, Charles, and Sidney Tarrow. 2006. *Contentious Politics*. Oxford: Oxford University Press.

Tismaneanu, Vlaimir. 2007. "Is East-Central Europe backsliding? Leninist legacies, pluralist dilemmas." *Journal of Democracy* 18(4): 33–39.

Tismaneanu, Vladimir, Marc M. Howard, and Rudra Sil, eds. 2006. *World Order after Leninism*. Seattle and Washington: University of Washington Press.

Tódová, Monika. 2013. „Polícia mala na Kotlebu dvanásť spisov, odsúdili ho len za haváriu." Accessed August 11, 2016. http://domov.sme.sk/c/7022142/policia-mala-na-kotlebu-dvanast-spisov-odsudili-ho-len-za-havariu.html.

Trencsényi, Balázs. 2001. "The 'Münchausenian Moment': Modernity, Liberalism and Nationalism in the Thought of Stefan Zeletin." In *Nation Building and Contested Identities: Romanian and Hungarian Case Studies*, edited by Balázs Trencsényi et al., 61–80. Budapest: Regio Books.

Turcanu, Florin. 2010."Right-wing extremism and its impact on young democracies in the CEE-countries. State, society, NGOs on Right-wing extremism in Romania." Paper presented at the conference of the Friedrich-Ebert-Foundation on "Right-wing Extremism in CEE-Countries", Budapest, 19 November.

Uitz, Renata. 2008. "Hungary." In *Populist Politics in Liberal Democracy in Central and Eastern Europe*, edited by Grigorij Mesežnikov and Oľga Gyárfášová, 39–68. Bratislava: Institute for Public Affairs.

Umland, Andreas. 2007. "Faschismus à la Dugin." *Blätter für deutsche und internationale Politik* 12: 1432–1435.

Umland, Andreas. 2008. "Rechtsextremes Engagement jenseits von Parteien: Vorkriegsdeutschland und Russland im Vergleich." *Forschungsjournal Neue Soziale Bewegungen* 21(4): 63–67.

Umland, Andreas. 2015. "Challenges and promises of comparative research into post-Soviet fascism: Methodological and conceptual issues in the study of the contemporary East European extreme right." *Communist and Post-Communist Studies* 48(2–3): 169–181.

Václavík, David. 2015. "Searching and Finding: A History of the Slovak Study of Religion." In *The Academic Study of Religion in Eastern Europe*, edited by Tomáš Bubík and Henryk Hoffmann, 55–86. Leiden: Brill.

van Biezen, Ingrid, Peter Mair, and Thomas Poguntke. 2012. "Going, going, ... gone? The decline of party membership in contemporary Europe." *European Journal of Political Research* 51(1): 24–56.

Van Der Brug, Wouter, Meindert Fennema, and Jean N. Tillie. 2005. "Why Some Anti-Immigrant Parties Fail and Others Succeed: A Two-Step Model of Aggregate Electoral Support." *Comparative Political Studies* 38(5): 537–573.

Vejvodová, Petra. 2014. *Transnational Forms of Contemporary Neo-Nazi Activities in Europe from the Perspective of Czech Neo-Nazis*. Brno: Muni Press.

Verseck, Keno. 2016. "Halb Osteuropa hasst diesen Mann." Accessed February, 26. http://www.spiegel.de/politik/ausland/george-soros-diesen-mann-hasst-halb-osteuropa-a-1078614.html.

Vetter, Reinhold. 2016. "Gezeitenwechsel. Polens Rechte erobert die Macht." In *Gegen die Wand. Konservative Revolution in Polen*, edited by Deutsche Gesellschaft für Osteuropakunde. Special Issue of *Osteuropa* 66 (1–2): 19–36.

Virostkova, Lucia. 2016. "New Slovak Government in Convalescence." *EU Oberserver*, April 25. Accessed September 1, 2016. https://euobserver.com/beyond-brussels/133199.

Vodicka, Karel. 1994. "Wie der Koalitionsbeschluß zur Auflösung der CFSR zustande kam." *Osteuropa* 44(2): 175–186.

Von Beyme, Klaus. 1988. "Right-wing Extremism in Post-war Europe." *West European Politics* 11(2): 1–18.

Von Beyme, Klaus. 1994. *Systemwechsel in Osteuropa*. Frankfurt/Main: Suhrkamp.

Von Beyme, Klaus. 1996. "Rechtsextremismus in Osteuropa." In *Rechtsextremismus*. Special Issue of *Politische Vierteljahresschrift*, edited by Jürgen Falter, Hans-Gerd Jaschke und Jürgen Winkler, 423–442. Opladen: Westdeutscher Verlag.

Von Beyme, Klaus. 2015. "Transforming Transformation Theory." In *Transforming the Transformation? The East European Radical Right in the Political Process*, edited by Michael Minkenberg, 13–26. London: Routledge.

Vyhlásenie, SP. 2016. "Vyhlásenie SP—My nie sme kotlebovci!" (January 30). Accessed August 11, 2016. https://pospolitost.wordpress.com/2016/01/30/vyhlasenie-sp-my-nie-sme-kotlebovci/.
Walczak, Agnieszka, Wouter van der Brug, and Cahterine de Vries. 2012. "Long- and Short-Term Determinants of Party Preferences: Inter-Generational Differences in Western and East Central Europe." *Electoral Studies* 31(2): 273–284.
Walicki, Andrej. 2000. "The Troubling Legacy of Roman Dmowski." *East European Politics and Societies* 14(1): 12–46.
Weßels, Bernhard. 2003. "Die Entwicklung der Zivilgesellschaft in Mittel- und Osteuropa: Intermediäre Akteure, Vertrauen und Partizipation." In *Zivilgesellschaft: Pfade, Abwege. WZB-Jahrbuch 2003*, edited by Wolfgang van den Daale, Diester Gosewinkel, Jürgen Kocka, and Dieter Rucht, 173–198. Berlin: WZB.
Whitefield, Stephen, and Robert Rohrschneider. 2009. "Understanding Cleavages in Party Systems: Issue Positions and Issue Salience in 13 Post-Communist Democracies." *Comparative Political Studies* 42(2): 280–313.
Williams, Michelle Hale. 2006. *The Impact of Radical Right-Wing Parties in West European Democracies*. New York: Palgrave.
Wilson, Robin, and Paul Hainsworth. 2012. *Far Right Parties and Discourse in Europe: A Challenge for Our Times*. Brussels: European Network Against Racism.
Wippermann, Wolfgang. 1983. *Europäischer Faschismus im Vergleich, 1922–1982*. Frankfurt (Main): Suhrkamp.
Wittenberg, Jason. 2015. "Conceptualizing Historical Legacies." *East European Politics and Societies* 29(2): 366–378.
Wodak, Ruth. 2015. *The Politics of Fear: Analysing the Rhetoric of Radical Rightwing Populist Politics*. London: Sage.
Wolff, Larry. 1994. *Inventing Eastern Europe. The Map of Civilization on the Mind of the Enlightenment*. Stanford: Stanford University Press.
Zick, Andreas, Beate Küpper, and Andreas Hövermann. 2011. *Die Abwertung der Anderen. Eine europäische Zustandsbeschreibung zu Intoleranz, Vorurteilen und Diskriminierung*. Berlin: Friedrich-Ebert-Stiftung.
Zubrzycki, Geneviève. 2006. *The Crosses of Auschwitz. Nationalism and Religion in Post-Communist Poland*. Chicago: University of Chicago Press.

INDEX

A
Accommodation, 2, 57, 76, 79, 134
  See also Co-optation
Acquis communautaire, 106, 115
  See also Eastern Enlargement
Action Front of National Socialists (ANS), 87
AfD, *see* Alternative for Germany
Agenda setting
  effects, 29
  levels, 29
Ágh, Attila, 21, 137, 138, 139
Akkerman, Tjitske, 26, 122, 129
Alliance of Free Democrats, 85
Alliance for the Future of Austria (BZÖ), 87, 103, 124
All for Latvia! (VL), 75
  coalition government, 128
  electoral performance, 103
  ideology, 75
All-Polish Youth, 73, 86, 92, 95
Alpine populism, 17, 112
  See also Populism
Alternative for Germany (AfD), 24, 96
Anderson, Benedict, 16, 44

Andreescu, Gabriel, 82, 86, 90, 136
AN, *see* National Alliance
ANS, *see* Action Front of National Socialists
Anti-pluralism, 138
Anti-Roma sentiment
  in Hungary, 83
  See also Gypsy crime
Anti-Semitism
  in Bulgaria, 77
  and the Catholic Church, 79
  in Eastern Europe, 84, 113
  in Hungary, 85, 137
  in Romania, 76, 86, 137
  See also Islamophobia
Antonescu, Crin, 24, 61, 69, 71, 77
Arrow-Cross, 76–78, 82, 144
Art, David, 10, 24, 26, 81, 83, 85, 104, 105
Asylum seekers, 2, 49, 111
  See also Immigration; Refugee
Ataka, 103, 124
  coalition government, 127–128
  effects, 131–133
  electoral performance, 101

Ataka (cont.)
  ideology, 73–75, 77, 87–88
  mainstreaming of, 68, 104
Attitudes, anti-elitism, 16, 17
  anti-system, 16
Auers, Daunis, 72, 74, 80, 100, 113, 128
Austria, 45, 53, 58, 81, 85, 93, 102, 111, 125
Austrian People's Party (ÖVP), 125
Authoritarianism, regimes, 37
Autocracy, 37
Autonomy, territorial, 14, 45, 50
Avramov, Kiril, 77, 86, 127, 131–132
AWS, see Solidarity Electoral Action

B

Backes, Uwe, 16, 17
Backlash, ethnic, 111
Bale, Tim, 122, 123, 136
Balkan route, 50
  See also Refugee
Baltic States, 50, 53, 68, 72, 74, 80, 84, 91
Barbu, Eugen, 69
Bargaining costs, 123
Bargaining processes, 30
Bayer, Zsolt, 78–79, 82
Beichelt, Timm, 3, 4, 24, 41, 49, 50, 55, 56, 61, 73, 106
Belgium, 46, 58, 82, 102, 111
Beneš decrees, 83
Berlusconi, Silvio, 123
Betz, Hans-Georg, 13, 17, 24, 85, 112
Bíró Nagy, András, 10, 78–79, 83, 136, 138
Blackmail potential, of the radical right, 31, 134, 147
Blood and Honour, 69, 72, 74

BNP, see British National Party
Border, issues, 3, 82
  questions, 6, 65
  See also Irredentism
Borderlands, of the European Union, 39
Brandt, Willy, 82
Breakdown' theories: debunking of
British National Party (BNP), 87
Brubaker, Rogers, 36, 44, 46, 48, 50, 129, 145
BSP, see Bulgarian Socialist Party
Bulgaria
  constitutional conflict, 50
  cultural nation, 61
  ethnic diversity, 52
  party system, 57, 132
  radical right, 11, 63, 68, 73, 76, 83, 90, 108, 147
  Turkish minority, 73, 84, 104, 132
  See also Ataka
Bulgarian Socialist Party (BSP), 127–128, 132
Bunce, Valerie, 37, 103, 126
Bustikova, Lenka, 3, 11, 39, 56–57, 77, 83, 115, 130, 141
Buzatu, Gheorghe, 77
BZÖ, see Alliance for the Future of Austria

C

Canovan, Margaret, 16
Capitalism, and modernization, 19, 21
  See also Transformation
Capoccia, Giovanni, 17, 61, 129
Carter, Elizabeth, 12, 16, 18, 23, 26, 27, 85, 105, 125
Catholic Church, 27, 47, 64, 71, 79, 141
  See also Catholic values
Catholicism, ideology, 76, 86, 90, 144

See also Catholic Church
CCS, *see* Committees Christianity-
 Solidarity
CD, 124
 See also Christian Democrats; Center
  Democrats
Ceauşescu, Nicolae, 24, 61, 69–70
Center Democrats (CD), 87
Chapel Hill Expert Survey, 133
Christian Democracy, party
 families, 58
 religion, 86
 See also Catholic Church
Christian Democratic People's Party
 (KDNP)
 electoral alliance with Fidesz, 87
Christian Democrats (CD), 123
Christianity, 20, 86, 87
Christian National Union
 (ZChN), 70, 72, 79
Christian People's Party
 (CVP), 124
Church
 Orthodox, 61, 63, 86, 144
 in Poland, 27, 90
 and radical-right ideology, 46
 in Romania, 60, 82, 86, 130
 state-church-relations, 136
 See also Catholic Church
Cinpoeş, Radu, 24, 82, 84,
  102, 116, 127
Citizens' Congress (Latvia), 80
Citizens for European Development of
 Bulgaria (GERB), 104, 127–128,
  131, 132, 147
Citizenship, 19, 50, 104
 dual citizenship in Bulgaria, 104
Civil liberties and rights, 14, 45, 60,
  76, 132, 139
Civil society
 in Eastern Europe, 60, 90
 in post-communist context, 114
 and the radical right, 11, 29, 30
 uncivil society, 60
 See also Participation
Cleavages
 in Eastern Europe, 55, 56, 88
 ethnic, 4, 100
 model, 27, 56
 and movement mobilization, 27, 53
 in party systems, 4, 6, 36, 53, 55,
  57, 65, 129, 146, 149
 patterns, 6, 58, 65, 105, 146
Coalition governments
 in Austria, 123
 in Bulgaria, 7, 11, 124
 in Italy, 125
 in Latvia, 7, 11, 75
 in Poland, 7, 11
 in Romania, 7, 11, 63, 127
 in Slovakia, 7, 11, 63, 127, 129, 130
Coalition potential, 31
 See also Sartori, Giovanni
Coalition for Republic – Republican
 Party of Czechoslovakia
 (SPR-RSČ), 69, 71, 100, 103
Coja, Ion, 71, 77
Cold War, 68, 123, 148
Collective action, 27–29
Collective identity
 of the radical right, 25, 116
 See also Movements
Committees Christianity-Solidarity
 (CCS), 87
Communism
 collapse of, 60, 99
 and fascist ideology, 69, 77
 historical legacies, 36, 76
 national-accommodative, 57, 76
 and radical-right parties, 22, 42
Confederation for an Independent
 Poland (KPN), 70
Conflict structures, 28, 61
 socioeconomic, 57, 115

Conservatism, 19, 36, 75
Consolidation
  democratic, 3, 4, 50, 55, 64,
    68, 91, 99, 126, 147
Conspiracy theories, 27, 71
Constitutional ban
  of Fascist Party in Italy, 125
Constitution conflicts
  in Bulgaria, 50
  in Estonia, 50
  in Hungary, 50
  in Poland, 50
  and right-wing extremism, 17
  in Romania, 50
  in Slovakia, 50
Context factors
  cultural, 43, 48, 53
  political, 6, 7, 65
Convergence
  of party systems, 3
  between Western and Eastern
    Europe, 96
Cooperation
  between radical right and
    mainstream, 116, 147
  between radical right
    parties, 147
Co-optation
  in Hungary, 116, 134
  in Poland, 134
  of radical right agenda, 90, 134
  in Slovakia, 134
Cordon sanitaire
  in Austria, 125
  in Czech Republic, 115, 129, 147
  in Italy, 125
  in Slovakia, 84, 115, 116, 147
Corruption, 59, 115
Counter-discourse, 27
Counter-mobilization, 11
  and East West difference, 11
Croatia, 137

Crown of Saint-Stephen, 138
Cultural mixing, 15
Cultural resonance, 26–27, 44
Culture, 6, 19, 22, 26–27, 36, 44, 60,
    63, 64, 70, 141
  political, 6, 22, 26, 64
Culture wars, 57, 141
  See also Identity politics; Value wars
CVP, *see* Christian People's Party
Czechoslovakia, 6, 45, 50, 63, 64, 70,
    76, 81, 126
Czech Republic
  cordon sanitaire, 115, 129, 147
  racist crime, 94–95
  radical-right movements, 91
  and Slovak minority, 63
  See also SPR-RSČ
Czurka, Istvan, 71

D
Danish People's Party (DF), 17, 85
Danko, Andrej, 75, 79, 131
De Lange, Sarah, 79, 123, 132
Democracy, overload of, 19
Demarcation
  in Czech Republic, 100, 116
  in Estonia, 100, 116
  in Lithuania, 100, 116
  in Romania, 100, 116
Democracy
  challenges to, 7, 144
  consolidation of, 3, 4, 20, 37,
    50, 55, 64, 68, 91, 99,
    126, 147
  crisis of, 19
  liberal, 13, 21, 23, 37, 46, 105, 141,
    144, 148
  quality of, 2, 7, 29, 57,
    75–90, 127, 134
  representative, 16
  trust in, 6, 60, 64–65

See also Deliberative democracy;
    Eastern Enlargement; Liberal
    democracy; Illiberal democracy;
    Militant democracy;
    Modernization;
    'Post-democracy'; Radicalization,
    of mainstream; Transformation
Democratic dilemma, 33
Democratic values/principles, 2, 115
Democratization
    and nation building, 14, 45
    re-democratization, 21
Demos, 14, 44
    See also Ethnos
Denmark, 49, 102, 111, 125
DF, *see* Danish People's Party
Direction – Social Democracy
    (Smer), 126–127, 130–131,
    134, 147
Diversity
    ethnic, 43, 45, 52, 113
    of regimes, 40
    religious, 111, 112
Dmowski, Roman, 64, 70, 72, 74, 76,
    79, 86, 144, 145
Dollfuß, Engelbert, 81
    See also Austria
Downs, William, 30, 31
DPS, *see* Movement for Rights and
    Freedoms
DS, *see* Workers' Party of Social Justice
Dutch People's Union (NVU), 88
DVU, *see* German People's Union

E
Eastern Enlargement, 1, 91, 100
Eastern Europe, 1–3, 5, 6, 10, 11, 14,
    17, 20, 21, 22–24, 30, 35–39,
    41–46, 49, 50, 53, 55–61, 64, 68,
    70, 76, 82, 83–85, 87, 88, 91, 96,
    100, 102, 106, 108, 111, 112,
    114, 122, 128–130, 134, 137,
    140, 143–148
    See also Europe
EI, *see* Estonian Independence Party
Ekiert, Grzegorz, 37, 40, 61
Election results, 140, 149
    of radical right parties, 101, 140
    See also Voters
Electoral authoritarianism, 37
Electoral market, 26, 103
Electoral success, 5, 43, 53, 57, 59,
    78, 104, 108, 111, 113, 125
    of radical right parties, 43, 53, 57,
    104, 111, 114
Elites
    established, 28, 59
    traditional, 28
Empires
    Habsburg, 45, 63, 145
    Ottoman, 45, 61, 145
    Russian, 45, 145
Enlightenment, 20
Entrepreneurs, political, 21, 79
Estonia, 58, 60, 116
    constitutional conflicts, 50
    ethnic diversity, 52
    movement sector, 108–111
    nationalism, 72
    statehood, 63–64
    "war of monuments", 80
    weakness of radical right
        parties, 100, 102
    xenophobia, 53
Estonian Independence Party (EI), 74
Ethnic cleavage, 4, 100, 149
    See also Cleavage
Ethnic homogeneity, 14, 50, 108, 113
Ethnicity, 61, 144
Ethnic nationalism
    in Czech Republic, 63
    in Hungary, 45, 138
Ethnocentric prejudice, 54

Ethnocentrism, 23, 24, 84, 125
Ethnocracy, 16
Ethnopluralism
　mainstreaming efforts, 86
　See also Islamophobia
Ethnos, 14, 44
　See also Demos
EU membership, 4, 37, 100, 108, 115, 148
European Commission, 2
European integration, 2–4, 38, 141
European Parliament (EP), 73, 96, 123
European Union, 1–5, 37, 38, 46, 53, 55, 57, 70, 74, 91, 93, 99, 100, 108, 114, 115, 126–128, 141, 144, 146, 148
　See also Eastern Enlargement
European Union Agency for Fundamental Rights, 93
European Values Survey, 52
Europe of Nations and Freedom, 96
Eurostat, 49
Evans, Geoffrey, 55, 56
Exclusion, 12, 14, 18, 22–23, 46, 57, 77, 144
External homelands, 50, 63, 64, 145
Extreme right
　as political partners, 127
　See also Radical right
Extremism
　extremism theory, 13
　in Hungary, 108, 131
　ideological, 102, 108, 144, 146
　right-wing, 17, 93, 105

F
FANE, see Federation of National-European Action
FAP, see Free German Workers Party
Fascism
　in Bulgaria, 77, 86
　clerical, 63, 78, 86
　interwar fascism, 3, 38, 77, 105
　in Romania, 76, 77, 86
For Fatherland and Freedom/Latvian National Independence Movement (TB/LNNK), 72
FDP, see Free Democratic Party
Federation of National-European Action, 87
FI, see Go Italy!
Fico, Robert, 130
Fidesz, see Hungarian Civic Alliance
Financial crisis, 4, 148
Finland, 93, 111
Fluidity
　of party systems, 57, 70
　of radical right parties, 88, 116
FN, see National Front
For a Better Future Hungarian Self-Defense, 118
Fortuyn, Pim, 129
FPÖ, see Freedom Party of Austria
Fragmentation
　ethnic, 59
　political, 24
　religious, 111
Framing
　frame competition, 104
　See also Narrative shift
France, 48, 49, 81, 82, 85, 102, 111
Free Democratic Party, 86
Freedom Party of Austria (FPÖ), 24, 85, 96, 125
Free German Workers Party, 87
Free market economy, 140
Freezing hypothesis, 55
　See also Lipset Seymour M.; Rokkan, Stein
Front National (National Front - Belgium), 17, 85
FrP, 101

See also Progress Party (DK); Progress Party (NO)
Fundamentalism
 Religious, 79, 145
 See also Islamophobia; Religion
Fundamental Law (Hungary), 138

G

GERB, *see* Citizens for European Development of Bulgaria
German Offices for the Protection of the Constitutions, 17
German People's Union (DVU), 71, 101
Germany
 Nazi Germany, 64, 78, 86
 See also National unity
Giertych, Roman, 139
Globalization, 19
Go Italy!, 125
Government participation
 of radical right, 7, 73, 134, 135, 147
 See also Coalition government
Green parties, 19
Grid/group model of political boundaries, 15, 56
Griffin, Roger, 16, 18
Group-based Enmity, 15
Gyárfášová, Ol'ga, 75, 79, 83, 92, 115–116, 126
Grzymała-Busse, Anna, 48, 64, 79, 136
"Gypsy crime", 73, 83, 104, 135
 See also Anti-Roma sentiment

H

Habermas, Jürgen, 19
Haider, Jörg, 125
Hegemony
 American, 77
 Soviet, 4, 82
Heitmeyer, Wilhelm, 15

Herfindahl Index, 112
Heterophobia, 23
Hlinka, Andrej, 78, 126, 130
Hlinka's Slovak People's Party (HSĽS), 75, 78
Hobsbawm, Eric, 44–46, 76
Holy Crown, 138
Homogeneity
 cultural, 14, 108
 ethnic, 14, 50, 51, 108, 113
 national, 16
Homogeneous nation, 14, 42, 144
Homophobia, 23
 See also Minority issues
Horthy, Miklós, 24, 78, 82
Howard, Marc M., 41, 60, 65n1, 91
Human rights
 values, 115
 See also Minority issues
Hungarian Civic Alliance (Fidesz)
 government participation, 135, 147
 media reforms, 137, 138
Hungarian Democratic Forum (MDF), 71, 133
Hungarian Guard (MG), 73, 78, 92, 96, 118, 119, 145, 146
Hungarian Justice and Life Party (MIÉP), 2, 71, 73, 78, 82, 83, 86, 88, 91, 132, 134, 135, 137, 145
 See also Militant democracy
Hungarian Self-Defense Movement (MÖM), 69, 72, 74, 87
Hungary
 constitutional reforms, 2, 78, 138
 ethnic diversity, 52
 greater Hungary, 82
 radical right, 2, 5, 24, 63, 68, 71, 73, 81, 83, 86, 88, 90, 91, 102, 108, 115, 116, 132, 134, 137, 138, 142, 144, 145, 147, 148
 Roma minority in, 96, 146

Hungary (cont.)
  See also Arrow Cross Party;
    Co-optation; External
    homelands; Fidesz; Hungarian
    Guard; Illiberal politics; Jobbik
Hybrid regimes, 37
HZDS, see Movement for a democratic
  Slovakia

I
Identity
  national, 21, 27, 43–45, 47, 48,
    63, 64, 76, 80, 85, 86, 90, 106,
    144, 145, 147
  See also Collective identity
Identity politics, 21, 57, 131, 134,
  141, 147–148
  See also Culture wars; Value wars
Ideology
  fascist-autocratic, 24
  nationalist-communist, 24
  See also Catholic Church;
    Catholicism; Radical right
Ignazi, Piero, 16–19, 105, 123
Illiberal, 46, 79, 126, 127, 148
  See also Illiberal democracy;
    Religious fundamentalism
Illiberal democracy, 38, 138
Illiberal politics, 38, 79
Immigration
  European public opinion, 49
  as political issue, 49
  See also Border; Insecurity; Refugee
Impact of the radical right
  on party competition, 53, 108, 146
  policy impact, 136
  societal impact, 100
Implementation, 7, 61, 106, 115
  of radical-right policies, 7
Independence
  movements, 72, 81
  national, 4, 45, 72, 86
  See also Revolution
Independence March (Warsaw), 95
  See also All-Polish Youth
Individualism, 14
  See also Universalism
Industrialization
  industrialism, 19, 22
  post-industrialism, 19, 22
In-group and out-group belonging
  distinctions, 14, 15, 43
  See also National identity
Inglehart, Ronald, 19, 21, 28,
  57, 114
Insecurity, 6, 38, 65
  See also Immigration
Integration, European, 2–4, 38, 141
Inter-war period, 6, 18, 46, 48, 64,
  69, 70, 78, 145
Interaction
  between mainstream and radical
    right, 7, 12, 30, 115, 130
  between parties and movements,
    7, 100
  patterns of, 30, 114–119
Interaction effects, 29, 30, 122,
  130–136
Internet and radical right, 93
Ireland, 47–49, 52, 112
Iron Guard, 69, 71, 76–77, 144
Irredentism, 6, 65, 81, 82
  See also Border
Islam
  See also Religion
Islamophobia, 54, 85, 88, 114
  See also Anti-Semitism;
    Ethnopluralism; Mainstreaming
    efforts
Issue politics, 22
  See also Minority; Post-industrialism
Italian Social Movement (MSI), 23,
  68, 101, 123

Italy, 27, 48, 49, 52, 58, 81, 85, 101, 102, 111, 125, 129, 130
IV Republic(France), 139, 140

J
Janos, Andrew, 6, 20, 38, 39
Jesse, Eckard, 16, 17, 61
Jobbik
  anti-democratic agenda, 77
  and Christianity, 86
  electoral campaigns, 134
  gypsy crime, 73, 83, 104, 135
  and the Hungarian Guard, 73, 78, 118
  relationship with Fidesz, 2, 82, 83, 86, 104, 132, 134–139
  relationship with MIEP, 2, 73, 78, 82, 83, 86, 88, 132, 134, 135, 137
  See also Arrow Cross Regime; Treaty of Trianon
Jowitt, Kenneth, 20, 39–41, 148
JSN, *see* Netherlands Youth Storm
Judt, Tony, 6, 38, 48

K
Kaczyński, Jarosław, 128, 140, 141
Kasekamp, Andres, 72, 74, 80, 84, 100, 113, 128
Kasprowicz, Dominika, 73, 86, 90, 92, 118, 128, 136
KDNP, *see* Christian Democratic Party
Kitschelt, Herbert, 11, 12, 15, 16, 18, 20, 23–26, 28, 40–41, 55–57, 76, 81, 83, 93, 96n1, 105, 106, 115, 130
Klingemann, Hans-Dieter, 12, 60
Kopecký, Petr, 60, 90, 91
Kopka, Artur, 132, 139, 140

Kossack, Oliver, 32, 91, 114–116, 126–128, 132–136, 146
Kotleba, Marián, 75, 79, 118
Kotleba – People's Party Out Slovakia, 75, 118
KPN, *see* Confederation for an Independent Poland
Kréko, Péter, 78, 90, 92, 118
Kukiz' 15, 74, 75, 118, 140
Kulturnation, 44
Kurski, Jacek, 140

L
Laizism, 140
  See also Religiosity
Language laws, 50
  See also Minority issues
Latvia, 46
  ethnic diversity, 50, 52, 113
  government coalitions, 128–129
  movement sector, 108–110
  nationalism, 72
  statehood, 63–64
  Ulmanis regime, 80
  xenophobia, 53
Latvian National Independence Movement, 72
Law and Justice (PiS)
  government participation, 73
  programmatic shifts, 147
  relationship with LPR, 73, 104, 132, 135, 140, 145
  See also Radio Maryja
Law and order, 31, 122, 123, 128, 136
  See also Right-ward shift; State
LDPR, *see* Liberal Democratic Party of Russia
Leadership
  in radical right groups, 15, 96
  of radical right parties, 103–104
  See also State

League of Polish Families (LPR), 2, 72–74, 79, 87, 92, 104, 118, 128, 131–135, 139, 140, 145
Legacies
 contextual' and 'textual' legacies, 30
 historical, 4, 36, 42, 61, 76, 146
 Leninist, 43, 148
 of non-democratic past, 22
Legion of Archangel Michael, *see* Iron Guard
Legitimacy
 delegitimization, 29
 mobilization of support, 26
 See also Leadership
Leninism, 36–37, 39–43, 148
Le Pen, Jean-Marie, 82, 85
Liberal consensus, 38
Liberal democracy, 21, 23, 37, 38, 46, 138, 148
Liberal Demoratic Party of Russia (LDPR), 22, 70
Liberalism, 17, 29, 36, 45, 56, 76, 141
Lipset, Seymour M., 16, 17, 55, 56, 146
List Pim Fortuyn (LPF), 101, 129
Lithuania, 49, 52, 62, 63, 100–102, 116
Lithuanian Nationalist Union (LTS), 100, 101
LN, *see* Northern League
Lobbying, 30
Lost territories, 50, 79, 81
 See also Revisionism
LPF, *see* List Pim Fortuyn
LPR, *see* League of Polish Families
LTS, *see* Lithuanian Nationalist Union
Lutheranism, 46
 See also Catholicism; Orthodoxy; Religion

M
Macierewicz, Antoni, 140
Mainstreaming
 efforts, 85
 of the radical right, 7, 125, 136
 See also Ethnopluralism; Islamophobia
Mainstream left, 2
Mainstream right
 and *cordon sanitaire*, 116, 125, 147
 programmatic shifts, 147
Mainwaring, Scott, 59
Majority-minority relations, 48, 50
Mareš, Miroslav, 31, 63, 81, 84, 88, 91, 92, 100, 129
Market liberalism, 17, 56, 76
Marshal Antonescu Foundation, 77
Masaryk, Tomas, 63
Matica Slovenska (a cultural association for language and culture - MS), 91, 130
Mayer, Gregor, 78, 90, 92, 96, 130, 137, 138
McAdam, Doug, 12, 27, 29
MDF, *see* Hungarian Democratic Forum
Meciar, Vladimir, 63, 130
Media
 mass media, 22, 136
 and the radical right, 22, 136
 reforms in Hungary, 137–139
 reforms in Poland, 95
 See also Radio Maryja
Merkel, Wolfgang, 19, 38, 60, 123
Mesežnikov, Grigorij, 68, 75, 78, 84, 92, 126, 130, 131
MG, *see* Hungarian Guard
MIÉP, *see* Hungarian Justice and Life Party
Milieus, 12, 25
 sub-cultural, 12

Militant democracy
  Censorship, 61
  See also Party ban
Minkenberg, Michael, 3–4, 11–16, 18–20, 22–28, 30–33, 36, 39, 42, 53, 61, 70–72, 81–83, 85, 90–93, 100, 105–106, 111, 114–116, 122, 125, 136, 137, 142n1, 146
Minority
  National, 33, 82
  Rights, 33, 76, 115, 122, 148
  See also Minority issues
Minority governments, 11, 114, 128, 129, 131, 132, 137, 147
  and radical right parties, 11, 114, 129, 131, 137
Minority issues
  in Eastern Europe, 61, 148
  in Hungary, 61
  See also Anti-Semitism; Immigrants; Islamophobia; Language laws; Roma
MNR, *see* National Republican Movement
Mobilization, 13, 19, 20, 24, 26–33, 37, 39, 44, 50, 53, 57, 60, 78, 79, 83, 84, 88, 91, 93, 97n3, 99–119, 146
  See also Movements; Movement sector
Modernity, 6, 13, 14, 19, 45
Modernization, 5, 10, 12–14, 18–22, 53–65, 106, 111
  See also Transformation
Moldova, 61, 82, 144
MÖM, *see* Hungarian Self-Defense Movement
Moral norms, 21
  See also Value wars
Most-Hid, 124, 127, 131
Most similar systems comparison, 5

Movement for a Better Hungary, *see* Jobbik
Movement for a democratic Slovakia (HZDS), 63, 68, 126, 130
Movement for the Reconstruction of Poland (ROP), 70, 72
Movement for Rights and Freedoms (DPS), 127–128, 131, 132
Movement party, 25, 93
Movements
  organizational strength, 7, 68, 108
  radical right, 3, 7, 12, 18, 25, 31, 40, 75, 87, 91, 100, 116, 145
  social movements, 19–20, 25, 26, 71, 90
  See also Mobilization
MS-FT, *see* Social Movement – Tricolore Flame
MSI, *see* Italian Social Movement
Mudde, Cas, 2–4, 10–11, 13, 14, 15, 17, 23, 26, 29, 42–43, 53, 60, 72, 83–84, 85, 86, 91–92, 96, 100, 104–105, 111, 113, 115, 122, 143
  conceptualization of the populist radical right, 10, 22, 76
  impact of the radical right, 2, 22, 136
Multiculturalism, 19, 106
  See also Immigration; Refugee
Multinational empires, 6, 45, 47, 145
  See also Nation-building
Muslims, 52, 85, 86, 95, 114
  See also Immigration; Islamophobia; Multiculturalism; Religion
MW, *see* All-Polish Youth

N
Narrative shift, 104
  See also Framing

NA, *see* National Alliance
Nation
  Cultural, 44, 61, 64
  Ethnic, 44, 45, 61, 63, 138
  Political, 44
National Alliance (NA), 75, 80, 96n1, 128–129
National Democratic Party of Germany (NPD), 81, 82
National Democrats (ND), 74
National Front (FN), 96
National Front Party of the Fatherland (SN), 70, 72
National identity, 21, 27, 43–45, 47, 48, 63, 64, 76, 80, 86, 90, 106, 144, 145, 147
  See also In-group and out-group belonging; Nation-building; Religion
Nationalism
  and the communist past, 22
  emancipatory, 16
  ethnic, 45, 63, 138
  ethno-centrist, 18
  integral, 16
  and the mainstream, 61, 65, 72, 115, 146
  See also Fascism; National identity; Religion
National Movement (RN) (Poland), 74, 92
National Movement for Saving the Fatherland (NMSF) (Bulgaria), *see* Political Party Attack
National Party (NS) (Czech Republic), 17, 75, 86
National-Radical Camp (ONR), 92
National Republican Movement (MNR), 101
National Socialist German Workers' Party (NSDAP), 27
National unity, 44

See also Germany
Nation-building, 5, 6, 27, 30, 41, 43–53, 57, 64, 76, 78, 144, 145
  See also National identity; Nationalism
Nationhood
  cultural, 64
  ethno-cultural, 145
Nativism, 15, 76
  See also Immigration; Xenophobia
Nazism, 18
  See also Germany, Neo-Nazism
ND, *see* New Right; New Democrats; Nederlandse Volksunie (Dutch People's Union)
Nederlandse Volksunie (Dutch People's Union), 87
Neoliberalism, 19
  neo-liberal politics, 19
Netherlands, 48, 49, 52, 82, 85, 93, 95
Netherlands Youth Storm, 88
Network, 25, 33, 72, 90–91, 93, 127, 131, 132, 142
New Democrats (ND), 74
New Free Slovakia (NSS), 87
New Hungarian Guard, 118
New Left, post-materialist, 20
New National Party (NNP), 87
New Politics, 53, 55, 106
  See also Old Politics
New Right (ND)(Romania), 71, 74, 82
NF, *see* National Front
NOP, *see* Polish National Rebirth
Norris, Pippa, 24, 27, 114
Northern League (LN), 96
NO, *see* National Resistance
Nostalgia
  for communist past, 22
  for despotic regimes, 76, 144
  in Hungary, 76

NPD, *see* National Democratic Party of Germany
NSDAP, *see* National Socialist German Workers' Party
NSS, *see* New Free Slovakia
NVU, *see* Dutch People's Union

O
Office for the Protection of the Constitution, 93
Old Politics, 55
  See also New Politics
ONR, *see* National-Radical Camp
Opportunity structures
  cultural, 27
  institutional, 105
  political, 53, 104
  See also Cleavages; Party competition
Orbán, Viktor, 2, 137, 138, 139
  government of, 137, 138
Orthodox Church
  in Bulgaria, 61, 63
  in Greece, 61
  in Romania, 61, 63, 86, 144
Ost, David, 42, 70
ÖVP, *see* Austrian People's Party

P
Pamyat, 22
Pankowski, Rafał, 10, 24, 30, 64, 68, 70, 71, 79, 86, 90, 92, 95, 115, 128, 132, 133, 139, 140
Participation
  of citizens in democratic process, 19
  political, 20, 60
  of radical right parties in government, 68, 127, 137, 139
Partitocrazia, 123
  See also Cordon sanitaire
Party ban, 61
  See also Constitutional ban; Militant democracy
Party competition, 40, 53, 55, 57, 59, 104, 105, 108, 146
  See also Cleavages; Opportunity structures, and the regime divide
Party families, 16
  See also Christian Democracy
Party of Freedom (PVV), 96, 129
Party for Greater Romania (PRM), 22, 69, 77, 87, 90, 100, 127, 145
Party membership, in West and East European countries, 58
Party positions, 132
  GAL-TAN continuum, 132
Party system
  Differentiation, 105
  East European, 3, 11, 53, 58, 86, 87, 104, 132, 146
  Fluctuation, 7, 11, 103
  impact of radical right on, 3, 11, 29, 108, 129, 147
  polarization, 106
  under-institutionalization, 59, 91, 103
  West European, 87, 129
Path dependency, 39, 41
Piłsudski, Józef, 64
Pirro, Andrea, 11, 74, 77, 79, 82–84, 87, 104, 115, 131
PiS, *see* Law and Justice
Pluralization
  cultural, 111
  ethnic, 7, 113, 119
  religious, 111–112, 125
  See also Modernization
Poland
  ethnic homogeneity, 50, 108
  See also Illiberal politics; Inter-war period; IV Republic; Radical right in; Radio Maryja, and the regime divide

Polarization, 28, 33, 38, 55, 106, 132, 141
  of party systems, 132
Police, 29, 31, 77
Policy-making
  effects, 30, 122, 136
  levels, 29–30
Policy shifts, 136–142
Polish National Rebirth (NOP), 69, 87
Polish National Union (PWN-PSM), 22, 69, 72, 87
Political culture, 6, 22, 26, 64
Political parties
  features, 99–100
  mainstream, 90
  radical right, 90, 103, 118, 147
  See also Co-optation; Cordon sanitaire; Movement party
Pop-Eleches, Grigore, 40, 60
Populism
  and the radical right, 18
Portugal, 47, 54, 112
Post-communism, 4
Post-communist, 2, 4, 11, 20, 22, 37–44, 48, 50, 57, 60, 61, 70, 77, 88, 114, 121, 127
'Post-democracy'/'post-democratic', 19, 148
Post-industrialism, 19
Prejudices
  ethnocentric, 54
  stereotyping, 84
PRM, *see* Party for Greater Romania
Process model, 114, 115, 122
Professionalization, 58
  of populist parties and movements, 18
Progress Party (DK - FrP), 87, 103
Progress Party (NO – FrP), 103
Prosecution
  of radical-right actors, 31

Protest, 7, 17, 18, 68, 119, 128, 137, 139, 141, 146
Protocols of the Elders of Zion, 140
PSD, *see* Social Democratic Party
PSM, *see* Socialist Party of Romania
Public discourse, 135, 147
Public opinion, 5, 11, 49
PVV, *see* Party of Freedom
PWN-PSN, *see* Polish National Union
Pytlas, Bartek, 11, 21, 30, 42, 48, 55, 58, 70, 71, 82, 84, 89, 104, 115, 132, 134, 136, 137

R
Racism, 15, 23, 69, 72, 74, 137
  racist crime, 94, 95
Radicalization
  of the "mainstream", 147
  of public discourse, 147
Radical right
  Characteristics, 4, 11, 42
  class composition, 88
  in coalition government, 129
  as collective actor, 6, 10, 25, 35, 144
  competitor parties, 31
  electoral performance, 24, 68, 103
  electorate, 88
  ethnocentrist, 23, 69, 72, 74, 87, 109–110
  fragmentation of, 24
  government participation, 122, 134, 135
  "in Hungary", 83, 145
  ideology, 15, 46, 90, 137, 146
  interaction with other parties, 25
  in Latvia, 7, 11, 46, 50, 72, 74, 80, 92, 101, 102, 124, 128, 135
  mainstreaming, 7, 85, 136
  marginalization of, 134

movement strength, 107, 108
and nearby-competitors, 7, 31, 83, 104, 115, 134
parliamentary presence, 135
party strength, 107, 108
in Poland, 2, 5, 7, 11, 27, 38, 55, 72, 90, 102, 108, 118, 134, 137, 145, 147
policy making, 31
radical right in Bulgaria, 73
religious agenda, 86, 87
religious-fundamentalist, 23, 144
in Romania, 11, 37, 45, 50, 63, 68–71, 76, 77, 82, 84, 86, 90, 91, 100, 108, 108, 127, 129, 130, 134, 136
in Slovakia, 7, 11, 27, 62, 70, 83, 92, 102, 115, 126–130, 134, 137
See also Coalition governments; Mainstreaming, of the radical right; Mobilization, Media; Movements
Radio Maryja, 71–72, 75, 79, 86, 90–92, 132, 133, 139, 140, 145
Reform Party (RP), 124
Refugee
refugee crisis, 4, 148
Regime
references, 42, 80
regime change, 2, 4, 9, 36, 40–42, 45–48, 57, 76
regime divide, 21, 55
Vichy, 81
See also Transformation
Regime diversity, post-communist, 40
Regime divide, 21, 55
Religiocentrism, 15
Religion, 18, 41, 63, 76, 85, 86, 114, 144
See also Catholic Church; Catholicism; Lutheranism; Laizism; Orthodoxy

Religiosity, 140
See also Catholic Church; Catholicism; Laizism
Religious identity
fusion with national identity, 46–47, 64, 86, 108
Representation, in parliament, 45
Repression
impact of, 29
of radical right, 108
See also State repression
Return of history, 3, 38–39
Revisionism, territorial, 76, 81, 83, 144
Revolution, 6, 17, 19, 26, 44, 64, 71, 125
Right, ethnocentrist, 96n1
See also Radical right
Right-ward shift, 122, 128
See also Law and order
Right-wing extremism, 17
Right-wing populism, 16
Right-wing radicalism,
see Radical right
RN, *see* National Movement
ROC, *see* Romanian Orthodox Church
Rokkan, Stein, 55–56, 146
Roma, 50, 73, 76, 78, 83, 84, 88, 92, 96, 104, 119, 145, 146
See also Anti-Roma sentiment; Gypsy crime
Romania
constitutional conflict, 50
ethnic nation, 61
interwar fascism, 77
radical right in, 11, 37, 50, 61, 63, 68–70, 76, 77, 82, 83, 86, 90, 91, 92, 100, 108, 115, 126, 127, 129, 130, 132, 134, 136, 137, 144, 147, 148
Romanian Orthodox Church, 86, 88, 144

Romania (*cont.*)
   See also Iron Guard; Orthodox Church; Party for Greater Romania; Roma
Romanian Communist Party, 69
Romanian Cradle (VR), 69, 71, 72, 74, 87
Romanian Legion, 76, 144
Romanian Orthodox Church (ROC), 87
ROP, *see* Movement for the Reconstruction of Poland
RP, *see* Reform Party
Rucht, Dieter, 14, 26, 29, 105, 136
Russification, 50
Rydzyk, Tadeusz, 71

S
Salience, 55, 104, 131
Samoobrona (Self-defense), 68, 124, 128, 131–132
Sartori, Giovanni, 31, 134, 147
Scapegoating, 53
Scheuch, Erwin, 12
Schweizerische Volkspartei (Swiss People's Party), 129
Scully, Timothy R., 59
SD, *see* Sweden Democrats
Second Vatican Council, 46
Secularization, 114
Separatist forces, in Bulgaria, 82
Shafir, Michael, 22, 70, 71, 77, 80, 127
Shirinovsky, Wladimir W., 70
Siderov, Volen, 77
Skinheads, 69, 72, 74
Sládek, Miroslav, 70, 84
Slota, Ján, 75, 79, 83, 86, 130
Slovak Motherland, 91
Slovak National Party (SNS)
   attitude toward Hungarians, 81

electoral performance, 75
impact, 130
opposition to minorities, 76
See also Hlinka, Andrej
Slovak National Union (SNJ), 69, 72, 87
Slovak Republic
   constitutional conflict, 63
   ethnic minorities, 63
   Hungarian minority, 5
   radical right in, 5
   See also Catholic Church; Roma; Slovakia; Slovak National Party; Slovak Republic; Treaty of Trianon
Slovak Supreme Court, 118
Slovak Togetherness (SP), 69, 72, 74, 118
Slovenia, 48, 49, 52, 60, 85, 91, 102, 137
Smith, Anthony, 14, 36, 45
Social change, 12–14
Social class, 21
   and electoral decisions, 89–91
Social Democratic Party (PSD), 70, 134
Socialism, 3, 18, 22, 36, 39, 42
Socialist Party of Romania (PSM), 69, 70, 124
Social movements, *see* Movements
Social Movement – Tricolore Flame (MS – FT), 69, 72, 74, 87, 101
Socio-cultural conflict, 21
Solidarity Electoral Action (AWS), 70, 101
Soros, George, 85
Soviet Union, 8n1, 64, 74
Spain, 23, 27, 93, 111, 112
Spatial shifts
   in Bulgaria, 133
   in Hungary, 133

in Poland, 133
in Romania, 133
in Slovakia, 133
SPR-RSČ, see Coalition for Republic –Republican Party of Czechoslovakia
SP, see Slovak Togetherness
State, 2, 3, 5, 7, 11, 14–17, 19, 22, 23, 28–31, 33, 38, 39, 41, 44, 47, 48, 50, 53, 56, 57, 60, 61, 63, 64, 68, 71, 74, 76, 78, 79, 81, 83, 84, 91, 95, 106, 108, 114, 116, 125, 128, 130, 137–141, 145
See also Law and order
State-church relations, 136
See also Catholic Church; Religion; Religiosity
State interventionism, 140
State repression
isolation of radical-right, 116
See also Repression
State socialism, 3, 22, 39, 42
State vigilance, 11, 95
Status Law (Poland), 82, 137
Stigmatization, 84
Stratification, 89
of right-wing radical party voters, 89
Street politics, 11
Subcultures, 27, 68, 91, 144
racist, 68
SVP, see Swiss People's Party
Sweden, 47–49, 93, 95, 105, 111
Sweden Democrats (SD), 103
Swiss People's Party (SVP), 88, 103, 124, 129
Switzerland, 47, 102, 112, 123
Symbols, 26, 42, 76, 78, 79, 144
Systems
electoral, 24, 27, 106
most similar, 5
Széchenyi Square (Budapest), 138
Szydło, Beata, 140

T
Taggart, Paul, 16
Tarrow, Sidney, 12, 25–28, 53, 136
TB/LNNK, see For Fatherland and Freedom/Latvian National Independence Movement
Terrorism, 145
Tilly, Charles, 12, 25, 39, 41, 136
Tismaneanu, Vladimir, 36, 40
Tiso, Jozef, 63, 78, 86
Tixier, Jean-Louis, 82
Totalitarian, 38
Traditions
national, 44
religious, 27, 90, 106, 147
Transformation
in Czech Republic, 5, 49, 60, 63
See also Communism, historical legacies; Eastern Enlargement; Modernization; Post-communist; Regime divide
Transition
post-communist, 4, 56
See also Modernization; Transformation
Trianon (Treaty of), 48, 64, 71, 82, 104, 137, 145
Trust, 6, 59–60, 65
Tudor, Corneliu Vadim, 69, 77
Turkey, 82

U
Ukraine, 71, 137
Ulmanis, Kārlis, 80, 96
Ultranationalism
ethnic, 80
religious, 23, 80
Uncivil society, 60
Union of Greens and Farmers (ZSS), 124

United Kingdom, 47, 95
United States of America, 40, 44, 56, 60, 77
Universalism, 14

V
Value change, 19
Value wars, 21
 See also Culture wars
Varna airport incident, 77
Vatra Romaneasca (Romanian Cradle), 69, 71, 72, 74, 87
Velvet revolution, 6, 64, 71
Verfassungsschutzbericht, 93
 See also Office for the Protection of the Constitution
Vichy, 81
Violence
 racist, 92, 95
 of radical-right movements, 11, 92
VL, *see* All for Latvia!
Volatility, electoral, 7, 59–60, 102, 104, 118, 144, 146
Volksnation, 44
Vona, Gábor, 73, 83, 138
Von Beyme, Klaus, 3, 21, 24, 56
Voters
 of radical right parties, 88, 130
 See also Election results
VR, *see* Romanian Cradle

W
Weber Max, 19
Wehrhafte Demokratie, 17
Weimar Republic, 27, 38, 46, 148
Weimarization, 3, 38
Welfare chauvinism, 18, 126, 141
Welfare state, 19, 57, 76, 125
Wilsonian order, 38, 41, 48
 See also World War I
Wittenberg, Jason, 39, 41
Workers' Party, 100
Workers' Party of Social Justice (DS), 100, 103
World War I, 38, 41, 45, 46, 48, 63, 76, 144, 145
World War II, 6, 21, 46, 48, 63, 64, 75, 77, 78, 79, 82, 86, 131, 145

X
Xenophobia
 Baltic States, 53
 and East West difference, 53
 measurement, 52

Y
Yugoslavia, 5, 50

Z
ZChN, *see* Christian National Union
ZSS, *see* Union of Greens and Farmers
Zubrzycki, Geneviève, 73, 79, 140

The manufacturer's authorised representative in the EU is Springer Nature Customer Service Centre GmbH, Europaplatz 3, 69115 Heidelberg, Germany. If you have any concerns regarding our products, please contact ProductSafety@springernature.com

Printed and bound by CPI Group (UK) Ltd, Croydon, CR0 4YY

23/03/2026

02076663-0001